The GUINNESS Guide to 20th Century Homes

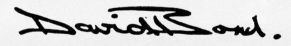

David Bowl

DEDICATED TO MY MOTHER – RENEE JARRETT

Editor: Alex E Reid

Design and layout: Jean Whitcombe

Chapter opening drawings by David Bond

© David Bond and Guinness Superlatives Limited 1984

Published by Guinness Superlatives Limited
2 Cecil Court, London Road, Enfield, Middlesex

'Guinness' is a registered trade name of Guinness Superlatives Limited

British Library Cataloguing in Publication Data:

Bond, David, 19-- –
    The Guinness guide to 20th century homes.
1. Dwellings – History – 20th century
I. Title
643'.09'04   TX301

ISBN 0-85112-413-5

Typesetting by Crawley Composition Ltd, Crawley, Sussex
Printed and bound in Yugoslavia by Mladinska Knjiga, Ljubljana

THE GUINNESS GUIDE TO
20TH CENTURY HOMES

GUINNESS BOOKS

CONTENTS

PREFACE

The hereditary idea of home making has existed throughout recorded history all over the world and has ranged from simple mud huts to the building of impressive palaces. During the 20th century the wide gulf in the standard and sizes of homes has narrowed; fewer palatial residences have been built but better housing for the majority has been achieved on an unparalleled scale in many countries and there are more home owners than ever before.

The home environment is important to most people; it is often associated with significant stages and developments in life. Childhood homes frequently make a deep impression which sometimes remains an enduring influence. The first independent home away from parental supervision usually marks a milestone in growing up, and the striving to achieve the differing ideals and aspirations for a family or individual person's home background often stretches from young adulthood to the retirement years.

The turbulent events of this century, world wars, far reaching political, economic and social changes together with great advances in technology have mde fundamental alterations inevitable to homes and home life in an amazingly short space of time. These developments have been reflected on a visual and superficial level by the changing fashions in interior decoration and clothes which have both followed a close and paralleled time scale of evolution.

Fussiness and over-decoration characterised the homes and the clothes of the affluent established world at the beginning of the century. Simpler lines gradually came in as technological developments and social reform gathered pace. Garish colours and transitory design crazes mirrored the jazzy unstable years after the First World War, to be followed in turn in the later 1920s by streamlined modernistic styling as hopes for a bright, progressive future grew. Disillusionment, fears of war, and the effects of the Second World War fostered nostalgia for the fashions of the more stable world of the upper classes during the 19th century. Expansion and widespread prosperity from the 1950s to the 1970s encouraged progressive, youthful and casually modern concepts for homes and clothes.

The less buoyant atmosphere of the later 20th century has slowed down the pace of fashion changes and once again reflects the character of the period with quieter less extrovert styles and nostalgia for the romanticised designs fashionable in earlier decades. Hopefully more optimistic times will soon return and exciting new trends for the styling of homes will emerge before the end of the century.

Acknowledgments

I would like to thank Vogue Library for their assistance in enabling me to collect so much information from their extensive collection of past issues of *House and Garden*.

Many thanks also to Liberty's and Heal's for access to their unique archives and to Habitat for their invaluable help and information concerning past and present merchandise.

I would like to express gratitude to the many friends who have provided magazines, newspapers, catalogues and views relating to 20th century homes, and special thanks to Jill Hart for her considerable help in preparing the manuscript.

Acknowledgment is made to the following for the reproduction of illustrations on the following pages:
Illustrated London News 9, 17, 31, 33, 47 (top), 48, 49 (bottom), 51 (bottom), 52/3, 57, *63* (top), 81, *83*, 88/9, 113; Popperfoto 16, 121 (top), 160/1

The author and publisher wish to point out that the following illustrations have previously appeared in HOUSE & GARDEN magazine and are the sole copyright of The Condé Nast Publications Limited:

p. 139 – photographer, Michael Wickham; p. 143 – photograper, Anthony Denney; p. 145 – artist, Dennis Loxley; p. 148 – Dennis Lennon with wife and family; photographer, Hans Hammarskiöld; p. 151 – Bernard Klein's home in Scotland; photographer, Ray Williams; p. 155 – Ronald Fleming's house in London; photographer, Anthony Denney; p. 165 (top) – Pevensey Gardens, Worthing; designer, David Brock; photographer, Michael Wickham; p. 165 (bottom) – house in Cambridge Road, Twickenham; architect, Alexander Gibson; photographer, Michael Wickham; pp. 166/7 (middle) – Cephas and Helen Howard's house; designer, Timothy Rendal; photographer, Michael Wickham; p. 171 – John Galliher's home; photographer, Ray Williams; p. 172 – chair design, Prof. Arne Jacobsen; artist, Rosemary Grimble; p. 173 (top) – chair designed by Roger Dean; photographer, Peter Rand; p. 173 (bottom) – chair designed by Robin Day; artist, Rosemary Grimble; p. 174 (bottom) – Don and Marilyn Higgins' house; designer, Marilyn Higgins; photographer, Ray Williams; p. 176 – Stereo headphones by Sony; photographer, James Mortimer; p. 177 (top) – photographer, James Mortimer; p. 185 (top) – designer, Olive Sullivan; photographer, Ray Williams; pp. 194/5 – Helen and Desmond Preston's home; photographer, David Massey; p. 196 – Christopher Wingrave's home; photographer, James Mortimer; p. 211 – Sean Langton's home; photographer, Duncan McNeill; p. 216 (top) – chairs by Hille International; photographer, Dudley Mountney; p. 216 (bottom) – designer, Floris van den Broecke; photographer, Dudley Mountney.

The 1900s

In 1900 Queen Victoria's long reign still had one year to run. Britain ruled one of the most extensive Empires the world had ever known and many people looked forward confidently to a progressive new century.

Very few could have envisaged the momentous events of the near future: even the prophetic writer H G Wells with his inventive imagination hardly surpassed in fiction the realities of the 20th century. World wars, social, political and economic upheavals – combined with the speed and scale of technological developments – were soon to affect every aspect of people's lives including the homes they lived in.

At the beginning of the century the basic concept of most upper class homes was firmly established and had altered surprisingly little, particularly in Britain, for about two hundred years. Apart from changing fashions in interior decoration and the introduction in the second half of the 19th century of more modern forms of plumbing and lighting, homes at the top end of society continued as before with a town house and at least one impressive country house.

Town houses were usually built in the well known pattern of terraces and squares facing communal gardens for the exclusive use of the overlooking houses. To save ground space they were built tall and narrow with brick or stucco fronted brick exteriors. The predominant style of architecture was still a version of the neo-classic style which had been adopted in Britain during the 17th century.

Some variations in the outside design of town houses had been briefly fashionable in the later 19th century. Ornate Gothic, Jacobean and Dutch facades had all been popular fads. London's Cadogan Square and nearby Pont Street contain good examples of these styles built in the 1870s and 1880s, some of them were designed by the British architect Norman Shaw who was well known for reviving period influences. By 1900, although slightly different in detail from the town houses built in the earlier part of the 19th century, neo-classic or, as it was by then known, 'Georgian' exteriors were once again fashionable.

The inside lay-out of most of these houses also followed a well established plan. The family living rooms and the formal reception rooms were on the ground and first floors; bedrooms, dressing rooms and nurseries on the upper floors. The servants' rooms and living area, the kitchens and the many extensions to the kitchens, store rooms, pantries and wine cellars were all in the basement. Further servants' sleeping quarters were in the top floor attics. Wide, impressive, front staircases were for the use of the family and guests; a network of narrower much plainer back staircases for the servants. The ordered day-to-day life of this kind of London house at the beginning of the century was well portrayed in the British television series *Upstairs Downstairs*.

Stabling with living accommodation over the stables was built at the back of the big house in a narrow street or mews. Other members of staff, the coachmen, grooms and their families belonging to the main houses lived and worked in the mews, which also often contained a few modest shops, one or two pubs and possibly a working blacksmith's forge.

The mews was full of life and colour; Edwardian children must have loved watching from their bedroom and nursery windows. Men and older children were busy with the horses and carriages, preparing them for use or putting them away. Riders and coachmen smartly dressed for outings came and went, there were regular deliveries of hay and fodder, small children played in the streets and mothers were busy in their homes or going to and from the shops.

One of the early motor cars and a chauffeur in uniform would have caused great excitement in the mews of the early 1900s. The noise and smell of the high open car with its sinister looking driver in leather helmet and goggles would have been a frightening experience for many of the carriage horses who were still unused to motor traffic. The first family cars for the rich and adventurous had arrived and were one of the early signs of the changing 20th century.

Many upper class families regarded the town house, although large and well furnished by most standards, as the family base for stays in the city particularly during the London summer season with its many social events. These were especially lavish and glittering during the reign of Edward VII who enjoyed and encouraged the grand social life of the period.

The family country house was usually felt to be the real home, many of which had been built in the heyday of the landed gentry's fortunes and were by 1900 usually at least a few generations old. Some were already of architectural and historic interest.

Most country houses were two or three times larger than town houses and often beautifully set in extensive grounds or private

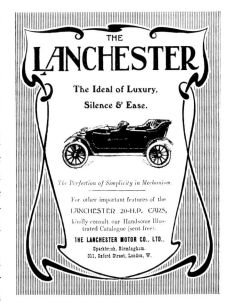

The sight, sound, and smell of the early 'Horseless Carriage' was a frightening experience for many horses at the beginning of the 1900s

parks, well maintained by a team of attentive gardeners. Grand houses were roomy enough for large parties of weekend guests many of whom were accompanied by their own personal servants. Apart from the wide range of indoor activities sporting interests such as hunting or shooting were often available.

Country homes tended to change even less than town houses. Modern forms of lighting and heating were introduced more slowly in the country, transitory fashions in furnishing and interior decoration followed in town were far less popular and sometimes considered unsympathetic to the character of the house and perhaps a little *nouveau riche* or vulgar. In many homes, fortunately for posterity, furniture, paintings and ornaments remained the same from generation to generation apart from occasional additions brought back from foreign tours or stays in the Empire.

In John Galsworthy's *The Forsyte Saga*, Soames as an elderly man in the early 1920s remarked to his sister Winifred that in his opinion stable society was already in decline having reached its peak at the end of the previous century. The stable society of the solid middle class to which he belonged certainly seem to have been at their most influential in the early 1900s.

By the second half of the 19th century the industrial revolution had caused a considerable shift in the composition and distribution of society. Several countries including Britain changed from being a predominantly rural community into a predominantly urban one. Peasants left the land to work in the grim city factories where they lived in very poor housing conditions. Industrialisation, together with the expansion of empires all over the world, proved far more beneficial to the middle classes who administered the growing

GARDENS of BAILRIGG near LANCASTER for HERBERT·STOREY·Esq THOMAS·H·MAWSON 2nd ARIBA · GARDEN · ARCHITECT ·

economies. Their numbers increased and formed an important new section of society, class conscious enough to be divided into the upper, middle, and lower middle class groups. Despite temporary slumps and booms it was an expansive and progressive age for them compared to earlier or later periods.

In three generations many families went up the social scale – starting as tradesmen they moved on into professional occupations and on again to become investors and buyers of property and land. They sometimes crowned their progress by marrying into aristocratic families some of whose fortunes were already declining by the end of the 19th century.

The thriving middle classes were undoubtedly the most important consumers of the time and there was tremendous scope for providing them with suitable homes. By the turn of the century one of the greatest booms ever known in domestic building was under way.

The character of cities changed quickly as suburbs grew and sprawled out in all directions. In London, districts such as Cricklewood, Clapham, Fulham and Putney were transformed in less than 20 years from the city's quiet outskirts to become the built-up inner suburbs with miles of modest terraced houses and semi-detached villas.

Further out of London areas like Chislehurst, Kingston Hill and Wimbledon altered from semi-rural backwaters into the more

Large, impressive looking houses in a variety of revived period styles were built for the prospering upper classes on an unsurpassed scale during the first decade of the century

prosperous but less densely developed outer suburbs.

Similar developments were taking place on the edges of most of the provincial cities. Liverpool, now so sadly declined, was bustling and prosperous in a way rarely seen in more recent decades apart from in South East Asia. Liverpool suburbs grew and merged into one another between Liverpool and Southport; and on the opposite side of the River Mersey the dormitory town of Wallasey was reputed to be one of the fastest growing towns of its type in the country.

Middle class houses built in the 1900s are today easily dated as 'turn of the century' or Edwardian. When they were built it would have been difficult to say what was the predominant contemporary style. It was in fact a time of revivalism in popular architecture. Although reviving earlier styles goes on throughout history no other period has revived so many at the same time. British architects seemed to have produced a whole range of tributes to all the well known styles of the previous three or four hundred years. The 1900s was the last decade of Britain's supreme power and influence – perhaps the nostalgic looking-back to the domestic architecture of its most powerful and historic centuries was expressive of the closing years of the age.

The great variety of fashionable house designs was certainly a big help to the Edwardian builders who catered for a wide range of tastes, aspirations and income levels – and to the established middle classes who shunned any ostentatious show of wealth and who were looking for the under-stated and accepted good taste of the period. Deceptively modest looking houses in a Tudor or Elizabethan cottage or farmhouse style were built. Some were designed or inspired by well known architects of the time such as C F A Voysey or Rennie Mackintosh. A variety of gables, sweeping roofs and natural brick or whitewashed rough cast walls with small paned windows were the characteristics of these quiet looking houses. The

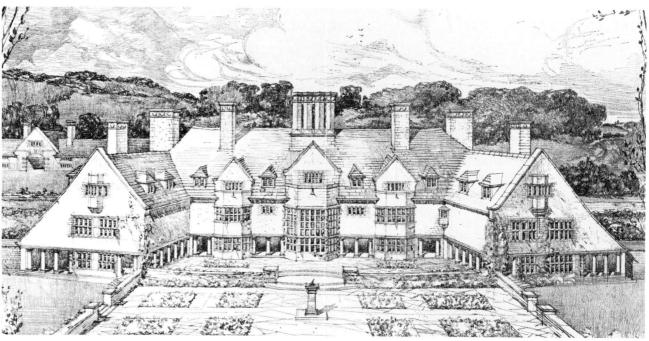

style was particularly popular and remained an important and lasting influence until the middle of the century.

For people wanting a more definite show of prosperity versions of Jacobean manor houses were built with prominent chimneys, ornate windows with lead strips edging the glass panes, and sturdy wooden front doors heavily hinged and studded. An alternative design for this market was the neo-Georgian 'Squire's house' with large bay windows and substantial classic columned porches.

Individually designed houses such as these would have cost from £2000 to £4000, probably less than the annual income of the many successful professional or businessmen who commissioned them. The comparatively low cost of building combined with low taxes and an expanding economy helped to encourage the middle class to buy more ambitious homes.

For the very ambitious and the more pretentiously affluent who wanted plenty of show for their money, even grander more expensive houses were built, sometimes unhappily and rather randomly combining bits of all the fashionable period styles and topping them with a few Gothic spires for good measure. A similar design approach was taken with some of the new blocks of flats known as 'mansion blocks'.

Flat or apartment living at all levels of society had been established in the major cities of Continental Europe, North America and to a lesser extent in Scotland during the 19th century. It was initially far less popular in England where flat living had tended to be associated with the poorer classes who were often houses in tenement blocks to be near the factories of the newly industrialised cities. Gradually in the late 19th century a few large imposing looking blocks of mansion flats were built in London for the middle classes. The Albert Court complex near the Albert Hall built in the 1870s was one of the first. By the 1900s many more were being built in provincial cities as well as in London. The living accommodation varied in size from modest bachelor flats of three or four rooms which still always included a servant's or maid's room, to impressively large family apartments containing as many rooms as the average family house of the period.

Flat living suited the lives of many of the young urbanised Edwardians who were more worldly and outgoing than many of their Victorian parents' generation. Prosperous city life had become

Left, a 1900s version of a grand Jacobean manor house with tall prominent chimneys and ornate small paned windows

13

Below, suburban villas often made a proud feature of their pleasant colourful gardens which were a source of pleasure to many families who had migrated from gloomier inner city areas

more sophisticated, people enjoyed dressing up and lunching and dining out in the many new luxurious hotels and restaurants. The big department stores were coming into their own with a wider than ever selection of tempting home and imported consumer goods. Stores and shops were within walking distance of the fashionable residential districts and entertainment was available a short cab ride from home with more theatres and enticing music halls to choose from than ever before.

Although there was a considerable boom in building new blocks of flats and individually designed houses for the very prosperous, the largest market of all for new homes in Britain was the suburban house for the middle to lower middle class.

Because of the need to produce houses quickly at a competitive price fashionable period influences had to be used more sparingly for larger scale developments.

Small areas of Tudor style timbering on the upper floors and one or two gables were the style features on one group of houses. Nearby houses might have followed some of the Georgian influences; partly fronted in red brick with a porch supported by pillars and a polished wood or white-painted-panel front door.

Both styles of house would probably have included some stained glass windows. They were a much admired feature in many new

Left, sizeable new blocks of apartments like these in London's Kensington were usually described as Mansion flats!

Below, more modest homes sometimes shared with the adjoining house greatly modified versions of the fashionable period designs, such as gabled roof and some Tudor style timbering

suburban homes. Small stained glass panes were put across the tops of living room windows or made into small square or octagonal windows next to, or as part of, the front door. More expensive whole windows of decorative glass were sometimes put at the side of the staircase or on a half landing at the top of the first flight of stairs where they would be a noticeable feature.

Less expensive new homes had period influences simplified still further. A gabled roof, one side of a front porch or a bay window were shared with the adjoining house. Speculative builders produced these acceptable small houses for the lower middle classes with very modest incomes of £150 to £200 a year. New bungalow cottages in 1906 containing three bedrooms, a living room, kitchen and bathroom were for sale at £200. For another 45 guineas they were offered complete with furniture 'in simple good taste', linen, plate, cutlery, china and glass.

Gardens were usually complementary to the size and cost of the house. Many of the larger houses of the outer suburbs had grounds rather than a front and back garden. These houses were set back from the road, partly concealed by mature trees and shrubs and approached by a short curved drive bordered by well laid out lawns and flower beds. A conservatory joined one side of the house and further laid out lawns spread out at the sides and the back of the

15

building. Some houses had their own tennis court, a croquet lawn and possibly stabling. Most had a vegetable garden discreetly tucked away near the less attractive looking kitchen areas and functional outbuildings.

Land was more expensive in the conveniently situated suburbs slightly nearer the city with their frequent public transport services and good selection of local schools and shops. In these districts gardens were smaller and the houses were clearly visible from the street with quite short front gardens but larger more pleasant gardens at the back which often joined the wall of a similar length garden at the bottom preventing the houses from being too closed in or overlooked.

These middle level, middle class homes were a great joy to their early occupants many of whom had come from gloomier terrace houses in the smokey districts closer to the town centre. Bringing their families into the newer, greener and fresher suburbs to live in a lighter more modern house with a fair sized garden was a source of pleasure and achievement for them.

Because of the increasing cost of good land for building, cheaper houses had to be built much closer together with tiny front gardens a few paces long from the garden gate to the front door and small plots for back gardens about the length of two small living rooms. Many enterprising families managed to make them into attractive lovingly cared for gardens but neighbouring houses at the sides and back were

Left, in marked contrast to the affluent homes of the upper classes the poor frequently lived in dilapidated slum properties

Below, the early sky-scrapers were beginning to alter New York's sky line, and although starkly modern by the standards of the time, neo-classic columns were often used to decorate the top of the buildings

sometimes oppressively close.

Home ownership increased quickly during the 1900s although it still formed a small proportion of the population compared with later decades. Early in the 1900s mortgage availability increased to 90 per cent and for the first time brought the possibility of owning a house within the reach of families with lower middle class incomes.

Many of the new houses, however, were built to rent on renewable short leases, rent varying from £45 a year for modest family houses to £75 a year for a more spacious businessman's home. Some families who could afford to buy were quite happy to rent their homes: houses did not appreciate at anything like the rate they were to do in later years and they were not always considered the best investment for savings or capital. Other forms of investment were sometimes preferred where a regular income or additional income was produced.

Housing for the working class and the poor was pitiful by later standards and a condemnation of an age that had produced such expansion and wealth. The best that can be said about the poorer homes of the 1900s was that the worst was over and they were at least a little better than the horrifying conditions of the early industrial revolution.

Social consciences were stirring and the beginning of a more planned and progressive approach to working class homes had started. During the first decade of the century some considerably better larger scale developments of flats and small houses were built. However, by far the largest proportion of the population still lived in very poor cramped conditions. Even the smallest gardens were rare in the poor districts of towns and cities. Nearly every town had its dismal area of slum dwellings where families lived in tenement blocks or shoddy houses with bad sanitation.

Better off workers lived in rows of modest terrace houses rented for about 7/6 to 10/- (37½p to 50p) a week. Accommodation consisted of a small front room or parlour, a kitchen/living room and two or three small bedrooms. Very few houses had bathrooms: baths were taken in a tin tub in front of the kitchen fire, filled with water heated on the stove. Lavatories were still usually outside the main house in an attached extension or across the small back yard and were sometimes very cold in winter.

Many of the tenants of these very modest houses took a great pride in their homes. Front doors opened straight into the street: keeping the front step clean and the door handles and knockers brightly polished was a point of honour. If the woman of the house was ill a neighbour would often keep the step and door up to standard to ease any unnecessary anxieties. Inside the house curtains and furniture were clean and well maintained. The family wash, done on Monday mornings and without the aid of modern detergents, was hung across the back yard where it could have been subject to comparisons and criticisms and was usually spotlessly clean.

Although the miles of newly built small houses spreading out into the country were particularly characteristic of Britain in the 1900s, in other parts of the world especially in Europe and North America large scale domestic building was also taking place. Individual houses

17

for the prosperous, designed in revived architectural styles, were being built in large numbers and apartment building was increasing even more quickly than in Britain.

In North America, where tallish buildings like New York's famous Dakota Apartments had been built as early as the 1880s, the newer apartment blocks were even taller and rather less decorated. Period influences were confined mainly to the top of the building with rather fanciful sharp Gothic spires or with a miniature classic Greek or Roman temple complete with the roof and columns rather like a decoration on top of a wedding cake.

The quantity and variety of domestic building was phenomenal but even with the arrival of early high-rise homes no clearly modern 20th century style for the exterior of domestic buildings had yet emerged. Interior decoration, however, was already showing definite new trends, none more typical and controversial than the art nouveau style.

Art nouveau was fashionable as early as the 1890s and was strongly and memorably featured in the important Paris exhibition of 1900. Some people claimed the style had originated in England where it was sometimes known as the 'Liberty style'. London's famous Liberty's store was promoting versions of art nouveau by the turn of the century. They were, however, quite moderate in comparison with the more extreme French designs. It was a much more popular and widespread movement in France.

Art nouveau suited the France of the period, particularly Paris. It was the time of 'La Belle Epoch', a delightfully light-hearted, stylishly elegant and rather indulgent age for the well off. Art

nouveau furniture had a rather frivolous feminine appearance that was very complementary to the ultra-feminine women's fashions of the period. Furniture and decoration favoured curved, slightly voluptuous lines: designers were said never to use a straight line when it could be curved. There was much use of veneering, satin wood effects, pale woods and contrasting pale and darker wood inlaid. Carved wooden swirls and gilt tippings were sometimes used for added decoration giving some pieces of furniture a look reminiscent of French 18th century designs. Lamps and light fittings were also very decorated with elaborately twisted metal stems and deep shades in multi-coloured glass.

The new style was not universally popular; some people, particularly some of the Anglo-Saxons, thought it a very overdone almost decadent style. In the book *The House Beautiful and Useful* art nouveau is strongly criticised in one section on fashionable trends: 'the chaos in design has spread all over France, Germany, Austria and Italy upon which countries the creed of art nouveau lies heavily. There all respect for natural limitations in the materials has been cast to the winds. Wood is cut as though it were grainless and fibreless like cheese; metal is twisted into weird and unnatural shapes, chairs appear as clumps of gnarled tree roots, twisted boughs conspire to form a bedstead. Electroliers appear to be boxes suspended by innumerable strings; walls show trees with their roots in the skirting boards and foliage on the ceiling; sea serpents chase each other round

The nursery, left, and the living room, above, both show pleasant mixtures of two of the most fashionable styles for interior decoration at the beginning of the century; the furniture reflects the influence of the simpler lines of the 'Arts and Crafts' style and the colouring and patternings follow art nouveau design themes

19

The simple unadorned lines of the chair, table and bannisters all designed by C F A Voysey were very advanced for the 1900s particularly when compared with the fussy, over ornate furnishings general in most homes of the period

the walls and entrance doors are guarded by appalling dragons. Nowhere is the purpose of an article frankly and honorably expressed. The electric lights must masquerade in pools under nymphs or in the glowing horseshoe of a blacksmith's anvil; snakes twisted into ingenious knots for stair balusters threaten you as you ascend; the door knocker becomes a grinning satyr and even the carpet casts malevolent eyes upon you as you traverse it.' These over-critical comments were describing the most extreme and theatrical forms of art nouveau which were mainly used in commercial rather than domestic buildings and especially in fashionable bars and bistros. The well known Paris restaurant Maxim's is a good example of art nouveau in its more extreme form.

The moderate influences – the lighter looking furniture – curved stylised decorative features on furniture – light fittings and wall decorations combined with the use of softer diffused colours, blue greens, grey blues, pinky reds and dusty mauves and purples – all had a beguiling charm particularly when compared with the solid heavy interiors of the later decades of the previous century.

For people who did not like art nouveau in any form there was an alternative, important new style, far more to the liking of the less flamboyant – and particularly to many of the British. This was 'the arts and crafts style'.

The arts and crafts movement had its beginnings as early as the 1860s. It followed the new concept of art of the Pre-Raphaelites and the new, more ascetic attitudes to the qualities of life that were expressed by men like John Ruskin. It was perhaps part of a reaction against Victorian materialism. In the early days it was a rather lofty intellectual movement which believed in the revival of good, simple design and craftsmanship rather in the Medieval tradition of craftsmen and guilds.

William Morris gently commercialised the new trends and brought them to the notice of a receptive public with his famous William Morris patterned wallpapers and printed fabrics. He was quoted as advising would-be homemakers 'have nothing in your houses that you do not know to be useful or believe to be beautiful'; it was good advice for home interiors in any age.

The lines of art nouveau had tended to be curved and feminine; the arts and crafts style was straighter and more masculine. Furniture designs were inspired by traditional country pieces; tall dressers and sturdy hall cupboards in plain woods such as oak; high-backed carver style chairs with rush seating and fireside forms or long seats with high wooden backs and arms which were often built into inglenooks as fixtures.

Inglenooks, many with small windows each side of a wooden surrounded fireplace, in the new plainer style with an overmantle of simple cupboards and shelves, were frequently made the main feature in living rooms and spacious halls. To emphasise the unpretentious farmhouse style, ceilings were sometimes beamed and walls painted in creams or beiges with only a moderate selection of pictures and wall plates. Curtains were plain and undraped and floors covered in dark tiles or polished wood with quietly patterned rugs. Panelled or partly panelled walls were popular and considered an

additional quality feature in these under-stated homes. Liberty's catalogues regularly advertised a panelling service. Oak panelling for a room measuring 18 feet by 12 feet complete with matching panelled door was quoted at £25.

Voysey and the Scottish designer Rennie Mackintosh produced some of the most advanced designs for furniture and interior decoration and although very much in sympathy with the arts and crafts style, it was free from the more cottagey influences. Voysey's simple undecorated high close-set banisters could well have been designed by the contemporary stylists of the 1950s. Rennie Mackintosh's simple elegant designs also had a dateless quality; his exaggeratedly tall high-backed black hall chairs were some of the first truly modern examples of 20th century furniture. They are still copied today over 80 years later and the originals have become much sought-after collectors' pieces. Hill House at Helensburgh near Glasgow, built in 1902-4 and designed by Mackintosh, contains many good examples of early modern 20th century designing; particularly an all-white bedroom, clearly a forerunner in style of countless rooms which were to be so popular in the homes of the flighty 'bright young things' of the 1920s.

The modern furniture of the 1900s did not appeal to all the new homemakers of the time. Some of the newly affluent preferred revived period styles for the interiors as well as the exteriors of their new homes. Heavy Jacobean style cupboards, chairs and dining room suites were found in many of the larger suburban homes.

Jacobean furniture was large and substantial; it looked as if it was built to last. Massive sideboards were wide and high with heavily carved overmantels and panelled cupboards prominently hinged and locked with large elaborate keys. Deep topped dining tables were supported by bulbous legs and a network of thick wooden rails on which unsuspecting diners knocked themselves when sitting down or getting up. Chairs were high-backed and imposing looking, covered in leather or thick tapestry fixed on with many large decorative studs. The heaviness of the rooms was further emphasised with thick velvet or tapestry curtains.

In contrast to the baronial look of many halls and dining rooms, drawing rooms were lighter and more feminine with softly draped pelmets and tied-back curtains in pale colours. Rooms were filled with lighter reproduction furniture copied from the designs of later, more elegant, periods. French 18th century, Louis XV and Louis XVI were especially popular for these formal 'salon' type drawing rooms. The upright couches and chairs upholstered in soft coloured silks and velvets with slim arm rests and unobtrusive legs were ideal for showing off the elaborate hats and sweeping dresses of the fashionable ladies at afternoon tea parties.

For slightly less formal drawing rooms, English 18th and early 19th century styles were considered safe good taste: Chippendale, Hepplewhite and Sheraton were reproduced in large quantities for a very receptive market. Much of this furniture was well made and is still popular and sought after today.

Late Victorian fireplaces were usually fairly standard in style; living rooms and dining rooms had solid but inoffensive designs with white or grey marble surrounds decorated with miniature neo-classic columns and arches. Edwardian fireplaces were far more designed: they followed all the fashionable styles in interior decoration. Some were very over-designed and overpowering for the size of the rooms with heavy overmantels in wood starting high on the walls with a sloping roof effect below which were a complicated range of cut-out fretwork patterns: columns, arched shelves and cupboards with decorated glass doors; below the mantel shelf the area round the fire was decorated with two or three different kinds of patterned tiles.

Simpler but quite varied fireplaces were put into most middle level homes. Some designs had very small overmantels or plain surrounds often in painted cast iron which had been cast from a mould designed to copy the look of wood panelling. The main part of the fireplace was filled in with a wide area of fancy and plain tiles. Other styles reversed the emphasis and had larger real wood surrounds with high overmantels possibly with an inserted oval mirror, but a much smaller space for tiles or polished brass below. To complement the popular revival of late 18th or early 19th century house designs and the craze for matching reproduction furniture 'Georgian' chimney pieces in mass-produced cast iron or more expensive marble or wood sold very successfully for many years.

In contrast to the elaborateness of so many features of Edwardian homes, floor coverings were surprisingly unemphasised. Prosperous houses had richly patterned carpets but they were nearly always squares of carpet set on polished wood floors or darkly stained surrounds of wood. Simple patterned tiles were sometimes used for hall floors and plain dull red or grey larger coarser tiles for kitchens and pantries. By far the most widely used floor covering for all rooms apart from the principal living rooms was shiny linoleum in dullish serviceable colours and designs. Rich looking wall-to-wall carpets in long-piled light coloured carpeting and boldly patterned floor tiles in strong colours would have been a revelation to the early 20th century homemakers.

The 1900s was certainly a very style conscious decade with an unusually wide variety of fashionable designs for the well off to choose from. The one feature all the early 20th century styles had in common was the swing away from the clutter of Victorian homes. Books on interior decoration and sections in the well-respected *Studio* magazine all constantly advised lighter colours, less crowded walls and more floor space the show furniture to better advantage.

The changing attitudes were pinpointed in the *House Beautiful* written in the late 1900s. 'The sin of over furnishing is, however, a common one and the average drawing room is an excellent example of it. A multitude of small tables, chairs, palm stands and articles so disposed as to leave but narrow lanes through which one must tread one's way gingerly and warily is a common defect. The partition of wall spaces by three or four different treatments, the use of meaningless and unnecessary mouldings, the introduction of "cosy corners" and "nooks", the use of too many plants or flowers and a surfeit of pictures and ornaments are also frequent evils. In regard to ornaments the ladies are, I regret to say, great offenders. When one

considers the enormous amount of labour entailed day in and day out dusting and cleaning one can only marvel at the instinct which prompts them to crowd every available shelf and table to its full capacity with knick-knacks and trifles.' These comments, although rather scathing and pompous, did describe quite accurately the rooms still found in many homes.

In a series of books published in 1904 called *The Book of the Home*, clutter and overcrowding of the type criticised was a noticeable feature in the sections on interior décor. On a proposed budget of £500 for the furniture of a house containing a dining room, drawing room, library, five bedrooms plus a maid's room, the £80 15s 0d (£80.75) allocated for the drawing room contents was made up of the following:

A living room compiled by Liberty's store in London showing the popular use of panelled walls and Jacobean styling

Wilton carpet, 13½ft × 11¼ft	£8	5 0
Angora skin hearth rug	£2	12 6
Two pairs silk chenille curtains @ £4 4 0	£8	8 0
Two pairs frilled lace curtains @ 11s 9d	£1	3 6
Couch, two easy chairs, two occasional chairs, four other chairs	£26	5 0
Brass fender £1 15 6, coal vase 14s 6d	£2	10 0
Brass fire irons 18s 6d, rests 12s 6d	£1	11 0
Artistic dark mahogany cabinet	£3	17 6
Overmantel	£3	12 6
Three tables of various designs	£8	0 0
Mahogany cosy corner with silk cushions	£14	10 0
	£80	15 0

Typical mass-produced Edwardian fireplace incorporating a mirrored overmantel

In another section, Victorian ideas on the use of draperies were still suggested. As well as various complicated curtain drapes for windows and across doors, hanging curtain style drapery was shown over the beginning of the staircase to break up a narrow hall. Curtaining was also recommended for the back of an upright piano in case the plain wood back was shown when it was pulled away from the wall. Styles of fabric draperies for fireplaces were illustrated although some reference to this being out of date was made. 'At the present time any notice of draperies would be incomplete without a reference to the mantel board; however severely drapery here may be criticised in some quarters, it is undoubtedly popular with the ladies'.

There was obviously a considerable gulf between the progressive ideas of the designers and the firmly established taste of a large section of the population. *The Book of the Home* goes on to suggest overhanging wood decorations in a Moorish style for a staircase and a miniature oriental room set for a half landing; complete with curved arches, curtains, cushions, hanging lanterns and suitably oriental looking ornaments.

Ideas for colour schemes also seem heavily overdone by later 20th century standards. For a dining room with brown oak furniture the colours suggested were 'plain tan cartridge paper, deep frieze of convential poppies in red, tan and brown. Oak brown paint, plain red linen-plush or velvet curtains, red and brown carpet. Blue china bowls and plates on mantelpieces and shelf over door.' And for a drawing room with south or west aspect 'wallpaper sapphire blue, friezes of copper leather paper with shelf painted blue beneath it and blue and white china jars and copper bowls placed upon the shelf. Woodwork all painted dark blue, carpet in Persian design, curtains of deep rose coloured damask. Furniture Chippendale, fire irons and coal vase of iron and copper.'

The purpose as well as the contents of rooms was advised on particularly for larger homes where a library and a morning room was available as well as a dining room and drawing room. In some houses the 'boudoir' was a kind of limbo room for the lady of the house half-way between the living rooms and the bedrooms. Its purpose and character were more fully explained in the following way: 'A boudoir is similar to the morning room but on the principle and scale of a strictly private instead of a more public room; it is also practically the mistress's business-room from which the household management is directed and a particularly methodical lady may have a sort of office table or secretaire for a conspicuous feature, otherwise it may be merely a very dainty retreat for refined seclusion.'

Middle class houses contained a lot of bedrooms by present day standards; six family bedrooms and two attic rooms for the maids was quite usual. Families tended to be large compared with later generations; four to six children was considered an average size. Sadly, a comparatively high proportion of children died in infancy and although considerably less than in the early Victorian period, bereaved young couples were not unusual and they were too frequently reminded of their loss with empty nurseries and too many spare bedrooms.

Bedrooms in the 1900s, even in the more conservative homes,

A miniature oriental room set designed as a suggestion for use on a half landing

Musical evenings were popular in many Edwardian homes: piano playing was general and some families had a pianola like the one illustrated on the left

became lighter looking; walls were painted in paler colours, lemon yellows and light blues, wallpapers were usually less overpoweringly patterned. The heavily built late Victorian wardrobes, chests of drawers and the high-standing beds with solid brass bedsteads were gradually replaced by the lighter looking fashionable bedroom suites in modern or reproduction designs. Wardrobes, chests, dressing tables, lower beds with wooden frames and washstands were all designed in a matching style. Few houses had bedrooms with adjoining bathrooms or wash basins in the bedroom; the washstand with its marble top, washing bowl and jug filled as required with warm water by the maids was standard in most homes.

Quite prosperous houses with many bedrooms and a large family usually shared one bathroom and one lavatory; an extra outside lavatory was provided for the use of the servants.

Compared with other rooms in the house the bathrooms of the 1900s were given little attention. They seem to have been regarded by many as rooms for attending to functional necessities not to be lingered in longer than was necessary. Even in homes where great thought had gone into most aspects of interior décor, the bathroom was usually furnished with the basic standard mass produced fittings of the time. Some of it was very substantial with baths and wash

Draperies were still used in some homes and were sometimes arranged to cover the plain wood at the back of the piano

Ideas for decorative colour schemes in 1904; wall space was often divided into several sections and each area was given a different design treatment

basins set into wooden panelled frames – and for a show of affluence, gold taps – but mostly lacking in design imagination. An exotic art nouveau bathroom was quite a rarity.

In *The Book of the Home* a minimum size for a bathroom was stated as 8ft by 10ft or 11ft with a separate tiled alcove for the bath and the lavatory. Some of the Edwardian bathroom tiles were quite attractive with border effects of stylised flowers or long panels of floral trellis designs. For less expensive duller bathrooms shiny washable anaglypta paper was used for the lower half of the walls.

Impressive designer inspired kitchens and bathrooms proudly shown off to friends and relations as glamorous features of the home were several decades away in the future. Most kitchens in the early part of the century were functional and utilitarian, rarely seen by visitors and in prosperous households unfamiliar to some members of the family.

In working class houses where there was only one smallish living room or, as it was sometimes called, 'the front parlour' – well maintained but only used for special occasions or for receiving visitors of higher rank – the kitchen acted as the family living room with a couple of fireside chairs, a sideboard and a table for family meals or for working on. When the table was not in use it was usually covered with a dark cloth preferably in chenille velvet. Kitchens in larger houses usually looked less like a cosy living room but they were used by the cook and the maids as their general living area and there was a selection of wooden wing chairs for them to use off duty.

The dominant feature of nearly all kitchens was the black leaded kitchen range with a fire, ovens and hobs. Some ranges were large and rather monstrous looking with several hefty ovens, many hot plates and pull-out rails for drying clothes. The fire burning section of the range when not needed for heating the cooking ovens could be opened to make a cheerful fire and throw heat out into the room, or it could be adjusted to direct heat upwards to heat water for the bathroom.

Nearly all kitchens contained a good selection of sturdy built-in wooden cupboards and shelves, some forming country-style dressers for china; other more basic shelves and hooks were used for cooking utensils.

Most houses had an adjoining back kitchen, usually a back extension to the house containing a stone sink with wooden draining boards and a gas cooker as an addition or instead of the range. Cooking by gas was growing in popularity: it was cleaner in use and did away with the laborious work of cleaning out and maintaining the kitchen range. Some women, however, were not happy with gas; they preferred the flavour of slow range cooking and felt gas might have a detrimental effect on food and leave lingering smells in the kitchen areas.

Magazines were full of praise for the newer electric cookers; they must have sounded miraculously modern to the women of the time, free from smells, easy to use and control and far less trouble to clean.

Matching suites of bedroom furniture which still included a wash stand became increasingly fashionable during the 1900s

Electric stoves were rightly declared to be the cookers of the future.

As well as back kitchens, walk-in pantries were built adjacent to the main kitchen or back kitchen. In the pantry there was usually a small wooden cupboard with a mesh fronted door called a meat safe where perishable foods were kept waiting for use. To enable food to be kept longer some homes had a second lead-lined wooden cupboard, the ice box, the forerunner of the refrigerator. Large blocks of ice were delivered regularly for the ice box, usually by a local fishmonger. Shelves were built right round the pantry walls; food stocks could be quickly checked with a few glances and the wider lower shelves were kept clear for freshly baked bread and cakes to cool and for the popular Edwardian desserts like jellies and blancmanges to set.

Electricity introduced into homes late in the 19th century still provided only a small percentage of home lighting compared with gas and oil; but it was increasing steadily. Most new houses in urban areas where electricity was available were built ready wired; 'modern efficient electric light' was made an important feature in the many advertisements for new houses; its superiority to gas and oil was detailed. Gas was claimed to produce inevitable smells, mark walls and ceilings and give out some unwanted heat in warm weather. The time and work involved in maintaining oil lamps for the average house was pointed out: wicks had to be trimmed and lamps cleaned and filled.

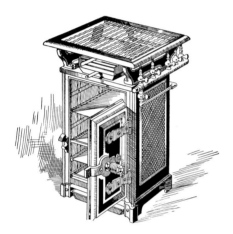

Standard gas cooker of the period

The predominant form of heating for most homes was provided by solid fuels; mainly coal or wood burnt in stoves or open fireplaces. In many homes maids got up early on dark mornings to cold houses; one of their first jobs was to clean out the previous day's fires and re-lay and light new ones in kitchens and living rooms; sometimes also in the halls, nurseries and bedrooms. During the day the fires had to be regularly maintained, the arduous job of looking after them continuing as part of a day's routine for many months of the year particularly in the countries of Northern Europe with their brief uncertain summers. To save work, gas fires were sometimes used in bedrooms and in the new labour-saving town flats.

Early forms of central heating were being introduced into progressive homes, usually in apartment blocks. Heating was provided from solid fuel burning furnaces in the basement; the heat was directed up into the rooms through small grills in the floors or alternatively through a network of hot water pipes and radiators. The development and adoption of central heating progressed steadily in countries with severe winters such as Canada and North America but much more slowly in Britain.

The idea that there would be an almost servantless society in less than two generations' time would have been hard for most people to comprehend at the beginning of the century.

Early refrigerator: wood cabinet into which large blocks of ice were placed

Servants of some kind had been a part of nearly all households, from the equivalent of a lower middle class level upwards, for many centuries although the concept of 'being in service' as it was often called had changed over the generations. In the Middle Ages service had a much wider meaning; being in service applied to the higher as well as the lower ranks of society. Noblemen were in the service of

Working kitchen with wall hooks and sturdy built-in dresser for pans and basic crockery

other noblemen for the protection of homes, working for the Church and to accompany then on the Crusades. Women of high rank were often in the service and protection of households similar to ones they had been brought up in. They were companions or attendants to the senior women of the house and helped with light domestic duties.

Below these closer personal services came the various other levels of service, ranging from those with specialised skills and status, to men and women attending to the menial tasks of the household.

By the 19th century the earlier concepts of being in the service of others had on the domestic level become somewhat down-graded. The tremendous expansion of the middle classes during the second half of the 19th century, which created a greater than ever demand for servants, may have accelerated the down-grading process. Some of the newly middle class, perhaps unassured in their elevated status, sometimes adopted a rather over-superior and patronising attitude to 'staff'.

By the end of the 19th century up to about 15 per cent of the working population were employed in domestic service; some were well treated and valued members of the household with comfortable living conditions; others harshly treated and exploited. A gradual drift away from domestic service into manufacturing industries started amongst the younger generation.

In *The Book of the Home* considerable advice is offered to middle class women on servants. There was already some reference to the 'servant problem' and the need to be firm but fair and just was emphasised. The general attitude towards servants was still, however, rather condescending almost as if dealing with a slightly sub-normal breed. On getting potential servants from institutions the following comments were made: 'The Marylebone Charity Schools and Institutions of that class turn out very respectable but seldom very alert or clever servants, their experience of life has been very limited and the cultivation of their faculties groovy. But some employers who are willing to spend time and trouble in training their own servants might consider these limitations rather an advantage.' The differences in servants' eating habits were also pointed out: 'Many employers, however, fail to realise that servants often prefer a

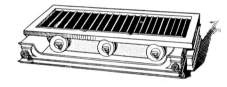

Electric ovens were beginning to be used in some homes

Plug-in electric kettles were still a great novelty

"The mistress of a young servant should begin early to train her in cookery and domestic economy."

Right, when compared to the over decoration used in many rooms in the home, bathrooms were usually quite plain and functional

"Every girl should have a comfortable and airy bedroom."

more highly seasoned coarser style of food than appeals to cultured palates. Liver and bacon, pork, tripe, stuffed sheep's hearts, all these and many other dishes of the same kind are often liked and there is no reason why they should not be allowed occasionally.' Disapproval of the way servants drank and ate is mentioned rather despairingly: 'Stewed tea is a beverage dear to the heart of the average maid and in most kitchens the little black teapot stands on the hob all day. It is shockingly unwholesome, of course, and together with sleeping in a stuffy atmosphere and eating at odd hours instead of proper mealtimes is responsible for much indigestion and ill health. The excessive tea drinking, however, is a practice almost impossible to check even by the exercise of the greatest tact.'

On the subject of servants' wages books and magazines agreed and were resigned to the fact that 'an upward tendency is steady and universal'. Wages for a general purpose maid, known as a 'general', were given as £10 to £14 a year in the country but as high as £15 to £20 in the London area. Good house and parlour maids were quoted

slightly higher, £15 or £16 a year in the country and £20 to £22 in the cities. Cooks' rates of pay were higher still; a 'plain' cook from £18 to £25 and a 'good plain' (good soups, entrees and pastry were sometimes mentioned in advertisements) ranged from £25 to £70 a year.

The status of servants in the home and their day-to-day relationship with their employers varied considerably. In modest homes with only one resident maid working at least some of the time with the wives and daughters of the house and coming into regular contact with all members of the family in smallish houses, the overall relationship was usually fairly informal. In larger more prosperous homes, with two maids and a cook, servants were less close to their employers who were usually addressed as Sir and Madam and the children as Master and Miss. My father and his sister, used to life in a modest suburban house, found when they went to stay in the more affluent homes of relatives they were immediately elevated to the status of Master Dick and Miss Dot. Cooks were considered senior to maids in these houses although they all shared the same living area, took their meals together and often formed their own kind of separate family unit.

Grander homes with a team of servants had their own class structure. Butlers and housekeepers were the senior members: ladies' personal maids were above parlour maids, parlour maids superior to kitchen maids. Employers and their families were far more remote from their staff. Apart from consultations on general policies and plans for special dinners or receptions the running of the domestic side of the home was left to the butlers and housekeepers who often had their own living quarters separate from the other servants. They were firmly in charge of the rest of the staff who were sometimes rather in awe of their rank and personalities – particularly shy young maids starting out in domestic service.

There were very few labour saving appliances to help the maids of the 1900s. Cleaning had to be done manually or with very basic manually operated aids. Carpets were cleaned with simple carpet sweepers or brushed by hand with long and short brushes; floors were polished or scrubbed. Coal for the many fires and warm water for the bedrooms had to be carried up and down stairs. The large amount of family washing was boiled in a round tank heated by solid fuel or gas, then scrubbed by hand and wrung out by hand or squeezed through a wooden mangle and later ironed with heavy flat irons which had to be heated on the stove or kitchen range. A lot of ironing, particularly women's and children's dresses, blouses and underwear, had to be done with great care and patience. Easy care fabrics had not been invented: clothes were always made from natural fibres like cotton and linen and were often a mass of pleats, tucks, lace inserts and rows of small fabric loops and buttons.

One of the last chores of the day in many homes was the cleaning and polishing of the family's shoes and boots ready for the following day. Edwardians considered well polished shoes and boots important and the failure to present properly cared for footwear was frequently thought to be a sign of general laxness and unreliability.

Self improvement and self discipline were firmly instilled into most families. Aimless lazing around the house would rarely have been tolerated. Girls learned needlework and sewing, and both sexes were expected to read instructive books, many homes having large sets of encyclopedias and detailed books on history, geography and on the achievement of the Empire.

Active sports were very much encouraged and indoor games such as table tennis and billiards were sometimes available. In many larger houses, special billiards rooms were quite usual and very popular with teenagers and grownups alike.

Music appreciation and participation was a feature in many homes. Gramophones were still unusual and were considered by many people to be an expensive novelty: plain instruments with large horns were thought ugly in the drawing room and neater ones in a Sheraton style cabinet were, at 50 guineas, prohibitive to most families. Mechanical pianolas were found in some homes but the piano was the most general provider of music. Nearly all homes from a modest suburban level upwards had a piano in the principal living room. Singing or playing a musical instrument, particularly

Manufactured entertainment for children was almost unknown in the 1900s; conventional toys were the popular Christmas presents of the time

Children's party games were usually performed under parental supervision

the piano, was engaged in by at least one member of most families. Walking down quiet suburban streets in the afternoon, the sounds of, not always very good, piano practice often came from several different houses. Musical evenings were still very popular; friends and relations arrived with their music sheets which they coyly left in the hall in case they were persuaded to play or sing during the evening. Later, children who were supposed to be in bed sometimes sat on the landing floor out of sight listening to the singing, music and laughter of the grownups downstairs.

In some respects life in the home was closer and more family orientated than in more recent decades. There were more children and because there were very few manufactured entertainments families made up their own games and amusements. There was more playing together and involvement in group activities. Parents believed in greater overall supervision; manners and behaviour patterns were more forcefully and confidently taught. Although becoming less usual, some children, particularly in the country, still received their early education at home from resident male or female tutors in a special schoolroom.

Etiquette and élitist attitudes towards rank and status were accepted and perpetuated by many people, and were clarified for the unsure in manuals and books of the time. On the procedure towards newcomers in the district the following points were made: 'When newcomers arrive it is usual for a lady of good position in the neighbourhood to be the first to call. If she is satisfied as to their social status, if she makes a favourable report her friends follow suit.' And on the observance of rank when entertaining in the home several guide lines were given:

'In introductions an inferior rank is always introduced to a higher ranking person.'

'At luncheon parties, when luncheon is announced the hostess turns to the lady of highest rank and says "Shall we go down to luncheon?"'

'At dinner the host leads the procession with the lady of highest rank; remaining guests are paired according to rank.'

Etiquette at private parties and dances also followed an accepted code. Teenage boys and girls who attended dancing classes were also instructed on general etiquette at dances. The correct behaviour after dancing was as follows: 'When after a dance her partner has conducted her to her place, he and she bow slightly to each other and he at once leaves her. No man accustomed to the usages of good society would linger as it prevents other men from approaching who wish to ask her to dance. Some girls sit out dances with partners instead of dancing them. This is most incorrect.'

Stiffness and formality in many aspects of higher class social life, although to later generations sounding more like the world of Jane Austen than a part of the 20th century, did remain very much a part of home life until at least the First World War and in a modified form after the War. Many elderly people today remember clearly the very different social life in the homes of their youth.

Edwardian ideas on food and meals differed very much from those

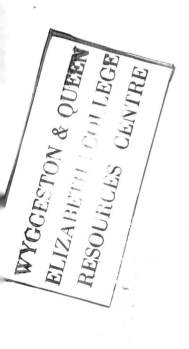

held by later generations. Theories on dietary balance, the avoidance of too many carbohydrates, high fat and sugar intake, and the striving to be a certain supposedly correct weight often thought so important today would probably all have been regarded as cranky if not downright eccentric by most people in the 1900s. Many of the poorer classes simply could not afford a nourishing diet of any kind; in poor districts thin unhealthy looking children were an accepted everyday sight; in very noticeable contrast prosperous families of the time often ate over-large heavy meals.

There were very few so-called convenience foods: more time was spent in the kitchen preparing and cooking. There was much more home baking of bread, cakes and pastries; vegetables needed more preparing, being nearly always fresh and available only in season. Meat was eaten more frequently and in larger quantities.

Meals were taken more formally at elaborately set tables. Families, particularly in England, sat down to a cooked breakfast every day; freshly made porridge, usually served with milk or cream and sugar, was followed by a fish course and/or a wide selection of eggs, sausages, bacon, kidneys, mushrooms and fried potatoes. Lunch consisted of at least three or four courses, frequently more if it was a luncheon party, and often included a baked or steamed pudding. Books of the period emphasised the importance of puddings especially in the winter; in *The Book of the Home* the middle of the day servants' dinner, as opposed to the family's lunch, was advised on in the following way: 'The bill of fare for the kitchen dinner is generally the same as that of the dining room lunch, but care should be taken that there is a sufficiency of wholesome plain food including a good substantial pudding.'

Tea, served in the late afternoon with a selection of bread and butter, toasted tea cakes or muffins, scones and cakes, was habitually taken in many homes. This would be in the drawing room in the

Life in most middle class homes was more formal and stratified than in the later decades of the century; children were subject to a stricter code of discipline and behaviour patterns

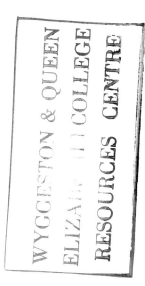
33

winter and in the garden, weather permitting, during the summer months. Afternoon tea was the most popular occasion for entertaining friends and acquaintances. Many women had specified 'at home' days for receiving visitors; carefully arranged not to clash with another 'at home' day in the same social circle.

Evening meals varied from suppers, lighter meals than the usual lunch, to elaborate dinners with many courses. The middle and upper classes always changed into evening dress for dinner, even for quiet evenings with the family. For dinner parties the dining table was usually decorated with shaded lights and flowers or leaf arrangements chosen according to the season. Women's magazines showed suitable artistic table decorations for each month of the year. As well as the range of large set meals which were quite usual in many prosperous homes, the day's intake of food was often completed with supper refreshments served in the late evening.

Attitudes to styles of food and ways of cooking, apart from amongst the travelled and sophisticated, were very insular by later standards. French cuisine had an established international following, sometimes with rather snobbish connotations; restaurants and private house menus were frequently printed in French even when the food described was in fact ordinary English dishes. The delights of so many other international styles of food were far less well known and through ignorance often condemned by a large section of the population; their wider appreciation had to wait for the age of mass travel and communication.

Homes and home life in the 1900s for the vast majority did not change dramatically from the last decade or two of the 19th century. Changes in almost every aspect of the home were under way but the pace of change that would really turn 19th century homes into 20th century ones had not accelerated as it was to do in the following decades.

Technological developments affecting the home only gradually gained pace during the 1900s; telephones, more modern forms of cooking, lighting and heating, considered unusually progressive at the beginning of the decade, were more common by 1910 but still not general. The predominant form of transport was generated by real horse power and the family carriage was far more usual than the family car.

Talented architects and designers with the sensitivity creative people often have for anticipating future trends were, however, already designing simpler more functional homes. And the development of 'modernism', as it was often called, was already in embryonic form in Germany and Austria where there were group activities to reconcile good design to the needs of industry. State sponsored design courses began for the early industrial designers. These were the forerunners of the famous 'Bauhaus' School that was going to revolutionise domestic architecture and design.

In America taller buildings were beginning to alter the skyline of New York and Chicago. These early sky-scrapers, although only moderately high by later standards, were to set the pattern for the cities of the future all over the world.

The 1910s

The 1914-18 war is often pinpointed as the clear-cut and abrupt end to one period in history, the Victorian and post-Victorian age. The definite close of one epoch can rarely be dated to a time span as short as 4 years, and although the shocks and great upheavals caused by the war accelerated the pace of change from one era to another more quickly than usual, considerable changes in most aspects of people's lives were already taking place in the pre-1914 years.

During the 1910s the speeding up of everyday life was becoming more evident each year, especially in the big cities. Pictures of city streets show a marked difference in less than 10 years: they had become clearly 20th century with the tremendous increase in the amount of motor traffic.

America was one of the first countries to become car orientated on a mass scale. Cars soon became invaluable in a large country where many people needed to travel considerable distances in the shortest possible time. Advertising began to promote the idea of the family

More homes had gramophones; portable and cabinet models were no longer quite such expensive novelties and the young generation loved to play the new ragtime records

Look inside the lid!

If it hasn't this trademark, it isn't a Victrola

You can readily identify the Victrola by the famous Victor trademark "His Master's Voice." It is not a Victrola without the Victor dog. This trademark is on every Victrola. It guarantees the quality and protects you from inferior substitutes.

The word "Victrola" is also a registered trademark of the Victor Talking Machine Company. It is derived from the word "Victor" and designates the products of the Victor Company only.

As applied to sound-reproducing instruments, "Victrola" refers only to the instrument made by the Victor Company—the choice of the world's greatest artists.

Look inside the lid—insist upon seeing the famous Victor trademarks. On the portable styles which have no lid, the Victor trademark appears on the side of the cabinet.

Victor Talking Machine Co., Camden, N. J., U. S. A.

Victrola

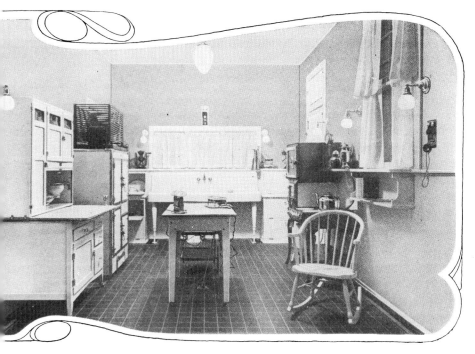

Some new American kitchens were noticeably more modern with electric cookers and electric refrigerators

car relating to the family home. Shiny new cars were often illustrated parked in front of impressive looking houses and pictures advertising pleasant new middle-level homes usually made a feature of an attached garage. The garage doors were often shown open proudly revealing the status symbol of a high standing black T-model Ford, one of the first and most famous big selling family cars of the century.

Technological advancements affecting the interior as well as the exterior life of the home were also gaining quicker and more widespread acceptance in America. Central heating was becoming more general and neater. More modern looking radiators were available, some with automatic time and heat regulators.

The electrification of homes had become more extensive: electric vacuum cleaners and all-electric kitchens with plug-in refrigerators and stoves which were still often described as 'electric ranges' were found in many of the modern new apartments and houses. The labour saving appliances lessened the hours of arduous housework and eased the need for domestic staff.

Gramophones were no longer an expensive novelty and were becoming increasingly popular with the young generation who liked to play the new blaring ragtime records day and night. Ragtime had originated in America and swept on to enjoy great popularity in Europe early in the 1910s. The first canned pop music had arrived much to the aggravation of many parents and older people. The latest popular music and songs had a differing appeal for each generation – loved by the young and hated by the old: a recurring feature of home life in each decade of the century.

In Britain the great boom in domestic building, so strong in the 1900s, started to peter out after 1912. The Land Valuation Act of 1911-12 had reduced the profit to be made on land. Early 20th century speculative builders had often made the highest percentage of their profit on the price of the building plots rather than the houses

Comparatively modern looking shower equipment and shower cubicles were already available

America was one of the first countries to become car orientated on a mass scale; advertisements began to promote the idea of relating the car to the home

built on them. Because of reduced profitability, fewer new houses and blocks of flats were built in the years just before the war. The availability of new homes started to lose pace with the needs of the market; the effects of the slow growth in building accumulated and proved to be one of the prime causes for the acute crisis in the supply of homes at the end of the decade.

After the wealth of designs for domestic architecture popularised at the beginning of the century, style changes evolved more slowly during the 1910s. Revived period influences still dominated house design and some over-elaborate versions were commissioned, but most of the admired new homes were quieter looking and more subtle and under stated in their interpretations of earlier periods.

In the *Studio Year-Books of Decorative Art* – some of the most authoritative guides on design – the trend away from richness and towards naturalness and simplicity was continually advocated. Traditional manor houses, farms and cottages provided much design inspiration, particularly in Tudor and Jacobean styles. Advanced architects had already promoted 16th and 17th century styles quite successfully from the turn of the century onwards, but they were usually fairly obvious 1900s adaptations. The newer movement developed by well-respected architects such as Mr Baillie Scott favoured a deeper form of revivalism rooted in the past traditions of building. Qualities such as the ability to harmonise with the countryside, the use of local materials, the scope for craftsmanship and the suitability of homes built for the vagaries of the British climate, were all greatly praised and valued.

The lack of a truly modern style was frankly admitted and not considered a disadvantage: more recent periods were thought to have lost touch with the national heritage in domestic building. The ideal suggested for a country or suburban house was a combination of old and new. The house would be Tudor in appearance with care taken to make sure the building looked mellow and not too new, but with 20th century improvements such as insulation, central heating, electric light and up-to-date kitchens and bathrooms skilfully and unobtrusively integrated for comfort and efficiency.

The refined and rather purist approach to using period designs had to be modified for the more price-conscious middle and lower levels of the housing market, but the influence of quiet country styles did show quite clearly at all levels. An example of a budget priced house shown in the *Decorative Art Year-Book* for 1914 illustrated well the kind of moderate sized detached family house in the fashionable cottage style. The house, built a year or two earlier, was reproduced from a design that won a prize for a £500 house. Attention was drawn to the following features: 'the outer walls are of multi-coloured sand stocks with wide joints. The roofs are hand made sand faced tiling, and the plaster-work is left rough from the trowel.'

There was a growing trend for smaller as well as simpler looking homes. Modern young married couples tended to have smaller families and needed fewer servants: some households no longer kept resident staff and managed with external daily domestic help. Bungalows, and semi-bungalows with two or three upstairs rooms became increasingly popular in the early 1910s; they were the forerunners of the countless similar homes built in the twenties and thirties and are often today wrongly dated as having been built in these later decades.

English cottage styles were more popular than ever. The Tudor design, above, was built in North America

There was a growing trend in Britain for smaller middle level homes, bungalows and semi bungalows became increasingly popular

Modern furniture like this display cabinet designed by Ambrose Heal began to anticipate the design developments of the 1920s

The excitement and controversy caused by the wide range of styles for interior decoration in the 1900s calmed down temporarily during the second decade of the century.

Exotic art nouveau which had been considered so daring in the early 1900s was completely out of date in fashionable circles by 1910. Its influence, however, lingered on at a more commercial level throughout the decade. Some manufacturers of furniture, stained glass, household fabrics and light fittings, used art nouveau styling details and colours for many of their standard products, and they were reproduced unchanged for several years.

To fill the void left by the demise from high fashion of art nouveau, avant-garde home-makers took up rather arty and transitory new crazes. The great successes of the Russian ballet inspired extreme fashions in clothes and in interior decoration. The living rooms and boudoirs of the ultra fashion conscious provided suitably stagey backgrounds for showing off the women's lamp-shade tunics worn over tightly draped hobble skirts. Walls were painted in deep rich colours; reds, golds, orange, deep blue and black. Animal skin rugs were strewn on couches and across floors; plain and patterned satin covers and cushions were over decorated with pipings and too many tassels. Deep light shades very similar in shape to the women's tunics were edged with sweeping fringes almost long enough to touch the tops of tables.

Vampish looking ladies reclined temptress-like on silk cushioned couches in these kinds of rooms listening to large-horned gramophones playing the latest tango records while they smoked Turkish cigarettes through long jewelled cigarette holders.

Other style conscious fads for the very fashionable included resurrected neo-classic influences from ancient Egypt, Greece and Rome. Classic columns edged with gilt leaves, friezes of Greek key patterns, torch-like wall lights and Roman couches were all revived.

In Paris the famous dress designer of the period, Paul Poiret, diversified into interior decoration, particularly curtainings and furnishing fabrics. His stylised flower designs and abstract patterns in bold colours appealed to some of the more advanced tastes of the time.

Although there were several new directions in interior design they were rather tentative developments compared to the confidently successful styles of 10 years earlier. The 1910s were in some ways a fallow period for the emergence of strong new design trends for the exterior or the interior of the home. It was exactly halfway between two famous style movements, the art nouveau of the 1900s and the art deco of the 1920s. The trends in designing that were gradually forming just before the First World War did, however, show some of the early characteristics of art deco and helped prepare the way for the acceptance of revolutionary concepts of design in the post-war years.

Also showing anticipation of the design directions of the future was some of the advanced modern furniture of the 1910s; especially some of the pieces produced in England, France, Austria and Germany, known as 'modernism'. The new style furniture was often severely criticised by many of the traditionalists of the time who were wedded to the idea that there could be no acceptable alternative to reproduction furniture based on the designs of earlier centuries.

Modern furniture had a comparatively simple appearance. Tall elongated lines were far less popular; sideboards, wardrobes and cabinets were lower and squatter looking with short legs or concealed stands giving a line flush with the floor. Cupboards and drawer fronts were either square and boxy or curved and rather bulbous; chairs followed similar lines and were deep box shape or round and tubby looking.

The idea that was to be developed so successfully in the later decades of the 20th century of simple unit style furniture sometimes built into rooms as permanent fittings was already beginning to be used by a few very advanced designers. A Paris bedroom and entrance hall designed by Rob Mallet-Stevens in 1913 showed the use of built-in seating units, beds and tables. These functional looking rooms were at least a decade ahead of their time in design concept. The last *Year-Book of Decorative Art* before the war singled these interiors out for special mention in the section on modern French architecture and decoration. 'Amongst the young architects of distinction there is Rob Mallet-Stevens – on journeying through

The eastern-looking lampshade above followed one of the fashionable style crazes of the period

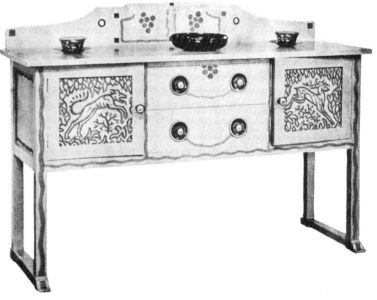

Decorative painting helped to liven up the plainer lines of some of the new furniture designs

The 1910s

Neo-classic themes were popular for the lampshades and bases shown above and on the opposite page at the foot

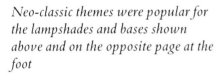

Paris one continually comes across interior and exterior fitments which by their simplicity and personality make it not difficult to trace their origin to his studios.'

In Germany serious attempts were already being made to combine the ideas of progressive modern designers with the needs of industry and its ability to produce and sell at reasonable prices. The Deutscher Werkbund Association who were foremost in this idealistic conception had a membership of over 1000 by 1913. Amongst the many new ideas pioneered through the group working of designers and manufacturers was the introduction of a range of up to about 800 standard modern shapes to cover many kinds of basic furniture. Although standardised they were available in numerous kinds of wood. Permutations in the combinations of the pieces of furniture and the individual arrangement in the home, lessened the possibility

Right, interior designed by Rob Mallet-Stevens in 1913 shows the early 20th Century use of built-in seating units

42

of dull uniformity and had the great advantage of being available cheaply enough for home-makers with modest incomes. The idea of marketing on a large scale a limited, but well thought out, range of home goods proved to be one of the most successful formulas for the rest of the century.

20th century ideas were beginning to show themselves in other areas of home décor as well as in furniture and household fabrics. Ornate metal work had been used in some homes from the mid-19th century onwards. Banisters, fireplaces and light fittings had all reflected many of the trends in interior design; art nouveau had made an especially strong feature of decorative metal work. The use of wrought iron, copper and brass continued strongly in the 1910s and followed the new trend in modern furniture for a neater more compact appearance, The growth in the use of central heating radiators, particularly in design conscious continental Europe, presented a new opportunity for its use. Plain functional radiators were boxed in with decorative metal grills often described in books of the period as 'heating mantles'. The heating mantles were

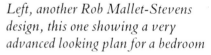

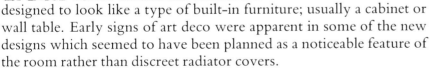

Left, another Rob Mallet-Stevens design, this one showing a very advanced looking plan for a bedroom

designed to look like a type of built-in furniture; usually a cabinet or wall table. Early signs of art deco were apparent in some of the new designs which seemed to have been planned as a noticeable feature of the room rather than discreet radiator covers.

Many surprisingly advanced and progressive ideas relating to the home often credited with starting in later decades had already made their début albeit in a rather diffident way in the years just before the beginning of the First World War.

A large proportion of the general public at the time were quite unaware of the significance or even existence of the developments that were under way and which would eventually affect most of their or their children's homes. The big change from Victorian clutter to lighter less crowded homes was still being assimilated. Many of the homes of the middle aged and older generations had been completely unaffected by all the new ideas and were still solidly late 19th century in their interior decorations and remained so in some cases into the

Above and below, pre-1914 glassware with a distinct look of the forthcoming art deco style

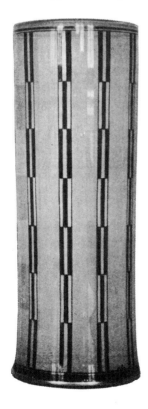

Right, metal radiator cover designed to look like an ornate cabinet

following two decades. Most younger home-makers were, however, following new trends in varying degrees and by the mid-1910s the interiors of their homes were usually lighter in the use of colour, the style of furniture and the number and selection of pictures and ornaments.

Comparing illustrations of middle class homes in 1900 and 1914 the change shows clearly and had been faster moving than in most earlier, comparable periods of time. But the adoption of extreme style in décor or the use of severely modern furniture was very limited. The overwhelmingly popular commercial styles were, as they had been in the previous decade, reproduction designs copied from a wide range of periods from Tudor to late Georgian.

London's well known store, Heal's, who prided themselves on supplying good value quality furniture for the middle classes, produced a brochure advertising reproduction furniture which they ran for several years. It showed about six suggestions for bedroom decorations and furniture each in a different period style. The printed fabrics for the curtains and bed covers were copied from original fabric designs of each of the selected periods.

Heal's extensive and studied approach to the needs of their customers included the equipping of the nursery. Regular catalogues

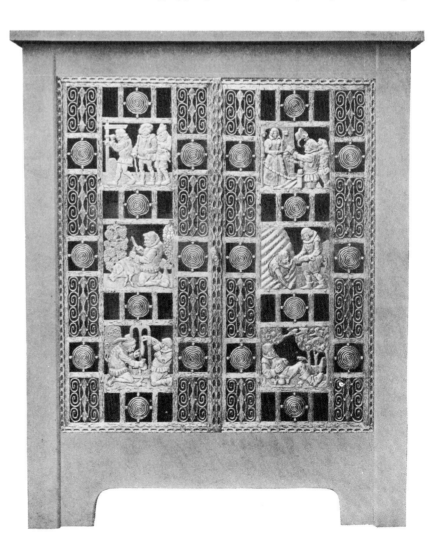

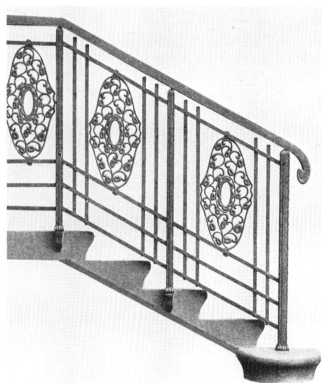

Fancy metal work was sometimes used to make banisters into a fashionable feature in the home

were issued showing children's furniture in a small sized nursery book. In the opening paragraphs tactful reference was made to the change from over-severe Victorian attitudes on upbringing to the more liberal approach to children's formative years that was gaining acceptance in the 1910s. The importance of environment was emphasised. Rooms with a bright aspect were recommended for nurseries, decorated with pale coloured walls and fitted out with Heal's specially designed simple furniture, free from sharp corners for children to knock themselves on and from unnecessary decorations to form dust traps. Simple children's wooden armchairs in oak were offered at 8*s* 6*d* (42½p) each, and a matching style play table for 16*s* (80p).

Homes for the poorer classes showed only a very modest improvement during the first half of the 1910s. There was some speeding up in the building of working class flats and houses, but the availability of a better home was still out of reach for the majority. The desire for a higher standard of living was growing; organised labour became more powerful and radical ideas on the improvement of life for the masses were gaining support amongst members of all classes. Extreme views suggested a major upheaval would be necessary to accelerate social changes. The 1914–18 war proved to be the drastic upheaval that propelled forward such changes.

Apart from those in the immediate areas of fighting, the beginning of the war did not directly affect civilians or their homes. Destruction of property, shortages of consumer goods and rationing came later in the war and were not as severe or prolonged as those of later wars. In the early months many people believed that it would be a short conflict. Men gallantly went off to fight in a foreign country while civilians waited, worried but safely at home.

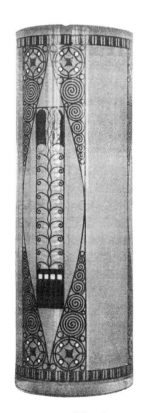

Abstract patterns like these were popular designs for flower vases

Many middle-level homes became less clutterd and favoured the use of lighter colours during the 1910s

Some of the first homes to be affected were the large houses of the upper classes. The casualties in the early major battles of the war were frighteningly and unexpectedly heavy. There were not enough hospitals to cope with the wounded or to accommodate men when they reached the convalescent stage. Many patriotic families with suitably spacious houses made them available for the duration of the war as additional hospitals, convalescent homes or rehabilitation centres. The family either moved out or kept the minimum amount of rooms for their needs.

Within a few months elegant reception rooms which had been used to fashionably dressed women and social chatter were stripped of their furnishings and decorations and crammed with hospital beds filled with wounded men. Stretcher bearers, harassed nurses and busy doctors came and went and anxious relatives visited their husbands and sons. Women members of the families whose homes had been converted often became directly involved in nursing or in the day-to-day running of the hospital or centre and worked unsparingly throughout the sombre war years.

The shelling of homes and the killing of civilians in towns on the south and east coasts of England caused shocks and much indignation from the British public. Although the destruction was light by later standards, the idea that civilians in their own homes could be reachable targets for a foreign aggressor outside the country was something new and horrifying for most people at the time.

The grim realisation of the facts of modern warfare became even more apparent later with bombing raids on London from Zeppelin airships. Air raids were not as heavy or as frequent as the bombardments of the Second World War but they were a feature of wartime life, particularly in London. Windows had to be blacked out at specified times and air raid shelters were made available in underground railway stations and the basements of public buildings and private houses. Signs indicating air raid shelters became familiar in many streets and air raid warnings were given by men on bicycles blowing whistles and wearing 'Take Cover' boards. After the raid 'All Clear' boards were displayed.

Punch made light of the effects of bombing and produced humorous cartoons on the subject. One well-known drawing showed a young officer near the front surrounded by devastated buildings reading a letter from home describing the horror of bomb damage; 'the other day we went to see the ruins of a house which had been bombed by a Zeppelin – you can't imagine what it was like'. *Punch* also produced many sketches showing new problems with domestic staff; the long talked of servant problem became a reality. Cartoons on the subject usually pointed out the new found cockiness and independent attitudes of maids and cooks and the long-suffering acceptance of the changed circumstances by their employers. Coarse looking maids with dominant personalities were shown bossily reprimanding the timid looking lady of the house in her own kitchen for being slow and unhelpful with the housework. Or a maid, well dressed for an interview, would be patronising her potential

Poor homes were often furnished in the most basic way. Following fashion was out of the question for many families

Reproduction style furniture continued to be one of the most successful designs of the period

employer with searching questions about the stylishness of the home and the status of the family.

The acute shortage of servants was caused by the redeployment of labour into essential war work. Men up to middle age volunteered and from 1916 were conscripted into the armed forces; women in the same age group also joined the forces, trained as nurses or worked in armament factories. Members of all classes worked together in a way that would have been inconceivable a few years before; class barriers were not broken down by the war but they were permanently lowered.

The total effects of the war began to be felt in nearly all homes as the conflict dragged on; bereavements were common in almost every street in the country. All the male members of some families from fathers to younger sons were killed. The arrival of a telegram or an official letter was dreaded in many homes and the sight of a telegram boy cycling down a quiet suburban street brought instant fear in case it was bringing bad news to some unlucky family. Newspapers published regular black-edged pages listing the latest casualties of injured and dead; anxious families read them carefully and were temporarily relieved from their anxieties if no familiar names appeared.

Britain as an island began to realise the vulnerability of her supply lines as enemy submarines destroyed a growing number of merchant ships. Essential supplies of raw materials and food were lost or delayed and shortages of all kinds became more severe. Many types of food were erratic in their availability or permanently difficult to obtain; looking for scarce items and queuing for provisions became a part of day-to-day life. It was the limited choice and the poorer and duller diet rather than the lack of food that concerned most families, particularly the comfortably off who were used to an abundance of food before the war. Margarine, which was much less refined than today, often had to be used instead of butter and tinned corned beef substituted when fresh meat was in short supply; this was considered a great hardship by families used to eating far larger quantities of meat than did most later generations. In the last 2 years of the war ration cards were introduced to cover basic items of food and many families turned parts of their gardens into plots for growing vegetables. Lovingly cared for, matured lawns and flowerbeds were replaced by rows of cabbages, cauliflowers and potatoes.

Despite the engulfing atmosphere of wartime life, interest and developments in domestic architecture and interior decoration although greatly reduced did not stop completely. In Britain house and flat building on an ever diminishing scale continued for the first year or two of the war; but the shortage of labour and suitable building materials increased month by month. Later, official restrictions were introduced and activity in domestic building was suspended for the duration of the war.

Slimmed down books and magazines on the home continued to be published. Interest and admiration for traditional English cottages and farms, with their solid local craftsmanship, already strong, intensified still further. The charms of simple cottage life, its harmonious relationship with the land, the joys of closely observing

48

Zeppelin bombing raids were a frightening new feature of the First World War

Opposite
Letters to and from home were an important link for the countless families parted by the war

the passing seasons, were all rapturised over in a romantic and sentimental way. The rosy view of gentle country life was perhaps a natural reaction to living through such a grim period in history.

Any showiness or richness in interior décor was generally considered very inappropriate for the time and often associated with the newly affluent, particularly the much despised war profiteers. When new decorations were done and new furniture bought as necessary replacements, or by newly married couples setting up home for the first time, the styles chosen were usually very low key. Shades of soft greys and blues were the rather appropriate popular colours for walls and furnishing fabrics. Furniture was usually in the simpler styles of period reproduction or designs that were a quiet mixture of period and modern influences.

Ambrose Heal produced some well received designs of this type for the Heal's family store. His designs for display cabinets and dining room suites had comparatively plain lines and often combined mahogany with simple inlays of ebony. Painted furniture was sometimes used to liven up the limited selection of available woods and was especially popular for lighter looking bedroom suites.

There were fewer planned alterations and additions to the inside of houses during the war, but many small unplanned changes reflected the different character of the home. Civilian hats and coats were replaced on hall stands by military caps, steel helmets, trench coats and nurses' capes. Sentimental colour tinted postcards showing soldiers dreaming of wives and children with messages of reassurance written on the back of the card were placed on many mantel shelves, usually next to the photographs of husbands and sons in military uniform. Further along the same mantel shelves rather brutal looking souvenirs from the battle areas were sometimes displayed such as lumps of shrapnel, bullets and parts of enemy shells. More delicate presents brought home by men on leave appeared in other parts of the house and included Belgium lace tablecloths covering family dining tables and French dolls propped on dressing tables and beds.

Children became very war minded: magazines and books were full

Officer at Front (reading letter from home). 'The other day we went to see the ruins of a house which had been bombed by a Zeppelin. You can't imagine what it was like!'

of war stories and illustrations which described great naval confrontations, fierce fighting in the trenches and the daring air battles of the new Air Force pilots. Older boys, particularly those at private schools, were usually in a military cadet force and appeared in uniform regularly. Younger boys loved dressing up in parts of their fathers' and elder brothers' uniforms; over-large helmets, military caps and belts with holsters were worn for boisterous war games which were staged in the home and garden despite protests from weary mothers.

Wives and mothers continually prepared homely and comforting items to send to their husbands and sons at the front. Some knitted garment, a pullover, socks or a scarf were always in production and if the ingredients were available cakes, biscuits and toffees were made specially. Parcels addressed to code numbered sorting offices, waiting to be posted, were a familiar sight on many hall tables.

Apart from the young men who left to join the European war most aspects of life in parts of the world well away from the fighting areas continued as before. Domestic building carried on and in some countries expanded considerably, particularly in North America. America did not become involved in the war until 1917 and, apart from the 2 war years, the 1910s were a progressive and expansive decade for many Americans. There was a growing feeling that a great future lay ahead for the North American continent which was already overtaking Europe in many areas of development.

Cities expanded rapidly and small towns were transformed in less than 10 years into sizeable new cities that were almost totally 20th century in character, and a marked contrast to most European big cities which had changed and evolved over the centuries incorporating their new buildings gradually into an existing pattern.

There was tremendous scope in America for architects and designers; sky-scrapers were multiplying and giving major cities a recognisably American look but the design of the new buildings still lacked a clear cut and impressively modern style. American buildings were known for their tall plain lines but the decorative features used on doors, windows and particularly at the top of the buildings were still inspired by European period designs. Houses also often followed styles already popularised in Europe, especially the English country style. Well-known English architects were commissioned by rich Americans to design impressive English looking homes. Tudor style manor houses with traditional half timbering, tall chimneys and small leaded light windows were built for successful businessmen right across America; they were even popular in the rather alien Californian climate where they were often built as homes for the early film stars. English houses, like English accents and English clothes, were considered to have a special classiness which appealed to many Americans at the time.

Although foreign styles were a strong influence, some types of domestic architecture were already considered traditionally American, particularly wood framed houses and 18th century colonial styles with their wide columned porches and first floor balconies. Colonial type houses of various sizes became a classic American design and have remained so up to the present day.

Many women helped to boost the war effort by working in the armament factories

POST·AND·M^CCORD·
INCORPORATED
·STEEL·CONSTRUCTION·
·ONE·HUNDRED·AND·ONE·
·PARK·AVENUE·
·N·Y·

Left, American cities unaffected by the war were expanding and developing a distinctly 20th Century look

Below, rationing was introduced in Britain during the later war years and shortages of all kinds became a part of day-to-day life

Different styles of balconies and sun porches were a feature of many American homes in the 1910s; most parts of the continent had the climate to enjoy them for several months in each year. After importing so many ideas for the home from Europe, America exported the idea of the glassed-in sun porch to Europe. In countries with fickle summers like England the opportunity to make the most of good weather, however fleeting, proved very popular and glassed-in porches and sun rooms were built in many new seaside houses just before the war.

The insides of prosperous new American homes were more spacious than an equivalent new English house of the period. Rooms were larger and more numerous, grounds and gardens more extensive. The concept of the English middle class home which had been so expansive at the beginning of the century was already contracting and becoming less ambitious; the American home, like the economy of the country, was still expanding.

Towards the end of the war a new idealistic mood for the future

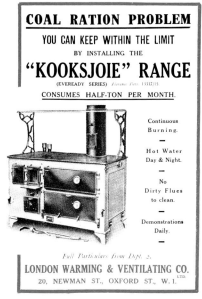

began to develop; a better world, it was thought, would emerge from the ashes of the old. Many people felt a higher standard of living and a good home for all would be a right in the new more enlightened post-war world. Gratitude to all classes for their efforts in the war was strongly felt and 'homes fit for heroes' became a slogan of the time.

In an article written in Britain just before the end of the war 'On designing cottages and small houses', new attitudes towards working class homes were pointed out: 'Foremost among questions needing immediate solution is the provision of dwellings for the workers. The unusual conditions of the past few years have brought many subjects once deemed of little or no importance into great prominence.'

A planned approach to post-war building had been considered essential as early as 1917. The possibility of an acute housing shortage caused by the lack of domestic building during the war and the higher expectations of the bulk of the population in regard to future housing, led to the forming of a special committee in July 1917 headed by Sir John Tudor Walters, MP. The committee was directed 'to consider the questions of building construction in connection with the provision of dwellings for the working classes in England, Wales, and Scotland, and report upon methods of securing economy and despatch in the provision of such dwellings.'

In October 1918 what was known as the Tudor Walters report was presented. Foremost in its findings was the need for 500 000 new homes immediately and to keep pace with demand a further 100 000 new houses annually. These recommendations could not be implemented straight away but they drew attention to the importance of mass housing schemes and successive governments in the twenties and thirties did undertake extensive building programmes.

As well as guidance on general housing policy and much practical advice on finance, the supply of raw materials and the basic types of accommodation required, the report also went into considerable detail on the architectural quality of the proposed new houses. Great importance was given to the desirability of large-scale building blending in with the local countryside and harmonising with traditional regional styles of architecture. A wide range of suitable

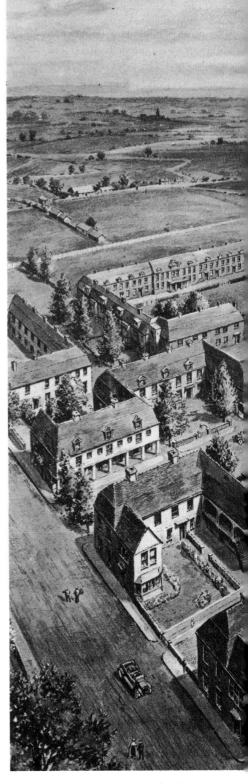

Left, early postwar houses built in concrete tended to look rather like army huts

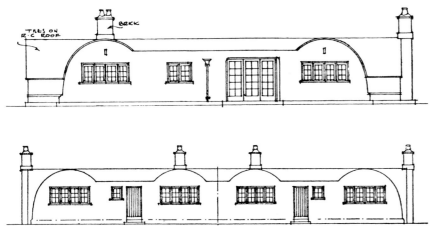

designs based on most of the well-known country styles in Britain was produced as a guide. The high value put on traditional cottage styling was an extension of the fashionable views of the pre-war years adapted to embrace the homes of all rather than the discriminating taste of the few.

On the suggested plans for room lay-out in the new mass housing schemes bathrooms were now always included. Sometimes a bath and wash basin were shown upstairs but many plans, very much in contradiction to the ideas of later decades, put the bathroom downstairs off the kitchen. The advantages in having the bathroom leading from the kitchen were thought to be the easier availability of hot water and the convenience of being able to use the bath for washing clothes. The only lavatory was nearly always placed downstairs and for some unexplained reason it was usually put off a back porch or lobby near the spaces allocated for keeping coal and leaving bicycles. A lavatory that was just inside was perhaps considered a transitional stage for families who had been used to life in a small terrace house built at the beginning of the century where the lavatory was nearly always in an outside building.

People's homes were expected to become more equal in the post-war world; the lower classes it was thought would enjoy larger more comfortable homes and the upper classes would be content with smaller simpler houses. These 1918 views were perhaps a little naïve but they began the trend towards better homes for the majority. The gulf between rich and poor homes started to narrow and although extravagant houses were built in the following decades they were rarely on the pre-1914 scale.

'Reconstruction' was the predominant theme in most parts of the world in 1919. There were many difficulties in reconstruction work during the early post-war years, particularly in Europe where the effects of total war had been severely felt and had left many shortages.

In Britain the housing problem was acute for the middle classes as well as for the workers. Speculative building for the middle market had been limited for nearly 10 years. This was caused by the combined effects of the Land Valuation Act which had depressed private building before the war, and the total stop to domestic house building brought about by the war. At the end of the decade there

Above, an idealistic plan for a postwar development of workers homes set in a pleasant rural landscape. Right, futuristic home designed and built in the mid-1910s and clearly anticipating the styles of the following decade

were simply not enough homes to go round. To aggravate this situation one of the major problems in starting extensive new building was the rapid inflation in costs. In less than five years building materials had risen by between 200 per cent and 600 per cent and labour costs by over 100 per cent. It was estimated that a very modest house built for £250 in 1914 would have cost £1000 to build in 1919. As a further discouragement in the provision of new homes the increase of the Rent Restrictions Act made it impossible to build new houses which could be let at an economic rent.

A home of their own was out of the question for many young couples in 1919 and they had to start their married life with the unsatisfactory choice of either living with parents and in-laws or renting rooms in private houses and possibly facing problems as lodgers, particularly if they wanted to start a family. Changed circumstances and the rather bleak outlook for housing in the early post-war years forced a general drop in the expectations of middle class home-makers. Those who were lucky enough to find and to be able to afford a house or flat were usually content with a considerably smaller, more modest home than they would have been willing to accept before the war.

A basic plan evolved for the lay-out of small post-war semi-detached houses which consisted of two moderate sized living rooms and a kitchen downstairs and two double bedrooms, one single bedroom and a bathroom upstairs. Houses with this accommodation became the acceptable standard sized home for a much wider range of families than ever before and remained so for several decades. The difference between the homes of the classes was still wide but the new working class and the new middle class houses were nearer in size if not in furnishings and equipment. The gap had narrowed although not on the scale envisaged by the idealistic social reformers.

The idea of a small neat house was quite cheerfully received. It was thought to be the realistic answer to the combined problems of shortages and inflation; magazines and books pointed out the advantages of the scaled down home. Less furnishings would be needed, running costs were more manageable, and domestic help could be reduced to the minimum and if necessary done without.

Although equipping the home was not quite as difficult as finding the home, many items were hard to obtain and the quality and selection were often poor. In the first *Studio Year Book of Decorative Art* written after the end of the war plenty of advice on furnishings was offered to people setting up home.

Simple, plainer looking furniture was recommended for the small new homes; design features combined some of the boxy lines of the modern furniture stylists of the 1910s with the influences of traditional country pieces. Cabinets, dressing tables, and chests of drawers had simple panelled doors, functional handles and sensible short or medium length stands and legs. Decorative detailing was confined to discreet inlays or simple raised mouldings and beadings using the same basic wood as the one used for the main part of the piece of furniture. Suggested ideas for chairs and tables were clearly inspired by well-known styles; wooden carver chairs with wide curved arms in the 'Windsor chair' style were very popular. And

drop leaf 'Pembroke' style tables helped to save space in the smaller living rooms and dining rooms.

Simple built-in furniture in the form of sideboards, cupboards and wardrobes was recommended to help make the best use of limited space and also to save money. The alcoves at the side of the chimney breast were considered a particularly good area to box in. The wall at each side of the alcove often did away with the need for a wooden sided piece of furniture. Only the front part of a cupboard had to be built and, for even greater economy, hall and bedroom cupboards sometimes managed with only a front framework of wood, the door areas being filled in with curtains. Curtained cupboards were especially popular for bedrooms; apart from the added storage space, the curtaining for the cupboard, the bed cover and the window curtains were all made in a matching printed fabric. Although basic room colours for walls and carpeting were still rather subdued – soft blues, greys and mauves were still greatly used – printed fabrics had stronger accent colours in the patterns – clear blues, bright greens and orange were all fashionable. To disguise the low grade wood that was available for built-in furniture, cupboards were sometimes daringly painted in a bold colour picked out from the design of the printed fabric used for curtains and covers.

Economy and ingenuity were the practical themes regularly advised on for equipping new homes. Ideas were given to bring what was considered offensively old fashioned furniture up to date; drawings were shown illustrating how thrifty and industrious home-makers could transfer a turn of the century wardrobe which today would be considered a quite pleasant piece of period furniture

A suggested scheme for furnishing a living room in 1919; the impact of the grim war years had fostered a feeling for a quieter and more homely styles of décor

into something more acceptable to 1919 tastes. The following comments and instructions were made: 'The wardrobe illustrated was originally a Curtain Road production of the worst type made in satin walnut, a most unattractive wood. It was adorned with machine carved panels, more dreadful than the drawing would lead one to suppose and the panels had meaningless lines scratched on them. A narrow mirror occupied the place of honour in the centre door and the illustration testifies to the hopelessness of the general proportions. This dubious piece of furniture was taken in hand by the good lady into whose possession it came and she proceeded to see what could be made of it. She first removed the pediment and cut away half the cornice with a saw, reversing what was left, then, removing the drawer at the bottom, she proceeded to saw straight through the sides at a point about a foot from the floor. The mirror was taken out and refixed in the door the reverse way so it was still available for use when the door was open. Finally, two plain panels of wood about a quarter of an inch thick were obtained from the carpenter and nailed over the side panels; another piece with a small moulding worked round served to cover the door. The whole was then papered down and given several coats of white paint.'

The rejection of the styles of furniture popular 15 or 20 years earlier showed clearly how the tastes of the younger generation were becoming influenced by the modern trends in interior design. The scope for developing the new 20th century concepts further was obviously limited just after the war. A potentially receptive market, however, was developing ready for the really dramatic changes of the near future.

The growing feeling of anticipation for exciting new developments was often rather frustrated at the end of the 1910s. Although there was much theorising on the importance of design, and many plans were suggested for large scale domestic building, most of them had to be held in the blueprint stage while shortages and inflation blocked their immediate progress. Impatience at the lack of quick action to ease the pressing housing problems led to some practical suggestions for the speeding up of building programmes even if this meant producing a more basic type of home. One of the ideas promoted was the use of less expensive building materials and methods of construction. Concrete was recommended as an alternative to bricks and stone. The British Government amended the bye-laws which had limited the kind of building materials permitted for use in domestic building and the scope for other kinds of constructions was opened providing they were considered sound. The use of concrete was one of the more practical new ideas.

The concept of a house built from its foundations to the roof in concrete was difficult for many people to accept after centuries of traditional brick, stone and timber building. The public's initial reaction to concrete homes was rather cautious. They were often considered substitute buildings which could be quickly built to serve as temporary homes for a few years until conventional brick houses were available.

Magazine and newspaper articles tried to promote the properties of concrete as a serious alternative to bricks. It was described as being

practically indestructible, fireproof, weatherproof and needing little maintenance. The cost saving advantages were also pointed out. Parts of houses and bungalows for concrete structures were manufactured in a factory and delivered to the building sites for final assembling.

Architectural magazines drew attention to the scope for imaginative design styling, particularly the potential for fashioning and sculpturing into a far wider variety of shapes than would have been possible in the conventional building materials of the time. In practice, most of the early concrete houses lacked design imagination, were rather plain and in some cases almost barrack-like in appearance, especially some of the rows of workers' bungalows. Despite the versatility of the material it did not suit the fashionable cottagey styles which relied on the use of traditional local building materials for their character and charm.

The wider and more successful use of concrete came in the following decade when the distinctive lines of modern post First World War architecture emerged fully. As the century advanced, concrete and concrete type building materials became increasingly important and were eventually used to a far greater extent than brick, stone or wood. The extensive use of easily processed, quick to assemble materials helped to accelerate the growth of cities all over the world and gave them a degree of sameness and even of uniformity on a scale unknown in previous centuries.

By the end of the second decade of the century fundamental changes in the lives and homes of the younger generation had become a reality. Although important changes had been under way for about 30 years, the general acceptance of new ideas had been

The relief at the ending of the war was expressed in dancing inside and outside the home and the dance craze lasted throughout the fun loving 1920s

slow. During the early 1900s life for most people had continued in the 19th century pattern. Prosperous young couples setting up home in the 1900s were very aware of modern ideas of the time and if they lived in the big cities they probably had electric light, possibly a telephone and followed one of the new fashions in interior decoration and furnishings. But the changes in the home were still on a fairly superficial level: the type and size of the home, the number of servants, the ordered day-to-day life and the social activities continued very much as before.

An equivalent young couple in 1919 had a very different approach to home-making; a smaller, more compact. easier to run house or flat was preferred. Electric lighting, the telephone and more modern kitchens and bathrooms were considered priorities. Smaller functional kitchens with gas cookers rather than coal ranges and constant hot water heated by gas were becoming basic requirements for many people.

The accepted good taste for décor and furnishings was far simpler and lighter looking than most people could have envisaged 10 years earlier. The debunking of the design styles of the previous generation had started and the swing away from clutter and overcrowding which had been pioneered by advanced designers and authorities on design for so long had finally become the standard views of most of the modern young generation. Quality rather than quantity became the new approach to decorative objects in the homes of the fashion conscious; there were fewer and more carefully chosen pictures and ornaments. Good simple craftsmanship and design was admired. Pottery bowls and pottery table lamps were popular in many young people's homes.

Although presenting a fashionable home was important to the well-off post-war generation, they were less home orientated than in earlier decades. There were many more distractions to bring people out of their homes to enjoy the liberating post-war atmosphere. Private motoring was increasing quickly and many more people had the opportunity to enjoy a day's outing away from home. Cinemas were multiplying and cinema going became a regular weekly or twice weekly activity. Dancing was becoming more popular than ever: dance halls opened in nearly every town and young people, single or married, loved to dress up in the daring new fashions and dance to ragtime and early jazz music in the exciting, crowded atmosphere of the local dance hall.

Technological progress and social changes already gathering pace in the early 1910s and speeded up by the war, had caused many established ideas on the home and home life to be drastically revised or abandoned by the end of the 1910s. The opportunities for new ideas and completely new concepts on the homes of the future were opening up and preparing the way for one of the most exciting and progressive decades of the century. The ideal for the early post-war home in 1919, considered very modern at the time and greatly changed in one generation, was to be even more quickly outdated by the rapid developments that were to take place during the 1920s.

The 1920s

'The Roaring Twenties' have already been categorised in most of the popular social histories of the 20th century as a party interlude. The decade, in fact, like any other period had its problems and set-backs. Financial insecurity, growing unemployment and political unrest were recurring and unresolved in many parts of the world and spread a certain amount of disillusionment. Despite this many people still believed a better, more progressive world order would eventually emerge. There was a widely held view that mankind had already experienced its 'Armageddon', a terrible holocaust to rid the world of many deep rooted ills, and the recent war was often referred to as having been the 'war to end wars'.

The move towards an ultra-modern new age was reflected in many of the younger generation's homes as the decade progressed. Before the end of the 20s the shedding of late 19th century clutter and stuffiness which had been going on for 20 years was taken further than most people in 1920 would have thought possible. The chilly glitter of the first starkly modern homes emerged. They were unlike anything known in recorded history and had an almost clinical appearance which seemed to anticipate the futuristic 'brave new world' envisaged by modern writers of the time such as Aldous Huxley.

Changes had been slow to take place in the early twenties. The aftermath of the war, shortages and inflation, lingered on for several years and there were few signs of the new developments about to take place. Disappointment with the lack of progress and disapproval of the social shake-up caused by the changed circumstances of the time were expressed in an article written for the important *Decorative Art Year Book* in 1922. 'Among the wealthier section of the community the division of money from the more cultured elements into the pockets of a different class endowed with somewhat crude tastes and a limited appreciation of beauty in domestic environment has introduced a factor seriously inimical to architects and designers generally. It is doubtful whether at any time so little encouragement has been given by wealthy citizens to individual expression or intelligent progressive thought in relation to the aesthetic equipment of the home. On the other hand, the present generation has witnessed the steady growth of an educated middle class with a keen and cultivated appetite for beautiful surroundings but with a purse too slender for indulging its tastes.'

The rather condemning attitude towards the newly affluent sections of society was perhaps over severe and possibly influenced by the general dislike still held for war profiteers.

The redistribution of wealth certainly had an effect on the development of homes in the 1920s. Many of the long established upper class European families had their fortunes and sources of income greatly reduced through sweeping new forms of taxation and the general economic turmoil of the time. Large country estates frequently had to be sold or made over to the state. Town houses were often converted into flats or became lodging houses or small hotels.

In London many of the tall Victorian houses in the dignified squares of Kensington which had been occupied by individual

middle and upper class families until 1914 were changed into a warren of small homes. Each floor was divided into several bed sitting rooms. Young single men and women had their transitory homes next to older people trying to adjust to living in the reduced circumstances of a rented room or rooms. Sedate looking houses which had been used to an ordered day-to-day life were filled with discordant noise: giggling flappers and loud voiced young men played blaring jazz records; they cooked on small gas rings; and they rushed off to parties in open sports cars, slamming doors and revving engines at all hours of the day and night. Older fellow tenants shouted their complaints from upstairs windows and lamented the changes in society, particularly the behaviour of the lively young post-war generation.

Women were gaining a far greater degree of independence and equality mainly as a result of their participation in the war effort. In the changing social pattern of the early twenties some women became less confined to the domestic environment of the home and more involved in the commercial aspects of home-making. Enterprising women with the taste and flair for interior decoration, either through the need to earn a living or the desire to have a career outside the home, set themselves up as interior designers on a fee earning basis.

Many of their clients were the newly rich who lacked impressive collections of pictures and furniture and were uncertain and unformed in their tastes. It was very useful for the socially ambitious to be able to buy the kind of tasteful background that would enhance their position in society through the services of a competent interior decorator.

Home designers did not cater only for the brash new rich; their clientele was quite varied and cosmopolitan. Fashionable post-war society was more fluid and democratic; actors and actresses, sports personalities, musicians and businessmen were accepted by the establishment on a more equal level than in earlier periods – particularly if they were successful, newsworthy and amusing. Many members of the new smart circles often called 'café society' used the services of interior decorators to provide them with the professional's approach to styling the fashionable house or flat of the moment. They believed in consulting respected experts for the design of their homes as well as the design of their clothes. These new, less permanent, attitudes to style-conscious living fitted in with the rather restless brittle atmosphere of the twenties.

The responsibility and commitment to large permanent homes was less popular even for those who could afford to maintain them. People were far more mobile and diversion seeking; they travelled more frequently and further afield. The home bases tended to be much smaller and easier to manage. The ideal for the well-off young English was thought to be a service flat in London W1, a modest country house, preferably old and furnished with genuine antiques – referred to as 'the cottage' – and, to escape the rigours of the English climate, a small Mediterranean villa.

Many of the young middle classes followed in a modified form the bright pert attitudes of fashionable circles. Young women wanted to be freer and less encumbered and cars were a great aid to the more liberated way of life. They were frequently linked to popular types of homes. In a book of the time on modern homes called *The House Desirable* the link between the freedom offered by car owning and the home was described in the following way: 'The young wife of today who is not blessed or cursed with wealth does not pine for a double fronted house larger than that of her neighbours. Her ideal may be described according to the taste and fancy of the describer as a cottage and a car, a bungalow and a Baby Austin, or a maisonette and a Morris Minor. If she lives in the country, she has no desire for three acres and a cow; she would much prefer a quarter acre and a Cowley.'

Architectural styles in the early part of the decade tended to follow in a modified form the designs that were popular just before the war; mainly revived period influences in the country cottage and farm house style or the neo-Georgian town house design. Because of the tremendous increase in costs, the painstaking efforts to give the appearance of authentic Tudor or Stuart buildings usually had to be sacrificed to the needs of economy, and the provision of acceptable new homes took precedence over architectural merit in most of the domestic building of the early 1920s.

Although the general public were still content with the rather commercial use of mock period effects in the design of the exterior of their homes the enchantment with revived styles from the past which had been popular for so many decades was at last beginning to wane with forward thinking designers and architects. The need for a really contemporary style more in keeping with the ideas of the young post-war world was discussed regularly in architectural journals. As early as 1922 a few excitingly modern houses and blocks of apartments were being designed. A plan for a large villa in the South of France by the advanced stylist Rob Mallet-Stevens was an early example of the forthcoming modern styles; it was faced in white rough cast and featured box-like shapes, large windows, flat roofs and stark lines.

In the first half of the twenties changes in interior design were

This drawing from the Sketch Magazine *cleverly contrasted the old world cottage with its thatched roof and the modern woman of the twenties with her new short shingle hair style. The famous Lalique figures in glass like the one below were amongst some of the most appealing decorative objects of the period*

moving much faster than modern developments for exteriors. Style conscious homes already had a recognisably 1920s look. Exotic Eastern influences were popular for reception rooms and boudoirs. Tubby shaped satin covered couches and chairs were piled with varying sized cushions decorated with long tassles; lampshades had complementing tassle trimmings and bulbous fronted cabinets were over decorated with surface designs. The Chinese style was also very popular and ranged from whole rooms decorated and furnished with Chinese designs to the partial use of Oriental themes, mainly lamps, ornaments, wallpapers and furnishing fabrics.

The well known art deco style was at its peak in the mid-twenties; today the term is rather loosely used to bracket together all the new ideas in interior design between 1919 and 1939. The style had been quite well known since the early 1910s and might have become a prominent design movement in the mid and late 1910s if the First World War had not intervened. The important Paris exhibition of decorative arts in 1925 acted as the delayed focal point for art deco and helped to promote and commercialise the style more extensively just as the Paris exhibition of 1900 had popularised art nouveau – another style which had been developing for several years before.

Art deco and art nouveau were both feminine and slightly decadent styles, particularly at home in Paris and very reflective of fashionable life at the time. Art nouveau suited the pleasurable rather languid life enjoyed by the well off at the turn of the century. Art deco could have been the daughter of art nouveau grown up in the unstable jazzy post-war world.

Art deco was less defined in the use of clear outlines and silhouettes than earlier 20th century styles. It relied more on a conglomeration of effects. Colour and patternings were quite dominant and distracting with the use of bold abstract and flat stylised flower designs in vivid colours; orange was a very characteristic colour of the twenties, particularly a deep orange called 'tango'. It was frequently teamed with other strong colours such as bright blue, black or green.

There were more women drivers and they were discovering the freedom and mobility offered by car ownership. Below, detached corner houses at about £1425 freehold, would have been amongst the more superior new suburban homes offered by the speculative builders of the time

Although furniture design had a definite character easily dated to the period, variations in furniture shapes were quite limited. Curved rather squat lines predominated; chairs were usually curve backed with short or medium length legs. Couches followed similar lines or showed slightly fanciful neo-Roman influences with deeply rolled and decorated arm rests. Well-known actresses and vampish looking film stars were often photographed reclining on these kind of couches. Nearby side tables and coffee tables were usually round topped with matching rounded lower shelves. Cupboards and wardrobes often had a low deep set appearance with short, rather stumpy legs or with a base line almost flush with the floor level. The fronts were mostly widely curved and this sometimes gave a rather swollen appearance. Most of the design interest was concentrated on the use of surface decoration; contrasting inlays in wood and exotic looking tortoiseshell and snakeskin were used in expensive modern furniture – particularly in the designs of the fashionable French stylists. Metal work cupboard door handles and short legs fashioned into elaborate neo-classic motifs were sometimes made the eye catching features on some pieces of furniture.

The most appealing and enduring items in the art deco style were the decorative objects. These became such popular collectors pieces

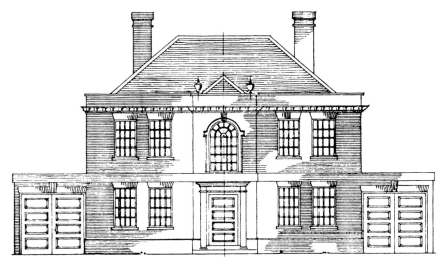

later in the century and for many people captured the light hearted, fun-seeking mood of the twenties more completely than the furniture designs of the period. Bronze or china figures of stylish women with accompanying pairs of elegant dogs, Isadore Duncan inspired neo-classic dancers and nude Olympic style female athletes holding oval lamp fittings were some of the best-known themes for ornaments together with vases and bowls decorated with vividly coloured geometric floral designs in shiny enamelled glazes. Rather more classic in character but very much of the twenties were the wonderful ranges of Lalique glassware.

Colourful jazz-age influences in the home were slow to affect the tastes of a large section of the conservative minded middle level home-makers. Reproduction furniture continued to sell in large quantities to a very receptive market; hefty Jacobean dining room suites were still proudly displayed in suburban houses. Modern trends in these homes were mainly confined to unobtrusive details: lighter colours and patternings in curtains and furnishing fabrics, a few brightly coloured cushions, some fringed lampshades and possibly one or two modern looking figurines or ornaments. The more up-to-date decorative pieces were usually bought as Christmas and birthday presents by well-meaning younger friends and relatives and helped to give some much needed lighter touches to the rather stolid interiors that still predominated in many homes of the period.

During the second half of the decade the long delayed and much needed second building boom of the century finally got under way. Although new homes were built for all sections of society there was less concentration on affluent houses for prosperous businessmen with large families. Clients of this kind were far less evident than they had been during the more expansive 1900s. Speculative builders in the 1920s and 1930s focussed their main attention strongly on the more modest middle market providing homes for men working in fairly secure administrative occupations with small families.

The younger married couples of the twenties were the first generation born and brought up with post-Victorian values and ideas. There had been a certain levelling out in class divisions to form the new middle levels in society. Children from working class backgrounds were better educated than ever before and many more people from modest backgrounds managed to lift themselves above

ELEVATION

FIRST FLOOR PLAN

GROUND FLOOR PLAN

A modest family house still showing some of the country cottage influence in its styling but including the growing requirement of an attached garage

65

Typical jazzy patterning of the twenties

their working class origins. Others, born into prosperous turn-of-the-century businessmen's families, had to lower their aspirations in the unstable economic conditions of the post-war world.

The requirements of the potential clients of the 1920s were different from those of the earlier generation. The carefully regulated incomes in secure occupations and the devaluation of money values through inflation made most of the would-be home-makers extremely budget minded.

Inflation in building costs had reached its peak about 1921; after that it began to fall slightly. By the time large scale domestic building was taking place in the later twenties house prices were estimated to have doubled from their equivalent pre-war values. Prices for three and four bedroomed bungalows and houses ranged from about £750 to £2000. Books were published illustrating the kind of homes available in these price ranges and one well-known publication of the time was entitled *The £1000 House*. During the depression years of the thirties prices dropped further but they never reverted to the pre-1914 levels.

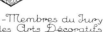

MERCIER FRÈRES
100, faubourg St Antoine
PARIS

Ameublements de Styles anciens & moderne Décoration-Papiers peints Tapis - Lustrerie

Hors Concours - Membres du Jury à l'Exposition des Arts Décoratifs

French interior designs were an important influence throughout the decade. The dining room furniture on the right with its rather squat outlines and lacquered surfaces shows the fashionable design trends frequently used

Many of the young home-seekers of the 1920s and 1930s had been brought up in Edwardian suburbs 5 or 6 miles from the centre of the big cities. These areas which had been thought so pleasant by their parents were already becoming the slightly shabby inner suburbs considered rather old fashioned by the younger generation. They preferred the semi-rural atmosphere of new outlying districts which were developing 10 to 20 miles outside the city centres. Rail services were extending and providing easy access to the outer suburbs; London's Metropolitan Line became one of the best known commuter train services. The new suburbs that sprang up on its outer fringes became rather affectionately known as 'Metroland'.

Metroland homes and home life had a special character which typified, and was unique to, modest middle England, half way between the two World Wars. Quiet tree-lined streets were edged with small detached and semi-detached villas with mock timbered upper stories, sloped cottagey roofs and leaded light windows. The general public had grown so accustomed to period style details in domestic architecture that most people tended to think of them as pleasant contemporary house designs rather than a haphazard mixture of styles from earlier centuries. Nearly all the large scale new housing developments followed very similar styles of design and types of accommodation; rooms were usually fairly small and a typical house plan had two modest sized living rooms, a kitchen, one bathroom and three or four bedrooms. Although there was a considerable amount of uniformity in the vast numbers of speculative builders' houses, subtle differences were noted and considered important by their early occupiers. Behind the bland almost identical exteriors there was sometimes a certain amount of petty snobbery and rivalry between neighbours over home details. A detached house, particularly a corner property with slightly more garden, even if it was very close to other houses, was considered much superior to semi-detached villas. Exact details of the size and

DANS UN BOUDOIR

Manufacturers reduced the size scale of their popular styles of furniture like this Jacobean dining room suite to suit the smaller living rooms of the new suburban houses

numbers of rooms were closely compared. A kitchen large enough to eat in – often rather grandly called 'the morning room' – and a small adjacent back kitchen, was rated more highly than one all-purpose working kitchen. Four bedroomed houses were thought more impressive than three bedroomed ones and three fair sized rooms definitely a cut above two bedrooms and a tiny possible third bedroom, usually described as a box room. A garage or room for a garage and the amount of garden were all further points taken into consideration when assessing the precise status of the home.

Small houses, almost indistinguishable in appearance from the other houses in the same street, were sometimes given rather unsuitable but impressive sounding names which were written on the front gates instead of the usual street numbers. Some suburban wives married to quite modest office personnel ordered items in local stores and shops to be delivered to 'Greenwood' or 'The Elms'. Later, bewildered delivery boys searched for the high sounding names amongst the rows of numbered suburban houses.

The interiors of many of these small homes still tended to follow the ideas and the size scale of the furniture which had been used in the larger family houses of the 1900s and early 1910s. The two small living rooms of the new houses were still usually furnished and decorated as a defined drawing room and dining room. Drawing rooms featured a display cabinet for showing prized ornaments and china, a piano and a large three-piece suite covered in patterned upholstery or loose, plain or printed fabric covers. Dining rooms had a heavier more solid appearance; the walls of modest sized rooms about 14 or even 12 feet square were sometimes panelled with real wood or a simulated wood panel wallpaper and furnished with a sturdy sideboard, dining table, matching chairs and leather armchairs. The size and amount of furniture used in many homes was too overpowering for the proportions of the rooms and furniture manufacturers were slow at first to adapt their designs to fit the growing popularity of houses with lower ceilings and fewer and smaller rooms. As the Metroland type of home multiplied all over Britain, manufacturers revised the design and size of many types of furniture. Some of the more progressive firms such as Heal's and Liberty's produced special ranges of quietly modern simple furnishings very suited to the new homes of the late 1920s. Other less enlightened furniture makers simply reduced the size of their well known reproduction styles; Jacobean dining room suites, Queen Anne walnut bedroom sets, bulbous armchairs and couches plus a wide range of old worldy cupboards. Dressers and chairs were made available in several different sizes.

Adaptations and modifications of traditional styles of interior decoration were still followed by a large proportion of the population; fashionable new styles were only adopted by a comparatively small fashion conscious minority. The search for a truly modern 20th century style had been only partly successful until the late twenties. Germany had been a pioneer in the modernistic movement and the famous Bauhaus group of designers formed just after the war developed a new rather purist approach to interiors. Extreme simplicity in design, emphasis on the functional aspects of

A very modern dining toom of the later twenties featuring the new tubular steel furniture

Plan your Kitchen by "UNITS"
and put the walls to work!

The kitchen unit, so usual in homes during the later decades of the century was a very advanced idea in the twenties

the home and the use of materials such as tubular steel and leather gave the new designers' work a starkly modern style. This was excitingly progressive to some of the young generation but very unsympathetic to the established ideas of many older people who condemned the revolutionary ideas for homes as strongly as they did the brief simple lines in fashionable clothes.

Punch cleverly illustrated the extremes in popular taste with a drawing showing two living rooms in a fairly standard block of flats, one was still completely late Victorian, heavily overcrowded with furniture, draperies, pictures and knick-knacks. A plumply rounded elderly couple sitting contentedly in the room were dressed in the covered up clothes belonging to the same period as the room decorations. The other living room was self-consciously modern with almost bare walls, tubular steel furniture and a youngish couple wearing the modern fashions of the twenties and smoking through long cigarette holders.

The completely different concept of the new homes of the later 1920s was very controversial and keenly discussed and debated. Many articles were written expressing the new ideals which were becoming known as 'The New Movement'. Some of the advanced views were described in the following way: 'The house of the future will be judged on a rational basis by its utility and convenience, by the degree of comfort it provides and the success with which it meets our needs and not by any superficial resemblance to a Jacobean manor house or other product of a past age. Its furnishings will be determined by common sense which is the essence of good taste and fitness for purpose which is the basis of all sound design. These are

Many comfortable middle-level living rooms like this one showed only slight influences from the fashionable styles of interior décor

the principles which animate the architects of the new school who seek to achieve their purpose by making use in a perfectly rational manner of the whole technique and resources of modern science and by freeing themselves from the servitude of ancient styles and using these methods to create a style suited to our needs and characteristic of the age.'

The reaction away from revivalism which had been developing for several years was firmly expressed, and represented a dramatic rejection of the much loved period styles which had been so highly praised 10 years earlier. The debunking of revising the styles of the past was pointed out clearly in another article at the time: 'Plagiarism amounts to a confession of incompetence; to copy the productions of historic periods is not to maintain the traditions of those periods which were in no sense opposed to rational change. For generations we have been false to the fundamental principles of good architecture and have abused a fine heritage. We are not even content with copies of old buildings as they originally appeared but set about to reproduce by artificial means the tones and textures imparted by age. Old world effects beloved by house agents have a high market value. We love an atmosphere of mellow age slightly tinged with decay, and if we cannot secure the genuine article we contrive spurious imitation. It is only when we enter our garage that for a time we are content with reality, with clean honest design and healthy aesthetics.

Garden chairs were often designed in the fashionable tubby shape

Contrasting colour inlay, worked into a step effect gave a simple decorative motif to the plainer lines of some of the modern furniture

So far we have not attempted to design our cars in imitations of Roman chariots. The new architectural movement which superficially seems to be such a violent departure from precedent is actually more closely related to the best traditions of the past than the meaningless compromises and dishonest practices of the period from which we are now slowly emerging.'

The modernistic houses and flats of the 1920s owed nothing to the styles of the past and were at last totally expressive of their own time. Constructions of concrete and concrete with brick were widely used and helped to fashion new and imaginative shapes in domestic building. The scope for imaginative design which had been suggested in the previous decade was developed far more extensively. The new homes had a frank open appearance with plenty of wood or steel framed windows in various shapes and sizes. Windows that curved round the corners of buildings were a much used feature; sun balconies and flat roofs for sun bathing or for city roof gardens added to the light outward-looking character of the new homes. Buildings were usually a combination of varying-sized box and cylindrical shapes. Houses and blocks of flats with curved porches, balconies and rounded – instead of squared off – edges often looked rather like a passenger ship of the period and were sometimes described as being in 'the ocean liner style'.

Uncompromisingly modern domestic buildings were more popular in continental Europe than in Britain. French versions, although not as purist in style, were slightly less stark and masculine than were German designs and looked particularly good in the warm sunny environment of the French Riviera. The new shapes looked more alien and far less at home in the British Isles where they were mixed in with traditional domestic architecture or standing in the soft countryside under rainy skies. Although not as well received generally as in some parts of the world, very good examples of modernistic architecture were built in Britain and greatly praised by the young devotees of the modern movement.

The insides of the new homes were as revolutionary as the outside designs. Every aspect was modern and different. Interior walls were free from any decorative moulding; they were either flat surfaced or rough cast and painted white or cream. Window frames were plain and functional, often in metal and sometimes left uncurtained or hung with unobtrusive light coloured blinds or very simple curtaining. Some homes, particularly flats, did away with the idea of a fireplace and relied for heating on radiators or a simple modern electric fire set in the wall. When fireplaces were used, designs followed the boxy or curved shapes of the modernistic style and dispensed completely with any kind of overmantel. Expensive fireplaces were fashioned in stone or marble and some designs had very understated design features such as a few rows of simple mouldings or a graduated step or sun ray effect at each side. Wooden slatted banisters, even of the most simple kind, were replaced by plain or curved boxed-in sides topped with a plain metal or wood hand rail. Some homes had art deco style metal banisters as a feature to relieve the starkness of the ultra-modern interior.

There was much use of built-in furniture; plain surfaced built-in

A high fashion design for a study in 1927, with glossy veneered wood and angulars shapes

wardrobes in bedrooms and a range of wall cupboards in dining rooms did away with the need for matching suites of furniture. Built-in bookcases were very popular, usually table high and designed with either the fashionable step effect or curved sweeping lines at each end. Wall pictures which had been in such profusion at the beginning of the century and steadily losing favour ever since reached a record low in popularity with the arrival of the ultra-modern styles of interior decoration. They were sometimes banished altogether and replaced by a few large unframed oblong or oval mirrors.

In the plain unadorned shell of the new homes, pieces of furniture stood out and became the focus of attention. Designers were committed to the idea that furniture must be predominantly functional, free from any trace of earlier periods and extremely sparing in the use of decorative effects. Metal, particularly steel, was one of the most modern materials used by the designers of the 1920s for glass-topped tables, bookcase units, simple all-purpose upright chairs and leather covered easy chairs and couches. Some of these designs have become 20th century classics and are reproduced today unchanged from the original styles of over 50 years ago; their ultra-simple lines have a dateless modern quality that appeals to many young people in the 1980s as strongly as it did to the 'bright young things' of the 1920s.

Stark functional interiors furnished with steel, glass and leather, although considered the ultimate in modern homes, were too uncompromisingly futuristic for most people. Many of the progressive young generation admired and appreciated the new revolutionary movement in design in an objective way but were not ready to live with it. They still preferred home surroundings that were a little softer looking. The warmer appearance of wooden furniture appealed to their less austere tastes.

The newer designs had shed the over-elaborate surface decoration of the typical art deco style of a few years earlier and concentrated on a more subtle approach to design, still very modern in concept but more traditional in the use of craftsmanship and materials. Light woods, sycamore, walnut and bleached or silvered oak were especially popular and helped to emphasise understated design styling and the reduced size of most pieces of furniture. Dining room suites, desks and wardrobes were boxy looking but less hefty and bulbous. Octagonal shapes were used for low tables; tiered step effects were featured on cupboards, bookcases and dressing tables which had three-quarter or full length mirrors centrally placed and deeply stepped down from various heights and sizes of shelves at each side. Other dressing tables had large circular mirrors set above a shallow flat-topped chest of drawers shape; rather squat looking matching stools made to an appropriate height for the dressing table mirror were available with most sets of bedroom furniture.

Ebony edgings on light wood, or whole pieces of furniture made in rosewood or lacquered wood gave similar basic designs a much more formal urban look, popular with people who wanted their homes to have a richer, less casual appearance.

Glamorous Hollywood homes and film sets used highly glossed furniture, particularly lacquer, to give an ultra sleek background for the modern sophisticated life style portrayed on and off the screen by the famous film stars of the time. Immaculately dressed women and men with neat brilliantined hair styles sipped their cocktails in rooms furnished with skyscraper-style tiered bookcases and cabinets made in toning coloured lacquer or in a single strong colour such as red edged with shiny black. The use of strong contrasting colour was especially effective for tables and desks with boxed in sides and low shelves.

By the late 1920s many of the prosperous young generation in western Europe and North America had not only become very fashion conscious in the presentation of their homes but also receptive to the idea of changing the style of décor every few years. They were influenced by the home background shown in films, advanced furniture designs and the well known interior decorators who set many of the popular style crazes. Syrie Maugham, wife of the famous author Somerset Maugham, was one of the best known decorators of the decade and helped to promote the idea of the luxurious modern house with all-white rooms. In some of her planned interiors not only were the walls and the modern furniture white but period tables and chairs were also disrespectfully coated with white paint to give extra impact to the overall composition of the room.

Enterprising departmental stores, realising the potential for faster changing fashions in home furnishings amongst the growing numbers of style-conscious young people who could not afford the

services of well-known interior designers, opened new departments featuring the work of respected stylists. Paris stores did this particularly well; Paul Follot worked for Bon Marché and Marcel Dyfrere for Galleries Lafayette.

Although the overall trend for interior decoration had become progressively more simple as the decade progressed, bathrooms were given far more attention than in the early decades of the century. In some wealthier homes they were often made a luxury feature with sunken baths, showers and elegant pedestal-style wash basins. Marble was widely used and large fashionably styled mirrors and suitably modern light fittings made some bathrooms the most design conscious room in the home.

Electricity had become the predominant form of lighting by the end of the decade and electric light fittings were newly important and noticeable features in many homes. Designs followed all the popular style directions; centre ceiling lights were often suspended by metal rods with the bulbs encased in one simple square or oval holder or in a more elaborate group of globe or box-like shapes. Wall lights, instead of, or as well as, a centre light, made in modernistic designs, were very characteristic of the late twenties. With the sharp decline in the use of pictures in many fashion conscious homes, there was plenty of scope for light fittings to be made the most important wall decoration. Oblong, fan and shell shapes in engraved, tinted or enamelled glass, held by silver metal holders were amongst the most popular shapes.

Table lamps varied considerably in style; in the early part of the decade many designs were over fussy with ornate metal work bases

The Mediterranean style villa was a popular influence on some of the more expensive domestic buildings of the twenties and thirties

and busily printed silk shades edged with fringing and tassles. Later, as plainer interiors became more general, lamp stands and shades were simplified; pleated linen or silk shades topped a more classic type of glass, china or pottery base. The most dramatic change in lamps was seen in the designs influenced by the severely modern style: low, squat undecorated shapes had square or octagonal panelled glass shades; or tube like strips of lighting were set starkly on metal frames which were fashioned into a variety of angular shapes.

The details of day-to-day life and equipment in the more progressive homes of the 1920s altered as much as the buildings and their furnishings. Manufacturers made the general public very aware of the much wider range of home appliances that were available with extensive promotional campaigns. Advertisements changed their style and emphasis; serious looking maids portrayed conscientiously cleaning heavily furnished, dark rooms with cumbersome equipment were replaced in advertising pictures by bright, carefree-looking young housewives vacuuming cheerful, less cluttered rooms or cooking happily in more modern kitchens on neater gas or electric cookers.

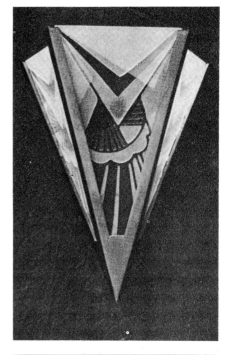

Attitudes towards food and cookery, particularly amongst the younger generation, changed; meals tended to be lighter, with fewer courses than the very ample quantities which had been served in the homes of many of the previous generation. People cared more about keeping their weight under control; they were more involved in active sports; the straight, flat lines of fashionable women's clothes required a very slim figure to be shown off to advantage. In Britain the traditional cooked breakfast was still general but the amount and selection of breakfast foods were usually smaller. Housewives, especially those without domestic help, were less prepared to be housebound by hours spent catering for the family and began the trend towards a simplified approach to preparing meals. There was less home baking; bread and other prepared foods were more frequently bought in and the availability of a wider selection of tinned food increased.

Domestic staff was still quite easy to obtain compared with the later decades of the century but the number of people prepared to work 'in service' had decreased considerably since 1914. Bulk manufacturers of every kind of home appliance concentrated on the young middle-level home with little or no domestic help. The new home equipment was beginning to have a clearly 20th century appearance. Electric refrigerators, washing machines, irons, kettles and sewing machines were all available for those who could afford them and were increasing in popularity each year. They were, however, expensive in relation to most people's earnings; a comparatively small electric fire cost £4 in 1925, higher than the average weekly wage of the time. The era when wide ranges of electrical equipment were taken for granted in most homes still lay in the future.

Apart from improved stoves and refrigerators, storage space in modern kitchens was revised and adapted to suit the smaller room sizes that were becoming general in most new homes. Rows of

Left, modernistic styling was very evident in these light fittings of the late twenties

built-in cupboards replaced pieces of kitchen furniture and magazines began to describe planned ranges of cupboards as 'units'.

The dressing table became the focal point in the modern woman's bedroom of the twenties. Although still sometimes disapproved of by the older generation, cosmetics were freely used by the young and women talked about 'putting their face on' before going out. The dressing table was a kind of shrine to the new artificial beauty: perfume bottles, scent sprays, face powder boxes, compacts and lipstick holders were all designed with great care and were strongly influenced by art deco patterns or the sleek modernistic style. Famous design names such as Lalique were sometimes commissioned to design bottles for expensive perfume. Many of these are now much sought-after collectors' pieces together with 1920s dressing table sets of matching mirrors, brushes and combs. These personal items, once used by flighty young flappers as they prepared themselves for an evening out, have a rather poignant, nostalgic appeal for the later generations of the century.

Punch showed drawings of women making up heavily in front of their long or circular mirror dressing tables with tolerant husbands or fascinated small children watching the ritual. One drawing from a 1927 *Punch* showed a shorn-headed, very modern mother made up ready for the evening ahead and a rather angelic looking small boy who had come to kiss his mother goodnight and reacted with the following comments: 'Well, goodnight, Mummy dear. I hope you'll enjoy your party. I can't kiss you because I've just had my bath.'

Applying make up became a new time consuming ritual in many homes

The 1920s

Gramophones, although available since the early years of the century, became far more general in the homes of the twenties. Elaborate cabinet sets designed like a piece of reproduction furniture were still expensive but there were many more reasonably priced, smaller, functional table models with wind-up handles. It was a great dancing age; the post-war generation, possibly as an expression of relief after the horrors of war, seemed determined to have a good time and to start dancing on the slightest pretext. The new dances, the Shimmy, the Black Bottom, and the most characteristic dance of the 1920s, the Charleston, were often practised at home, so that a competent standard could be reached before performing them in public. Social dancing to the gramophone was also popular in the home; friends who dropped in for cocktails or stayed to dinner were encouraged to dance to the latest 'divine' Cole Porter, Gershwin or Layton and Johnson record. Hits like 'My Blue Heaven' and 'Ain't She Sweet' disturbed quiet suburban streets and gardens on summer evenings as young revellers requested them again and again.

The 1920s marked the beginning of the family radio in the home. In the early years of the decade radios were still considered a novelty, being crystal sets and usually called 'the wireless'; broadcasts were listened to through earphones attached to the receiver. By the second half of the decade box-shaped table models had dispensed with the need for earphones and listening to the radio was becoming a part of everyday life in some homes. News bulletins, sports commentaries and dance music were followed regularly by the whole family. In Britain, the evening's broadcasting usually ended with dance music relayed direct from a well known restaurant or dance hall. London's famous Savoy Hotel was well known for its resident dance band and listeners were told they were being taken live to hear the music of the 'Savoy Orpheans'.

Made contented by
Western Electric
MODERN DOMESTIC APPLIANCES

Radio cabinets, unlike most of today's radios, were not designed as an unashamedly modern piece of equipment. The early sets were encased in a wooden shell designed to complement the general style of popular furnishings; various kinds of wood and mixtures of wood were available enabling people to choose a radio that blended in with their furnishings. Custom built radio cases were sometimes made to ensure an exactly matching style, such as a radio set in a Chinese lacquer casing to match a Chinese-style drawing room. Portable radios, rather like a box-shaped suitcase, were on the market by the late twenties and were regularly advertised in women's magazines as an ideal Christmas or birthday present for the fashionable young woman. Illustrations showed stylishly dressed women proudly carrying their portable radios as they arrived to visit friends for the evening or left their homes for a weekend in the country.

Home entertaining on a grand scale with many servants in attendance still continued in the years between the World Wars but on a far smaller scale than in the early years of the century. Difficult economic conditions made it impossible for many upper class households to entertain their guests in the lavish style of the previous generation. The trend throughout society was for smaller scale homes with minimum domestic help; large luncheon parties, formal dinners and elaborate receptions and balls were replaced to a great extent by much smaller, more informal parties.

The early evening cocktail party became a favourite form of entertaining. It was easy to arrange, economical in cost, and a considerable number of friends and acquaintances could be packed into the smaller rooms of the modern houses and flats. People expected a successful cocktail party to be noisy and crowded and to have an interesting cross-section of guests. As well as the organised party many fashionable homes had a specially designed cocktail cabinet or cocktail bar. Cabinets were in one of the popular styles in wood furniture or in modernistic mirror-glass and metal. The insides of the cabinets were often lit and the carefully planned range of shelves and racks for glasses and bottles were neatly displayed. The cocktail bar was a miniature version of a hotel bar with a counter in front and rows of bottles, lights and various styles of mirrors or a modern mural behind. Guests sat on high stools while their host prepared the popular cocktails behind the bar. They were often American inventions; 'A Side Car' or a 'Screwdriver' was mixed in a metal cocktail shaker and being able to prepare a really professional drink, properly shaken, like an experienced bar tender, was considered a great social accomplishment by the young people of the time.

Children's lives altered in the modern homes of the twenties. Young parents felt they were more enlightened in their approach to bringing up a family; discipline and fixed ideas on self-improvement were not as rigorously enforced; natural self-expression began to be encouraged. Children's day-to-day life was still simple and unsophisticated by later standards but the drift towards manufactured entertainment started. A steadily growing number of children listened regularly to the radio and gramophone; special children's programmes and gramophone records including the early self-

"It plays even as you carry it about . . ."

teaching foreign language 'Linguaphone' records were produced for the young. It was the first 20th century generation to have its early entertainment and instruction recorded and preserved for posterity.

There were more mechanical toys and families went out of the home more frequently for group activities and entertainment. City children enjoyed day trips into the countryside in the early motor buses; impressive looking public swimming baths built in the modern architectural styles were opened in many towns; and an ever increasing number of children were allowed to go to the cinema regularly to follow the adventures of their favourite hero or heroine in the latest episode of one of the long running serials especially made to appeal to young imaginations. Possibly because most families consisted of fewer children than their Edwardian counterparts, everyday life became less closely home orientated. External youth organisations provided the variety of company less readily available at home. Cadet forces, Boy Scout and Girl Guide groups began to have an increasing influence on children's lives and attitudes particularly in countries where growing State control and authoritarian regimes sometimes instilled political ideals at an early age.

The benefits of an outdoor life became more highly valued as urbanisation spread further into the countryside. During the building boom of the inter-war years, more people than ever before wanted a home with its own garden. But with the high cost of land suitable for domestic building speculative developers, in an effort to keep the price of new houses competitive, had to keep garden space to the minimum acceptable size. More homes had an individual garden but

Gramophones like this £50 cabinet model would have been considered an expensive luxury by most people

the average size was even smaller than the area around most of the homes built during the earlier building boom at the beginning of the century, particularly the space allocated for middle level houses.

Styles for gardens often reflected the fashionable house designs of the period. Cottage looking homes usually had complementary countrified gardens with crazy-paved paths, rose bushes and rockeries. Sundials were very popular and were usually made a centrally placed feature. Householders sometimes enlarged the deep country influence with small summer-houses and children's play houses rather whimsically called 'Wendy houses' designed as miniature versions of the main house; some homes went even further and disguised the garage in a cottagey shell and added still more twee touches with bird houses dotted about the garden.

In complete contrast to countrified old worldliness, the flat roofed large windowed modern houses were set in simple lawns with wide paths, cleanly paved courtyards and disciplined flowerbeds. The luxury feature in the grounds of these homes, particularly in warm climates, was one of the new status symbols, a swimming pool.

Two homes, a country house and a town house, had been an established way of life for the upper classes for many generations; during the 19th century the prosperous middle classes had also frequently become two home families and going to the country for the weekend became the accepted routine for many of the well off. The social shake up caused by the First World War and the financial insecurity which followed it meant some families could no longer afford to maintain two substantial properties; the style of one, or both, often had to be modified, with a flat instead of a town house and a cottage home replacing the large country house.

In contrast to the reduced circumstances of many of the upper classes, some middle level business and professional men together with those in certain administrative occupations became rather more prosperous and found they could afford a modest second home. Artisan style cottages were bought or rented and rashes of impermanent looking wooden bungalows were built dotted along the coastline or sprawling out from seaside resorts. The steadily increasing numbers of car owners brought new opportunities for family life; quiet country and seaside areas were invaded by weekend visitors from the city on a scale previously unknown. Modern motorways did not exist and narrow lanes and country roads built for occasional horse traffic were filled in the summer months with wide-bodied cars, hefty vans and motorbikes with attached sidecars. The first generation with mobility on a mass scale had arrived together with one of the unresolved and recurring problems of the 20th century, the traffic jam.

Schemes to provide new homes for the poorer sections of society fell short of the demand but they did improve more quickly than in the 1900s and 1910s. The idealistic concept of a good basic standard of housing for all as a right, which had been so earnestly expressed at the end of the war, faded a little as the years advanced. Most governments, however, remained committed to raise living standards for the working classes and radical political parties who campaigned for better housing gained mass support in many

Parties, dancing and following the latest fashions were an enjoyable way of life for many of the well off young generation

countries. Blocks of state-owned flats were built in increasing numbers. Although they were usually devoid of any unnecessary and expensive decorative features and had a fairly plain appearance which identified them as government-commissioned domestic buildings, they were often set amongst lawns and trees and were carefully planned by competent architects. The simple clear-cut designs compared favourably with some of the more haphazard developments of private housing and flats put up by speculative builders. Some of the better examples of state housing were proudly displayed by governments as the future pattern for workers' homes.

Blocks of state flats were not as popular in Britain as they were in other countries with a longer tradition of apartment living. Most British families were pleased with a new flat as an alternative to older, more dismal, accommodation but, given the choice, many preferred a council house with its own garden. Large estates of simple cottage-style houses were built all over the country; many of these small houses were well maintained by the tenants with lovingly cared for gardens which often had a small section for growing vegetables. Working class children brought up in the better environment of the new housing estates had a healthier and more outgoing start to life than earlier generations who had been confined to the poor inner city districts.

As well as the pleasure of an individual garden, the inside accommodation in the new council houses also represented a big improvement in living standards for most of the tenants. Furnishings and home equipment were still simple and basic compared with many middle class homes, but light rooms and a small modern kitchen and bathroom for each family was a great progression from the poor tenement blocks and terraced houses with their cramped conditions and outside lavatories which had been the predominant style of homes for the lower classes until the 1920s.

Britain's power and influence extended over several hundred years and reached its peak during the 19th century. Britain and British ways were emulated all over the world: its influence ranged from the organisation of armies and industry to social behaviour patterns, styles of dress and types of homes and home life.

North America, with its great resources, drive and vitality, started to catch up with Britain and western Europe early in the present century. The First World War left the old world weakened and in disarray; by the the mid-twenties America had taken the lead and from then onwards became the predominant country of the century. American influences were as widespread in the following decades as British ones had been in the previous century.

During the 1920s the general level of home equipment in America was already considered the most advanced in the world. The design evolution of modern appliances, refrigerators, washing machines, gramophones, radios and types of central heating were developed and improved each year. American products were exported all over the world despite the high cost of some types of equipment to the public in countries with weak economies and currencies. Modern appliances were used in a far wider cross-section of homes in America; the post-war boom was stronger and more enduring than in most parts of the world. Standards of living rose more quickly, wages were higher for comparable jobs and class distinction did not impede personal advancement.

European styles of architecture and interior decoration until the early decades of the century had been adapted to suit American climatic conditions and ways of life; this had gradually changed, and by the 1920s a very distinct American range of homes had emerged and became one of the strongest influences on the homes of the future.

American cities, particularly New York and Chicago, were already definitely 20th century in character, with high-rise buildings which were multiplying every year. Visitors from abroad still usually arrived by boat and were always impressed by their first sight of Manhattan's rising skyline, and the unfamiliar impact at night of hundreds of lighted windows shining from the many tall tower-like blocks.

Home in a high apartment was quickly becoming the established way of life for many New Yorkers. There were many more purpose-built blocks than in other major cities and the new homes catered for a very wide range of requirements and income levels. For the single person, or the newly-married couple living on a small budget, there were one-roomed apartments with a small kitchen and bathroom. Sleeping accommodation was provided with couches that were designed to convert into a bed or a ready-made-up bed which looked like a wall cupboard until it was pulled down to reveal the stored bed. Floor space in the fashionable districts of the inner city was expensive; only the affluent could afford roomy homes. Fashionably decorated penthouses with elegantly curved staircases down which stylishly dressed hostesses made their well-timed entrances to greet guests before directing them onto large balconies or roof gardens with panoramic city views, usually belonged only to the rich and successful.

In nearby poor apartment blocks, flat roofs were also used for summer life; tenants, made uncomfortable by the humid oppressive atmosphere in their small closed-in homes, shared the very basic communal area on top of the building with their neighbours. Although the settings were very different from the well cultivated

High rise apartments and traffic-filled streets had already become familiar to New Yorkers by the late twenties

and maintained gardens and balconies of the penthouses the views were just as impressive.

On the opposite side of the continent in California, well-publicised houses in a variety of styles were built at great expense for the film stars and the powerful film moguls. Style influences for these homes were taken from many different parts of the world and periods in history. Colonial style mansions with columned fronts, Ruritanian castles, old English Tudor manor houses and whitewashed Spanish haciendas were all near neighbours in the fashionable residential districts of Hollywood. Spanish style houses were the popular newer designs of the time; they had roughcast walls, curved arches and made much use of wrought iron for balconies, window grills and high gates inside and outside the house. Stabling, tennis courts and swimming pools were considered standard features in these homes and glamorous parties were often held round the swimming pool; lunches, cocktail parties and candle-lit dinners were all popular in the new élitist world of the Hollywood film makers.

Despite set-backs and instability the 1920s was in retrospect one of the more progressive and carefree decades of the century. Types of homes and ways of living that are still followed today over 50 years later had arrived in the twenties; small easy-to-manage homes and labour saving equipment were all considered important then as they are today.

The general public were very aware of the big changes in the progressive homes of the time and many of the new ideas were adapted by the prosperous in major cities all over the world. The cinema had become a very important influence and all sections of society saw the portrayal on the screen of the modern style home even if they had no prospect of living in one. Modernisation was very gradual for modest homes in most countries; it was still far too expensive for the masses.

The most confident mood for the future was in the late twenties; even some of the countries which had been through a period of great political and economic upheaval had a brighter spell. America was enjoying a buoyant phase and many people felt that at last the world was getting on course for a more progressive age with sustained industrial expansion, higher living standards and better homes. The Wall Street stock market crash in October 1929 and the collapse in world trading conditions that quickly followed it marked the abrupt end to post-war optimism and ushered in a very different more serious decade which was to be an odd mixture of progress and retrogression in many areas including the home.

The 1930s

The distinct change of character from the 1920s to the 1930s was far more speedy than is usual at the turn of a decade. It was caused mainly by the onset of the Great Depression which coincided exactly with the year 1930. The altered mood and the feeling that the 'party years' were over was well expressed in the introduction to the *Decorative Year Book* for 1932.

'In order to appreciate what is happening in decorative art we must first consider what in general is happening to the taste of the period. If it can be expressed in two words, those two words are "settling down". The "Jazz" period may be said to be over. Extravagance and grotesquerie were the spicing and seasoning demanded during the hectic phase of "post-war" which was filled with the feverishness of the war itself, and the high spirits produced by its termination – all this is on the wane.

'Night clubs, short-skirted women, the cruder type of negroid music, the jagged patterns of cubism, even the word "modern" itself begin to assume a period flavour and to rank as manifestations not of the present but of the immediate past.'

The slump affected people far more quickly than the slower and more controlled decline and recession of the later decades of the century. New domestic architecture and interior design in the early thirties began to retrench and adapt to the changed circumstances.

Potential home-makers, if they could afford a new house and new furnishings, were more careful and conservative in their tastes; the young generation still wanted contemporary style which reflected their own time but they preferred a more enduring decorous style which provided a quieter background than many of the harsher styles of the twenties.

The basic concept of the modern movement for simple functional lines in the exterior and interior of the home, which in its most extreme forms had been described as 'a machine to live in', continued but in a less self-conscious and aggressive way; the modern homes of the early thirties were more elegant and classic.

'Streamlined' became a new word for smooth modern styling. It

was used to describe a wide range of designs such as New York's latest skyscraper, the Empire State Building, long bonneted sleek cars and girls with good figures wearing well fitting swimsuits in the new elasticated fabrics. Streamlined homes had less angular, more flowing lines, flat roofs curved gently round corners and banks of windows, balconies and porches formed complementing rounded lines to give an overall unity of design.

The boom in providing small easy-to-run middle class homes in Britain which had gained momentum in the late 1920s slowed down temporarily during the worst years of the Depression but picked up more strongly than ever by the middle of the decade and continued until the outbreak of the Second World War. The main clients for the new houses were still professional and administrative men with small families who were relatively unaffected by the slump, particularly in southern England. The first half of the 1930s was one of the rare spells in the 20th century when the cost of living actually fell; people with secure jobs lived well and in some cases acquired more ambitious homes.

Although there were still potential buyers, speculative builders found they had to be more competitive with their prices than during the boom years of the earlier post-war period when the demand for new homes had far outstripped their availability. Several years of extensive building together with the accumulating effects of the Depression changed the property position from a sellers' to a buyers' market. Prices for equivalent houses and bungalows in the early thirties were about 10 per cent to 20 per cent lower than they had been 10 years earlier at the height of the post-war inflation.

The new mass market lay in the £500 to £1000 price bracket; costs were slightly lower in country and semi-rural districts where building land was cheaper and local amenities were far less extensive. A detached three-bedroomed house could be bought for as little as £750 and two-bedroomed bungalows were available from £450. In the large areas of development on the outskirts of the big cities costs were higher for similar types of property. Prices, however, varied and it was worth shopping around for the best value.

Two views of New York's skyline from Central Park showing the dramatic change in three decades, photographed, left, at the turn of the century, and above, in the early thirties

89

Gently curved corners and windows were popular style features of many of the new homes of the thirties: above, modest semi-detached suburban house; right, larger detached house in London's Chelsea

The Redway and Kneller Hall Estates at Twickenham approximately 20 minutes by train from the centre of London were typical of the keenly priced ranges of new homes which were being built in suburbs all over Britain. Two- and three-bedroomed bungalows were offered for £670 to £695 freehold, or on a mortgage with weekly repayments of 17/6 or 18/- (87½p to 90p) plus rates at 3/6 (17½p) a week. Houses on the same estates were priced at £649 to £995 freehold or 17/4 to 25/11 in weekly repayments. Advertisements pointed out the special features included in these homes. The growing importance given to providing good kitchens and bathrooms had become noticeable. Special mention was made of planned ranges of kitchen cupboards and detailed descriptions were given of bathroom fitments and wall tiles.

Other advantages for buyers emphasised in advertisements were deposits as low as £5 to secure a new home and no legal or road charges. Road charges were an anxiety in the minds of many people looking for new houses; young married couples who had strained

their financial resources to buy their homes were sometimes caught later for unexpected extra costs with demands for substantial contributions towards making up the new roads on the developing housing estates.

There were about four predominant design trends for popular homes, bungalows and blocks of flats in Britain. Homes in the modern style ranged from individual buildings, usually architect designed with the unadulterated use of flowing streamlined styling, to the more sparing application of contemporary features on modestly priced houses and flats. Design details in these homes concentrated on a more generous use of glass; windows were either widely curved at one or both ends or oblong shaped and made out of panes of smoked glass which looked like glass bricks. Windows in this design were usually put at the side of front doors, on landings, or by staircases. To add still further glass, front doors were sometimes made with a sunray effect worked in carefully angled panels; homes with the more extensive use of windows and glass were often described in advertisements as 'sunshine homes'.

A nautical looking house. Designs like this were often described as 'being in the ocean liner' style

The Spanish style with white-washed roughcast walls, fancy tiled roofs in terracotta or pale green, and arched doors and windows with wrought iron gates and balconies which had been so popular for the Hollywood homes of the early film stars in the twenties were adapted for a more general although still fairly affluent market. British businessmen's homes on the edge of industrial cities designed as Spanish villas looked a little incongruous without sunshine and palm trees, but were considered very glamorous by many people at the time and mellowed more gracefully into their backgrounds as the years advanced.

Georgian façades which had been popular since the first decade of the century continued to be a successful and commercial middle class style. There was an increasing admiration for the Georgian and Regency periods which were often romanticised in books, plays and films. The soft colours and the quietly elegant style of Regency interior decoration began to have a fresh appeal and became a growing influence on fashionable taste as the decade progressed.

The country cottage and the farmhouse design which had been one of the strongest and most enduring influences for three decades had begun to wane by 1930; they were no longer admired by the ultra fashion-conscious but they did remain amongst the useful commercial styles for speculative builders throughout the decade. Old world period features, however, tended to be used more sparingly than the detailed recreations of domestic Stuart and Tudor buildings which had been built with such pride earlier in the century.

Flats and apartment homes had increased steadily since the beginning of the century; during the 1930s, despite the economic situation, they were built on an unprecedented scale for all sections of society. Even the British, with their special affection for a house and garden, began to accept the idea of flat living as a convenient alternative way of life. The growth in apartment homes was part of a general drift towards a more communal way of life; fuel and labour costs were still comparatively cheap and the facilities that were often provided in flats rented from £90 to £150 a year were quite extensive.

The 1930s

Right and foot of page, brighter looking state housing with balconies and communal grounds

Above, fashionable curved lines adapted for new blocks of workers' flats

Apart from standard amenities such as central heating, constant hot water, general porterage and the use of maintained gardens, some new blocks of flats extended their amenities to include bars, restaurants, swimming pools and squash and tennis courts. Telephone calls went through a switchboard where messages could be taken and left and uniformed porters were on regular duty in entrance halls. These hotel-like homes were often called 'service flats' and were thought to be setting the pattern for the city housing of the future.

The provision, started in the twenties, of extensive well planned state housing, particularly large blocks of flats, developed even more strongly during the thirties. There was a growing commitment to build less austere flats that were more pleasant to look at than earlier state housing and, if possible, had individual balconies or faced onto communal gardens. Imagination was used to make interior plans, within the limitations of their budgets, more than just adequate. Kitchens with ranges of built-in cupboards and bathrooms with tiled walls which had become usual in middle-class homes were still considered quite luxurious features in the better type of state housing.

The difference between private and publicly owned blocks was still noticeable but had become less marked than in the previous decade.

The rent charged for state-owned flats was usually Government subsidised. For a three-roomed flat in one of London's new council blocks rent and rates combined were 10/- or 12/- a week (50p or 60p). It was estimated that families would have had to allow 4/- to 6/- (20p to 30p) per person for their week's food. These amounts of money seem incredibly small by later standards but they were in proportion to average weekly earnings of under £3 a week for workers lucky enough to have a job in the slump years.

The range of styles in interior decoration and in home equipment widened during the thirties; the pace of change accelerated for some sections but remained almost static for others. Many of the homes of the older generation who had married and set up house at the turn of the century still remained almost totally unaltered and unaffected by

Typical examples of budget priced speculative building in Britain during the thirties

"We'd love to have a Bungalow on your Estate, Mr. Crouch"

the changes which had taken place during their married life. The idea of remodelling kitchens and bathrooms, adding extensions to houses and replacing furniture and curtains because of changing fashions so popular later in the century would not have occurred to a high proportion of the population in 1930. Electric light and gas cookers had become general but by no means universal. Gas lighting, oil lamps and solid-fuel-burning kitchen ranges were all still in use, particularly in country districts, and many people today have childhood memories of home life 50 years ago which was only slightly different in character from the equivalent homes of the late Victorian period.

While some families still lived in an old-fashioned style, the younger more affluent sections of society had become completely 20th century in their approach to home making. Styles of interior

Price

£670
FREEHOLD

NO ROAD, LEGAL OR OTHER CHARGES

Also £695 Freehold (3-bedroom), 18/- Weekly Repayment. Rates, approx. 3/6 per week. Full details on request.

17/6 WEEKLY REPAY-MENT

In addition to Bungalows, houses of many types (including Crouch's famous Tudor designs) and various prices are available —£649 to £995 freehold, 17/4 to 25/10 Weekly Repayment

decoration popular with the fashion conscious were more subtle and sophisticated than they had been during the jazzy twenties. Modern interiors and exteriors blended together in a more complementary way; as the outside style of architecture became less angular, interior decoration followed suit and softened. Although completely modern styles were still liked, the overall impression was more understated; many of the designs of the modernistic period most admired in retrospect were from the early thirties rather than the mid and late twenties.

After the two extremes in fashionable colours during the previous decade, the vibrant shades of orange, green and red teamed with black or dark blue – so popular in many art deco designs – and the cold non-colours, white and cream with black or dark brown in the stark clinical interiors, colour preferences in the new decade reacted with a range of in-between shades. Plain painted walls predominated and cream roughcast was still greatly favoured but the trend towards more colour had started. Light tints, soft beiges, ash pinks, pale peach, silver grey, powder blue, eau-de-nil green and slightly deeper toned coral and turquoise gave a warmer more restful look to some of the style-conscious rooms of the early 1930s. Curtaining and furnishing fabrics endorsed the new direction with a similar colour spectrum or with the use of deeper toning shades to add further emphasis to the colour theme of the room. Tobacco browns, tans and deep chocolate were teamed with beigey walls, and deep blues, greens and grey were set off against a background of eggshell blues, greens and greys.

Perhaps because memories of over-busy garish patternings were still quite recent, plain furnishing fabrics were mainly used at the beginning of the decade. The tentative return to the use of patternings slowly started at floor level with the use of patterned rugs which became highlighted for special design attention and were sometimes made one of the most important features in fashionable rooms. Design themes were usually abstract, squares, oblongs, graduated and wavy lines and the use of dots were all popular. Colours were occasionally vivid red, yellows and blues but more

Latymer Court in Kensington, one of the many developments of smaller flats built in London between 1930 and 1940

generally safe tone-on-tone effects in light and mid shades with stronger flashes of brighter colour used to accent part of the patterning detail.

With the exception of mirrors and mirrored walls an unrelieved almost monastic bareness had been obligatory in the more extreme modern homes of the late twenties. Pictures were often considered obtrusive if not downright obsolete by the avant-garde with their enthusiasm for the functional as opposed to the decorative. With the mellowing change of mood in fashion, pictures were hung again although still rather sparingly; one carefully chosen contemporary portrait, or clever abstract which mixed neutrals with bright colours excitingly together in the style typified by painters such as Ben Nicholson, were made the focal point in a living room or bedroom.

Britain's well known couturier of the 1950s, John Cavanagh, remembers the home of an earlier famous British designer of the thirties in Paris, Molyneux; the colour scheme was completely neutral, beige walls, curtains and carpets were used as a quietly luxurious background to show off the colours of the designer's collection of paintings.

Murals instead of paintings were sometimes made the principal eye-catching feature in fashion-conscious rooms. Themes varied from so-called 'modern realism', epitomised by groups of serious looking workers, muscular athletes and the portrayal of active sports which were especially popular in Fascist countries, to romantic seascapes, dancers and couples in period costume beloved by the English. Walls behind cocktail bars were often decorated with slightly racy illustrations portraying Paris boulevards or promenades in the South of France. For the homes of the chic and sophisticated murals were painted as a modern art picture usually in the abstract or surrealistic style.

The popularity of light wood treated to give a special glazed or smoked appearance and the application of shiny darkened wood veneers continued to be used in many middle class flats and houses; fancy wood effects were used for dining room and hall walls, internal doors and built-in cocktail bars.

Veneered bedroom suites like this one in 'figured walnut' which included a millinery chest, priced at £18 15s inclusive, sold in large quantities

Many interior decorators prospered during the 1930s despite the world depression. Clients with money for an up-to-date home were still available and became more numerous during the economic recovery in the second half of the decade. With the general movement away from uncompromisingly set styles in décor, designers began to pioneer a new approach to the composition of the fashion-conscious room which was to gain greater acceptance as the thirties advanced and became in later decades one of the most established approaches to furnishing 20th century homes. The idea was to mix different styles and periods together to give a pleasantly individual look to each room. English antique styles were put with traditional Chinese screens, low tables, ornaments and lamps. In the same room nearby chairs, tables and bookcases in the modernistic style were in light wood or steel, leather and glass. An attractive assortment of different items was found to give an individual charm and a more permanent appeal which most people tired of far less easily than a fixed contemporary style. This, although the height of fashion for a short time, inevitably became dated and rarely reflected the personality and taste of the people who lived in the home.

The use of mirrored glass developed more extensively during the thirties. Mirrored walls helped to give an illusion of space in small roomed houses and flats. Modest sized entrance halls successfully gave the impression of added depth with a mirrored section at the end or along one wall. Bathrooms were becoming more luxurious than at any time since the days of the Roman Empire. The latest fitments were sleek and streamlined; baths and lavatories had low curved lines; mixer taps were beginning to be used and mirror glass walls and doors were often featured. Some were expensively decorated with engraved motifs of flowers, birds or fish. Tinted glass was considered very glamorous; it gave an extra dimension and an added femininity to mirrored walls and furniture; black and peachy pink tints were very popular, and apart from walls, they were also used for screens, low tables and bedroom furniture. They were often made in complicated, fancy shaped panels in various sizes and sometimes looked rather overdone and were thought vulgar by some people.

Ultra-feminine women's bedrooms combined the use of tinted mirror glass furniture with a considerable yardage of shiny satin which was used for draped curtains and pelmets, swathed dressing table tops, quilted bedspreads and deeply buttoned padded bedheads. These rooms were heavily influenced by Hollywood's fantasy film sets where *femme fatale* film stars such as Jean Harlow, Joan Crawford and Marlene Dietrich were frequently filmed or photographed reclining languidly, or pensively staring into dressing table mirrors.

Most middle level homes assimilated parts of the new trends in furnishings and décor. Creams, beiges and browns were the most popular colours but the wider range of pastel to mid-shades gradually gained favour. Light and veneered woods were generally used for modern furniture or rather unfortunate mixtures of modern and period. Dining room suites in oak with the boxy silhouette of the contemporary style often had sideboards with neo-classic mouldings, art deco style metal door handles, squat elephantine legs and spread feet. Simple square dining table tops with extending leaves were rather incongruously set on an elaborate network of Jacobean legs and stands. Figured walnut was popular for bedroom suites with basic square and oblong shapes which appeared decidedly top heavy set on gently curved early Geogian style legs.

These ugly rather bastardised designs were amongst some of the best selling mass produced furniture of the time.

The style range in soft furnishings developed during the 1930s; tubby shaped armchairs and couches were still used but newer designs were introduced which soon became widely popular. Couches and chairs with deeper longer seats were boxed in at the sides to form a wedge shaped line which gradually sloped backwards. They were covered in quietly patterned and coloured upholstery and sometimes had the side panels made in one of the fashionable styles of wood. Other chairs designed to take up less space, although still deep and comfortable, had wood arm rests

Glamorous Hollywood style bedroom with a generous use of shiny satin for padded bed ends, chairs, stool, rucked dressing table cover, curtains and draped pelmets

rather like an extended arm on a carver or Windsor chair. Divan beds were often used in the living rooms of small flats and had a row of firm cushions along the back so that they could be used as an armless couch or easily converted into an extra bed.

Seat units were another new space saving idea; 'settee units', as they were described in advertisements of the time, look surprisingly modern and could easily pass for a design of the 1980s. They were made as they are today with corner sections which had one shaped side and centre sections without arms and could be arranged as easy chairs, grouped together as a two or three seater couch or slotted into a corner to form a four-seater group of units. Corner sections cost £9 19s 6d (£9.95) and centre sections £9 7s 6d (£9.35); a total cost of around £40 for the complete set would have been considered expensive 50 years ago in comparison with a standard three-piece suite consisting of a couch and two easy chairs for around £15 to £30.

Fireplaces were still an important feature in most houses particularly in the living and dining room. The simple designs of the

period in plain marble or stone with a narrow surround in wood and an edging of steel or copper around the opening for the fire were fairly inoffensive in appearance; but many of the designs put into suburban houses by speculative builders were as unattractive as some of the mixed up styles of furniture in veneered woods which stood near them. There were several widely used types of designs. 'Beautiful and efficient all-tiled grates', as the advertisements proudly proclaimed, were made in patterns of glazed beige and brown tiles usually with a graduated step effect at each side. It is difficult today to understand their appeal but they were sufficiently popular for many people to feel compelled to remove neo-classic 19th century marble fireplaces and replace them with smaller far less impressive designs in tiles. The country cottage type of grate in slightly reddened natural brick with an arched front, and the scaled down baronial hall fireplace in stone which sometimes made a feature of pseudo-Gothic mouldings or a simulated shield cast from a much used mould were also popular in many homes. The brick, country-looking designs were usually put in living rooms where they were felt to be very suitably surrounded by flowery printed

Seat units, below, which could be arranged in various groupings were already available in the thirties, and right, tasteful furnishings in soft colours and light wood designed for a small living room in one of the new blocks of flats

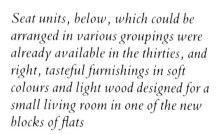

loose covers and curtains; the baronial style fireplace was found in the dining rooms to complement the heavy Tudor and Stuart influences which were still apparent in many sideboards, chairs and dining tables.

Although the majority of middle level homes had a general, if somewhat undefined, style of interior décor with quiet subfusc colours and fairly stolid furniture, the dash and sparkle of putting together rooms with contrasting items all complete in their own style but unrelated to one another was beginning to liven up some of the more adventurous of them. A piece of Regency or French Empire furniture, a modern glass topped or mirrored table, a Rococo framed or Venetian style glass mirror were some of the popular early examples of how characterful items were tentatively introduced to

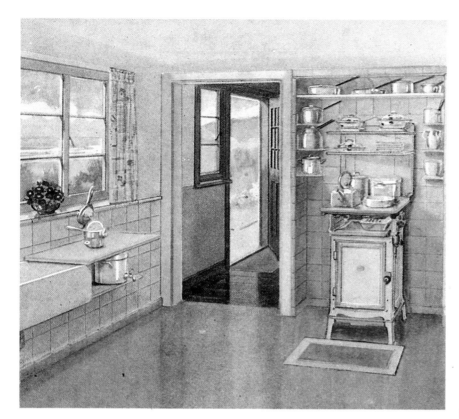

Kitchens were still often rather basic and plain looking with a stone sink and hefty gas stove

lift what would otherwise have been rather bland set looking interiors. The new approach was very modest in comparison with the room arrangements of the fashionable designers but the trend was spreading.

The modernisation of kitchens and the wider range of home and kitchen equipment continued to improve and became progressively more important features of the home. The spending of money on impressive reception rooms at the expense of kitchens continued in some houses but most of the younger generation considered a pleasant and functional kitchen to be an essential requirement. In a popular book called *Design and Decoration in the Home* written in 1933, the changed attitude towards kitchens was neatly pinpointed. 'I do not think very serious thought was given to the kitchen as a whole (apart from individual bits of equipment) until domestic service grew scarce. Now that most women have to do a certain amount themselves in the kitchen they are taking it more seriously. You will find the best kitchens of all where there are no servants.' This trend apparent 50 years ago grew even stronger during the later decades of the century.

The range of what would be considered basic equipment in a present day kitchen, gas or electric cooker, refrigerator, electric kettle, toaster and possibly a washing machine, in their earlier but recognisable forms, were all in use in some of the kitchens of the thirties. They were, however, still relatively expensive in relation to earnings; a medium size stove cost £14 or £15 and a family sized 'Frigidaire' refrigerator about £42.

A total range of built-in fitments, stainless steel sinks, draining boards, cookers, refrigerators and a carefully planned range of wall units for crockery, food and ironing boards, were put into some of the most modern kitchens and photographed for books and magazines. They were the forerunners of the planned kitchens of the future and did not become general in America until the following

Patternings were generally less popular in the early thirties but bold abstract designs for rugs like the one above and on the opposite page were sometimes used

Plastic casings were a new idea for cheaper radio sets

decade and were not usual in European family homes before 1950.

Although ultra modern kitchens were still a few decades away the radical change in the whole concept of the style and function of the kitchen had clearly started. As well as the improved status given to the room in the way it was planned – with good lighting, built-in fitments and modern equipment – the basic everyday household items, pots and pans, bowls, kettles and other utensils were also revised and brought up to date.

Housewives in earlier periods had put great value on their simple well-made range of kitchen ware, which was carefully cleaned and polished, hung on walls, generally preserved and was often passed on through several generations. The solidly put together cooking pots, kettles and irons were, however, rather cumbersome and heavy in use and took a considerable time to maintain.

With the steady decline in the availability of domestic help, particularly those willing to work as drudge-like kitchen maids, and the natural reluctance of a general-purpose maid or a young housewife to be over-burdened with kitchen chores, lighter, easier to manage ranges of aluminium pans, plug-in electric kettles and coffee percolators and new plastic bowls and containers were all quickly welcomed into the more progressive homes. Apart from the convenience of the modernised kitchen items, they were easy to mass produce and comparatively inexpensive to replace as improved versions came on to the market.

The comparative cost of home items in the thirties differed considerably from present day values, particularly when related to earnings at the time. The average weekly wage was still only a few pounds a week and an annual middle class salary of £1000 was considered impressive and more than sufficient for a comfortable standard of living. The majority of houses were sold for less than £1000 and pre-constructed garages made in sections were advertised for under £10. In contrast a Marconi radio in a veneered wood casing was priced at 11½ guineas (£12.07½). Fifty-two piece dinner sets in patterned china were available at £12 but a vacuum cleaner and attachments could cost as much as £27.

For the middle levels of society in Britain the use of income and relative costs have altered considerably. Fifty years ago food,

Tiled fireplaces were put into many homes and were often an admired feature

It's really fine!

Your guests pay sincere tribute to Gloria's inspired design

restaurants and entertainment were all cheaper; home equipment was less extensive and sophisticated, Continental holidays were not as widely taken, but expenditure in both these areas would have required a higher proportion of income than today. People's priorities were different; less money was spent on developing and improving the home possibly because houses and flats were not such valuable investments; prices did not appreciate at anything like the rate they were to do in the future.

Class distinction was more clearly shown through dress than in the later decades of the century, the middle classes cared more about looking ladylike and gentlemanly and more often preferred to spend money on good quality fashionable clothes rather than on bringing their homes and home equipment up to date.

Radios and gramophones became even more popular during the 1930s. Early in the decade radios were still expensive and the new radiograms, a radio and a gramophone combined in a specially designed piece of furniture, were considerably more expensive and were a much admired luxury feature in the home. Later in the decade radios were mass produced in plastic cases and were available at a much lower price; the great age of radio listening started in time to hear regular news bulletins on the deteriorating international situation as the threat of another world war grew. Governments encouraged the spread of the radio into as many homes as possible, broadcasting direct to people in their homes was a very effective channel for propaganda. The tremendous influence of the cinema on the general public also made the development of television accelerate; its potential as a new form of mass media was clearly evident. Regular television broadcasts to the general public began in Britain in 1936; early television could only be received in the London area and programmes which were introduced by announcers wearing evening dress were limited to a few hours each day. Very few families had a TV set until after the Second World War but people were very aware

Gloria
Panel Gas Fire

Gas and electric fires were sometimes fitted into a fireplace or a wall as a permanent and noticeable fixture

of the beginnings of television in the thirties and they were already excited by its obvious potential.

By the fourth decade of the century many of the directions relating to the development of homes in the future were already under way and advanced thinkers of the time were anticipating further revolutionary changes in architecture, interior design and social reform. Despite the many changes which had taken place, and with much theorising and debating over new ideas, several aspects of home life still followed in a modified form the long established pattern of earlier generations.

The reduction in the servant population and the steady increase in the building of flats and small houses designed for families with little or no domestic help was seen as a dramatic change in the twenties and thirties, it was in fact a developing trend, the arrival of the servantless age still lay in the future.

In the 1930s the front doors of quite modest suburban villas were often opened to callers by maids wearing their traditional uniform of black dresses, white aprons and caps. However, as a concession to the more modern times skirts were usually shortened to around the fashionable length and younger women sometimes had up-to-date hair styles. The maids in these houses still presented afternoon tea quite formally to the family and visitors in the new smaller drawing rooms; tea, bread and butter, sandwiches and cakes served on delicate china tea sets continued the social ritual which had been usual in the larger middle class Victorian and Edwardian homes.

Although reduced from pre-First World War levels, some upper class families still had an impressive range of servants. Apart from butlers, housekeepers and maids, many families employed a resident nannie. Nannies' age groups ranged from the very young in their first job to the well-past-retirement-age nannie who had sometimes stayed with the same family all her working life and had seen several generations through their formative years. Nannies' rooms were always within calling distance of the children's nurseries and bedrooms. Babies' and children's day-to-day lives were supervised by nannie who was often devoted to the young families in her care; she took most of her meals with them and firmly instilled basic manners and behaviour patterns.

Nannies, wearing a type of uniform consisting of a plain grey felt hat and a toning grey topcoat or cape, wheeling prams and shepherding neatly dressed small children were a familiar sight in Britain before the Second World War. On warm summer afternoons groups of nannies with their babies and toddlers were seen in London parks sitting under shady trees earnestly discussing the problems of children and employers.

Manufactured entertainment such as radio and cinema had become a part of most children's lives. It was still, however, quite a small part and much of everyday life particularly in the country continued in a natural unspoilt way, children relying on their imagination and inventiveness to create their own games and interests.

In the home they were also encouraged to be more self-reliant and resourceful. Many children, even if sometimes reluctantly, learned to play the piano and the sound of stumbling piano practice was still a

With a little word of thanks, hand her your gift-money

Place a modest tip at the side of your plate on leaving a tea-shop

familiar sound in many houses. Reading was far more extensive than in later decades; tales about Rupert Bear, adventure stories by Enid Blyton and Arthur Ransome, the Just William books, and the daring adventures of the dashing aeroplane pilot Biggles all had a tremendous following. Young schoolboys also looked forward to the weekly arrival of the latest comics, the *Beano* and the *Dandy*. The sound of comics dropping through the letter box, although not always welcomed by parents, was usually greeted with considerable enthusiasm by their young sons.

Children's parties were less sophisticated: a magician was occasionally hired, and for small children gramophone records like 'The Teddy Bears Picnic' were sometimes played; but most of the entertainment was generated by group participation in traditional games such as Hide and Seek or Consequences which were organised and supervised by grown-ups. Party food was less international in character and in Britain children wearing fancy paper hats sat around large dining tables eating a wide assortment of sandwiches, sugary cakes, trifles and jellies.

Many more items were delivered direct to the home in the 1930s. Tradesmen's entrances, indicating a side or back approach to houses from a modest middle level upwards, were clearly marked. Rather

WYGGESTON & QUEEN ELIZABETH COLLEGE RESOURCES CENTRE

Miniature hotel style bars, above, in a sleek and smart modern style were fashionable in some homes. After the bare walls of the modernistic style pictures and murals (left) made a welcome return as part of a more decorous approach to interior design

Afternoon tea was habitually taken in many middle-class homes in Britain

Does your Child know these signs of the Happy Healthy OVALTINEYS?

Angelic looking 'Ovaltine' children were always portrayed in the well-known Ovaltine advertisements

Dickensian looking teenage delivery boys wearing caps and lace-up ankle boots, cycling or on foot, with their heavy loads of provisions were still a familiar everyday sight making regular calls at houses in quiet residential streets.

Middle class housewives or a member of their staff often ordered the family requirements by telephone. Local shopkeepers saw their clients far less frequently than in the later more egalitarian decades. When a visit was made by a good customer they were usually greeted with special courtesy and attention; off-hand impersonal attitudes more usual today would have caused great offence 50 years ago. The sight of elderly women loading up their cars with boxes and carrier bags or staggering laden from the bus stop to their homes, now so familiar, would also have been seen as a sad decline in customer service.

Gardeners were far more readily available than today and a good sized garden was still considered an asset rather than a liability. Most middle level homes had at least some part-time gardening help; possibly as part of the general importance still attached to presenting a neat and disciplined appearance to the outside world, considerable attention was usually given to the maintenance of well-cared-for gardens, particularly in Britain.

The large elegant cars of the period belonging to the affluent were often driven by the family chauffeur. Well-dressed women and men were helped in and out of their cars; rugs were arranged round them in cold weather; and parcels, luggage and pets were carried to and from the car by the chauffeurs smartly turned out in a pseudo-military uniform of peaked cap, tunic jacket, riding breeches and polished gaiters and boots.

Social life and entertainment in the home generally quietened down during the thirties; because of the economic situation cocktail parties, dinners and dances were given on a more modest scale and not held as frequently. *Vogue* magazine in an article headed 'Chic and Cheap' informed its readers that it had become fashionable to entertain simply. The following reassuring advice on economy was given: 'One thing that this financial era has proved for ever is that, the lady who really enjoys entertaining her friends is not giving it up no matter what goes on – or off – in the stock market. The only real difference in the doing is that simplicity – which is smart any way you look at it – instead of being studied and expensive has become necessary and inexpensive.'

Lively exuberant behaviour was still enjoyed by the young but it was usually less frantic and wild. A slightly more formal mood returned; dancing was quite elegant and sophisticated with most of the dance steps nearer to floor level than the high kicking movements of the Charlestoning twenties; ankles and shins were less frequently knocked in the confined space available for home dancing; the raucous flappers had become as outdated as the firmly corseted stately Edwardian hostesses.

In a major effort to alleviate the scourge of mass unemployment and at the same time modernise and add international prestige to their countries, many governments sanctioned massive state sponsored building schemes. In Germany and, to a lesser extent in Italy, community centres, concert halls, post offices, sports stadiums and railway stations were built in a spacious grandiose style that was a mixture of modernistic designs and the classical periods; columns, doors and decorative mouldings were copied from ancient Greece and Rome. As if to emphasise the power and importance of the state over the individual, domestic building was in contrast quietly understated and functional. Wherever possible it was set in communal gardens with children's playgrounds, nurseries and schools adjacent to or nearby, helping to encourage a collectivised life outside the home environment from an early age.

Germany pioneered the construction of motorways in Europe, the autobahns, and began the trend towards fast and easy motor travel between cities. Hitler promised German families not only a good home but also a car. The famous beetle-shaped Volkswagen (the people's car), which was to be available for every home, was launched in the mid-thirties.

In America President Roosevelt also sanctioned, as part of his famous 'New Deal' to lift the country out of the Depression, extensive programmes of new road construction and public building. Spurred on by the Government private property development began to pick up in the second half of the decade. Pleasant looking middle level houses set in fair sized gardens were built in increasing numbers on the outskirts of many of the big cities.

Americans were becoming more confident about their own styles of domestic architecture which were generally preferred again rather than the adaptations of European designs which had been popular in the late 19th and early 20th century. There was a revived interest in the quietly mannered look of the early American colonial and New England styles which, although never completely eclipsed, had been somewhat underrated in the previous decades. Traditionally inspired houses were built with the extensive use of white painted wood boarding or a mixture of wood and brick. Centrally placed porches had white panelled front doors with a Georgian style fan-shaped window over them. Sash and bay windows were used downstairs and dormer type sash windows were set into sloping roofs for the upstairs bedrooms which gave many of the rooms the attractive lines of sloped attic ceilings.

Hollywood set many successful films about cheerful middle American life in these kinds of houses. As Europe drifted towards another war the portrayal of well-equipped comfortable American homes safely placed thousands of miles away from the potential war zones made a deep and favourable impression on many Europeans, providing much inspiration for their post-war homes in the 1950s.

In New York, as the slump lifted, the building of high-rise apartment blocks accelerated again. Lower structures became dwarfed and overshadowed by the new blocks and the owners of older buildings, realising the value of prime sites in densely populated Manhattan, sold them profitably for redevelopment. A similar, even more hectic, situation was to take place in Hong Kong's building boom in the 1960s and 1970s. Saving floor space had become an important consideration in the more moderately priced new apartments built in the later 1930s. Windowless internal

Uniformed nannies were important members of many upper-class households in Britain

bathrooms and cloakrooms became acceptable and another trend promoted in America was set for many of the homes of the future.

The swing away from the starkly modern, and towards a more relaxed, colourful mixture of styles in interior decoration developed more strongly as the decade advanced. The approach of a bright rather clinical futuristic age which had been confidently felt to be so near 10 years earlier appeared by the late thirties to be seriously postponed if not abandoned altogether, and the future began to look far less attractive than the past. Possibly because of the gloomy uncertain outlook the streamlined modernistic designs which had been seen as pointers to the dawning of a new age looked sadly out of date later in the decade; nostalgia for the designs of the past became a kind of escapism for the ultra stylish.

Period designs were once again admired, particularly early 19th century furniture. Even the Victorian age, which had been so ridiculed by the bright young things of the twenties, was looked at with renewed interest; selected items were brought down from the attic or borrowed from grandparents' houses and were thought chic and amusing additions to fashionable rooms which were becoming increasingly more highly decorated. At the same time a similar parallel development was taking place in women's fashions; dress designers were also busily reviving many of the ideas from the previous century.

Cream and pastel coloured walls were a safe good taste choice still preferred by many people for their homes, but the more adventurous began to use stronger colourings and patterns. The growing craze for Regency styles extended to wall decorations as well as furniture and architecture. Early 19th century colours were used in many fashion conscious interiors; deeper greys, saffron yellow and Wedgwood blue were all popular and Regency striped wallpapers in wine red with grey or beige were daringly used for some entrance halls, dining rooms and bedrooms.

The style which was to become so characteristic of the 1950s for different and contrasting coloured walls in the same room had also started. Colours, however, were usually less bold than the ones used in the fifties; a blue-grey tint with a pale lemon yellow, or ivory with pale greeny blue were popular colour combinations in the late thirties.

Printed curtain fabrics returned to favour and became a stronger feature in many rooms as the years progressed. Early in the decade designs had tended to be mainly simple abstracts on woven fabrics in rather insipid tone on tone colourings; beige on light tan, silver grey on mid grey and pale blue on deeper blue. In the second half of the thirties flower prints were reintroduced in positive shades; grass green, sunflower yellow and fuchsia pinks were printed on glazed or semi-glazed cottons to give extra clarity and impact.

Plain curtains were often given a richer look in colour, fabric and the way they were hung; velvets, slubbed silks and brocades in yellowy gold, royal blue or wine red were draped and swathed across the top in the 19th century manner and used as a dressy alternative to the plain boxed-in pelmets which had been standard a few years earlier. The revival of more highly decorated and coloured

Opposite page: more clearly defined patternings became popular for household textiles, and left, a rich and sophisticated design for a New York apartment cleverly combining modern styling with traditional Chinese furniture and ornaments

effects for walls and curtains was complemented by a marked increase in the use of pictures and mirrors; groups of pictures were hung again in halls and living rooms and mirrors set in curly baroque frames or designs with neo-classic gilt surrounds revived from the first half of the 19th century began to replace the modern unframed oval and oblong mirrors which had been so fashionable at the beginning of the decade.

The return to some of the plush, ornamentation and artificiality of the 19th century did not appeal to all the design-conscious younger home-makers some of whom felt obvious revivalism was retrogressive and out of tune with the spirit of the age. At the same time, cold modernism was already thought of as a brief outdated phase by many people.

Modern Scandinavian furniture with the use of light wood made into simple contemporary shapes helped to give distinctively modern rooms a pleasantly warm unpretentious character with which many of the more serious-minded style followers felt they could identify. Finland's designer, Alvar Aalto, produced ranges of classically modern furniture in birchwood, plywood and webbing; his laminated side units enabled chair and couch arms and legs to form one continual unbroken sweep and this advanced idea became more extensively used during the following decade.

The two new very different trends of the later thirties, 19th

Ornate 19th century styles of interior decoration returned to fashion later in the decade

century revivalism and Scandinavian modern, had their progress stopped by the Second World War. It was in fact a postponement rather than an abandonment; both styles formed the basis for important design developments in the early post-war years.

Also a war away from general acceptance and importance as a style direction were some of the most advanced designs in domestic architecture built at the end of the decade. Simple open looking houses and bungalows with clean cut lines and banks of windows were made more gentle looking than the earlier modern homes of the 1930s by the use of natural brick or local stone combined with weather boarding.

External international events affected the lives of many people during the 1930s to a greater extent than in most of the other decades of the century. Severe economic problems continued throughout the period. Nearly two million people were still out of work in 1938 and the dole allowance for a husband, wife and family was as low as 47/6 (£2.37½) per week. Many families still lived in desperately poor conditions. Late in the decade, as the world depression in trade and industry slowly receded, the threat of another even more destructive world war grew on the horizon. Many young married couples were so worried by the possibility of a world holocaust that they decided to postpone having children. The slump had already been one of the causes of the declining birth rate in many countries; the deteriorating international situation lowered it still further and there were many more childless homes.

The Spanish Civil War which lasted from 1936 to 1939 confirmed many people's worst fears that civilians would be affected more seriously than in earlier conflicts. Families sitting comfortably in their local cinemas watched with horror news reels showing death and destruction raining down on Spanish cities. A new addition to the home began to be thought of seriously; an air-raid shelter.

As early as 1937 books on new houses and flats included a chapter or a section which offered sound and detailed advice on the provision of air-raid shelters. The cost saving of building-in suitable types of shelters as new constructions were put up was clearly explained.

The much feared effects of persistent bombing were often rather played down by the governments of the day; it was pointed out that in the air-raids on Madrid only direct hits from high explosive bombs caused severe devastation. The widespread injury caused from blast which produced flying glass, splintered wood, dust and rubble could, it was claimed, be guarded against quite successfully by providing the right kind of shelters. Good ventilation and access through a door and an emergency exit were considered essential requirements; lavatory accommodation, a supply of drinking water and a wireless set together with tinned food and medical and surgical stores were also declared basic necessities. Internal rooms with thick reinforced concrete walls, preferably in a basement, were strongly recommended; for blocks of flats large areas were suggested as communal shelters for the use of all the tenants.

In private houses where the expense of an individually built indoor shelter room was too prohibitive, other less ambitious ideas were put forward as alternatives. Sealing windows and reinforcing with wood

and brick areas under staircases and in basements became a popular rather homely way of providing the family with an air-raid shelter, and the construction was often undertaken by enterprising 'do-it-yourself' fathers and grandfathers. To minimise the chances of being buried under rubble, should the home suffer a direct hit, outside shelters mass produced in corrugated iron and set partly into the ground in the back garden were preferred by many people; within a couple of years they had become the unexpected second homes for thousands of British families.

War over Czechoslovakia nearly erupted in the autumn of 1938; after a series of dramatic meetings in Munich peace was just preserved and the events of the time became known as 'the Munich crisis'. The European public, although temporarily relieved, soon began to prepare themselves seriously for the forthcoming war. The building of air-raid shelters was speeded up and families from grandparents to babies were fitted with gas masks; 38 million were issued in the autumn of 1938. Gas attacks which had been so horribly effective against soldiers in the First World War were expected to be used on the civilian population in future wars.

Civil defence forces and ambulance services were expanded and quickly trained to be able to deal with the effects of large scale air-raids. After the shock of the Munich crisis, recruitment for the Territorial Army grew quickly; fathers and sons sometimes joined together and uniformed men leaving for training or returning home from army manoeuvres became, after 20 brief years, once again a familiar everyday sight all over Britain. Conscription was introduced early in 1939 and the first young men were called up in the spring months; many of them, apart from short leaves, were to be away from their homes for the next six years.

The beginning of the Second World War did not produce the immediate destruction by bombing generally expected in Britain; but mass evacuation from the major cities resulted in unexpected changes in many people's homes and home life. Families with country houses or cottages moved to their out-of-town homes; fathers whose work kept them in the cities usually joined the family for the weekend. Some children, mainly from the more affluent classes, were sent to Canada or America for the duration of the war. The vast majority of young evacuees, however, came from the poorer districts of the inner cities and were sent to the rural and semi-rural parts of Britain; 600000 children were evacuated from London alone. Homes in safer areas with unused accommodation, particularly spare bedrooms, were eligible for the compulsory billeting into the home of children and expectant mothers.

The experiences of evacuees, particularly children, in unfamiliar home surroundings and the effect on the lives of the people into whose homes they were placed varied considerably; in some cases happy, long standing associations were formed; in other instances one or both sides were unhappy with the changed circumstances forced on them.

Blacked-out windows were far more rigorously enforced in the Second World War; black-out time was published in the papers every day and all households had to ensure their home was totally darkened

September 1939; London children awaiting evacuation to the safety of temporary homes in the country

during the specified hours. Auxiliary wardens patrolled the streets to enforce the complete effectiveness of the black-out period; failure to comply with the regulations could have resulted in prosecution particularly after a couple of warnings had been given to the offending home.

There were several popular ways to black-out windows; well-fitting, reasonably full curtains were lined with black material, black blinds were installed, or wooden frames with black paper stretched over them were made to fit exactly into each window. The everyday coloured or patterned curtains were then drawn across and during daylight hours, when the special black-out frames were not needed, windows and their curtains remained free from any heavy and obvious signs of wartime precautions.

Apart from the subjugation of Poland with the mass destruction of many homes and much of family life, the closing months of 1939 did not produce for the rest of Europe the fierce fighting that had been expected. People gradually got used to a wartime atmosphere of men systematically called into the Forces, darkened windows and food rationing. It was in some ways an anti-climax. Memories of the First World War were still quite recent for the middle-aged and the onset of the new war had not had the impact which had been expected. The drummed-up, heroic atmosphere which had been such a feature of the early months of the 1914-18 war was noticeably absent.

In the December issue *Vogue* magazine, cheerfully adapting to the changed circumstances, suggested a light-hearted and stylish idea to help lift the dull inactive period. A double page was devoted to what was entitled, 'I am a fun room'. Fun rooms included many of the amenities people usually went out of their homes for; a barrel of beer and mugs plus a dart board provided the atmosphere of a pub; cocktail cabinets and radiograms stocked with the latest dance records simulated a night club; and a curtained section enclosing chairs, a screen and a film projector offered a private cinema.

The 1930s was undoubtedly one of the most significant decades of the century: the two major problems which have recurred and remained unresolved, of recession and of war, both featured in the same 10 year span. Although major changes were to take place during the later decades many aspects of life including home development have followed on from their beginnings in the thirties. The striving to raise general living standards with better homes for the lower levels of society was an accepted ideal then as it is today. The end of the servant population and the building of compact well-equipped labour-saving homes was already an irreversible trend and gentler, more varied styles of architecture and interior decoration had emerged in their early forms. Despite the serious problems and distractions of the decade important new directions had started which would be resumed and developed further; hopes and plans had to be deferred until the arrival of a more peaceful and prosperous era.

The 1940s

Although only one decade divided the tougher, more severe life of the 1940s from the pepped-up optimism of the 1920s, the change of character had been so complete by the beginning of the Second World War that many already regarded the earlier decade as a remote period of frivolous behaviour and illusionary ideals. The fashions in clothes, interior decoration and architecture considered so modern and progressive less than a generation before were completely out of date and often thought ugly and ridiculous.

The serious world problems of the 1930s had forced a more realistic approach towards most aspects of life including the home. Realism became one of the most predominant characteristics of the 1940s. In the first half of the decade the mass destruction of homes and the turmoil caused to family life by the war was experienced by large sections of the world population; later, countless bombed-out families, demobilised Service personnel and newly married couples searched desperately for some kind of basic home.

The United States did not become directly involved in the Second World War for over 2 years; there was, however, a growing feeling that events would eventually pull the North American continent into the conflict as they had done during the First World War. In the meantime, life in the early years of the decade continued almost totally unaffected by the turbulent situation which engulfed most of Europe.

By 1940 America had completely emerged from the slump and was at the start of a prolonged period of unparalleled expansion and prosperity. Apartment and house building, which had picked up in the late thirties, carried on briskly and progressive new ideas in relation to the home were evolving. The trend which had started in the previous decade for a pleasantly contemporary style, less stark and boxlike than the modernistic houses of the early thirties, was developed further and gained more widespread acceptance in America.

New homes were constructed using local materials; timber-framed buildings, with concrete block foundations, featured the extensive use of wood boarding such as redwood, which was combined with regional bricks or stone. Roofs on the newer style houses usually sloped gently backwards to reveal a bank of windows and a sun balcony adjacent to the main living room or the principal bedroom. Rows of smaller windows for further bedrooms, bathrooms and kitchens ran across the narrower back of the building.

Double garages were often a standard part of these comfortable homes; the two- or even three-car household had become quite unremarkable in America by the 1940s. Fathers often had to drive considerable distances to get to their work; and a car was also needed by many busy mothers for their day-to-day life which was sometimes spread over quite large areas. Schools, shops and sports centres were usually further from home than in the more closely packed cities, towns and suburbs of Europe. American high school pupils in their late teens, much to the wonderment of their European contemporaries, frequently drove themselves to and from school in their own cars listening to the latest Glenn Miller record playing on their car radio.

The long-feared destruction of homes and the killing of civilians on a previously unknown scale became a horrifying reality in 1940

Garages, for some of the more progressive homes, were often joined to the main part of the house by a porch area which was sometimes large enough to provide a covered parking space for a car. Other very advanced homes built on hillsides or by the sea, particularly the west coast with its forward-looking population, had a rather futuristic appearance. Houses were built on raised stilts which were designed to give as many rooms as possible the benefit of spectacular views, and to provide, under the raised area, drive-in garages, laundry rooms, storage space and work rooms.

The inside plan of the new contemporary houses aimed to give the maximum feeling of space and openness; living rooms led directly into dining areas or were divided by a natural brick wall halfway across the room which sometimes housed a fireplace open at both sides of the wall. Kitchens formed one end of the dining room area or had some kind of partial division. The free and easy character of these casually modern homes with their intercommunicating rooms began to be described as 'open plan' and were early examples of the style used in many later mid-20th century houses built in the 1950s and 1960s all over the world.

In complete contrast to the casualness of open plan homes which were usually furnished with quietly modern wooden furniture and built-in units and cupboards, many of the fashion conscious houses and apartments in the major cities were decorated in a neo-Victorian style with draped velvet curtains, button backed mid-19th century chairs and couches and round side tables covered to floor level with plush looking cloths. Rich colours – burgundy reds, deep gold, purpley blues and bottle greens – were all emphasised and featured strongly in the ranges of plain and patterned materials which were used for wall coverings, curtains and furnishing fabrics. Films with opulent room settings in the fashionable period styles popular from the 1860s to the 1890s and especially the sets from the unforgettable film *Gone with the Wind* were an important influence on the taste of the general public.

In Europe the early months of 1940 were the lull before the storm; before the actual fighting of the war burst forth. Houses and flats under construction when the war began were usually allowed by governments to be completed if the work involved was not too extensive. Many shops and stores still had considerable stocks of furniture and household goods, and women's magazines continued to offer guidance on fashionable trends for new clothes and new homes. Brilliant yellow curtains in satin-finished velour were suggested for a living room painted in Wedgwood blue, described as 'Georgian blue'. A tubby looking fireside chair was recommended as 'cheerful and chunky as a peppermint humbug. Smartly striped in red and white satin; sensible shape, no arms to nudge your knitting. £8 10s 0d, from Fortnum and Mason.' Hollywood glamour was very evident in a bedroom set-up for non-shelter nights; 'therefore specially shining and beautiful, ruched satin headboard and spread, 9½ gns, ruched topped dressing table with easy-access shelves, 12½ gns; stool, 4 gns, all blue piped white'.

It was still possible for a spring bride in 1940 in France or England to have a brand new, prettily furnished home, although within a few

Prosperity had returned to America by the early 1940s and many pleasant looking colonial style houses were built on the edges of towns and cities

months the French home might have been invaded by German jackboots and the British house destroyed in the autumn blitz.

The speedy conquest of most of Western Europe came as an unexpected and frightening shock to the world, although the Spanish Civil War had prepared people for the spectacle of total war on the civilian population. The newsreels in the summer of 1940 showing the roads of northern France, less than 50 miles from the English coast, crammed with refugees pitifully struggling with suitcases and boxes of precious items from their homes, helping the elderly, comforting small children and trying to take cover in ditches and under trees when attacked by machine-gunners from the air, left the British in no doubt that their families and houses would soon be in the front line of attack. The ringing of church bells anywhere in Britain was forbidden: if they were rung it was to be taken as a declaration of enemy invasion, probably by combat troops parachuted from aeroplanes. The population was determined to resist the enemy and were cheered by Winston Churchill's famous radio speech pledging, 'we will never surrender'.

The expected invasion of the United Kingdom in the late summer of 1940 did not take place, but prolonged bombing of most of the major cities, as a softening up process, began in the autumn and continued for a year with the heaviest raids around Christmas time and in the spring of 1941.

Air-raid shelters became very much a part of home life in Britain. The insistent pitch of the air-raid warning sent families on many consecutive nights into their own shelter, or into a nearby public one. Nights under bombardment followed a set pattern; early in the

Secure comfortable American homes thousands of miles from the war zones represented an enviable world to many people and pictures of American fridges well stocked with food often produced sighs of wonderment from cinema audiences in severely rationed Britain

evening buckets and saucepans were filled with water in case the main supply was disrupted. A couple of packed suitcases with a change of serviceable clothing for the family were placed ready along with candles and some basic food; thermos flasks of tea or coffee were prepared; and as soon as the warning siren was heard, families took cover, grown-ups carrying suitcases and food, and children clutching their favourite books and cuddly toys.

The platforms in underground railway stations in London became the communal, nocturnal homes for many families. In the early winter evenings, even before the air-raid warning was given, mothers and children settled on rows of temporary metal bunks to ensure a place. Luckier families, with homes in the safer outer suburbs, would, on returning from day trips to the city, pass through the inner city stations which were gradually filling up with their night-time residents laden with bundles of bedding and suitcases of clothing.

Right and opposite page; two advanced designs for houses both showing a generous use of windows and balconies, and anticipating the popular 'contemporary style' of the following decade

Many homes had their own air-raid shelters some of which had been installed before the war began. Table shelters made with a heavy steel framework and top and metal wired sides were very popular. They were big enough to take a small family and filled most of the space in an average sized suburban living room. When not in use, children loved playing in them and used them as their special hiding place or den.

In Britain, rationing, although severe and very extensive, was generally well organised and reasonably effective as the fairest way of distributing the limited resources available. The smallest rations were in the later war years and in the early post-war period: stocks of consumer goods were completely exhausted and the accumulative effects of years when industry and economy had been almost totally geared to the war effort were inevitably felt on a market so long deprived of materials and manufacturing facilities.

Nearly every commodity found in the home was subject to some form of rationing or special allocation, particularly after 1941. New furniture, furnishing fabrics, fuel, and most kinds of food including sweets and chocolates were given a special allowance. Ration coupons for sweets and chocolates were called 'personal points' and entitled each person to between 3 and 4 ounces a month. Parents often saved their sweet rations for their children and some poorer, big families in need of extra money for essentials sold sweet and clothing coupons on the black market. Cigarettes, matches and alcohol were never officially rationed but were frequently in short supply, and many shopkeepers enforced their own restrictions and allocated their limited stocks to selected customers of long standing.

The approach to furnishing the home had to be completely revised and there was no longer any question of re-doing a house or even a room in an amusing new fashionable style. People with well equipped houses, unaffected by bombing, were considered extremely lucky and were often envied; their problems were confined only to a gradual increase in shabbiness and to difficulties in replacing worn-out or broken items.

The furniture made in Britain during the war was confined to a few Government-approved manufacturers. The wood used and the amount of workmanship and decoration allowed were strictly limited and subject to precise Government specification. The quality was, however, quite good and to avoid profiteering new furniture was price-controlled. The style of the limited range of wartime furniture, which was called 'utility furniture', followed the simple lines of the quieter, modern designs of the late thirties. Government controls were also imposed on the small amounts of household textiles that were produced and most home goods including furnishing fabrics, sheets, towels and blankets carried the Government approved utility symbol. Although limited in choice and fixed in price they were usually hard-wearing and made from natural fibres. Marks & Spencer's standards were often used as a guide for determining the quality levels imposed on manufacturers producing the utility ranges.

Priority for new furnishings was given to the bombed out and the newly married setting up home for the first time. Even the maximum allowance for new equipment was rarely enough and most new homemakers had to rely on pieces of furniture and household goods borrowed from or given by parents and friends. Sales of secondhand goods boomed and inflated prices were often paid for quite ordinary items of furniture and basic types of home appliances such as cookers and vacuum cleaners.

Georgian and Regency influences were one of the most fashionable trends for interior decoration

The mending, reconditioning and renovating of all kinds of home equipment was widespread in the war years; one of the slogans of the time was 'Make Do and Mend'. An age when appliances were not expected to last more than a few years, and were often thrown away at the first sign of a defect, would have been difficult for most people in Europe to imagine in the austere and deprived 1940s.

Despite the discouraging effects of rationing, restrictions and acute shortages, many resourceful women in Britain setting up home for the first time managed to produce surprisingly pleasant and individual looking interiors. Most walls were painted in a simple colour wash; furniture was a mixture of modern utility, often in light wood, and a variety of period pieces. Fashion-conscious young women tried to find mid-Victorian chairs and tables which they sometimes stripped down to the natural wood to give the period design a lighter look.

Curtain and chair cover materials were on ration coupons and although special allocations were sometimes granted, most home-makers were faced with the choice of buying new clothing or new furnishing fabrics: they were both covered by the same issue of coupons. Printed curtains with a countrified look – trellis patterns and sprays of flowers – were very popular and complemented the mixture of new and old styles of furniture, especially in rooms which featured light wood. If suitable new fabrics or coupons were not available, old materials or secondhand curtains were sometimes dyed a new colour to brighten up the fabric and, if possible, fit in with a planned colour scheme. Deepish shades such as wine reds, golden browns, and pine greens were the more successful dyed colours, and they also fitted in with the fashionable Victorian influence in décor. To add further emphasis to this trend – and to help disguise fabrics which had not dyed as evenly as had been hoped – curtains were sometimes tied back or, if there was sufficient material, matching draped pelmets were arranged.

Fireside chair, cheering and chunky as a peppermint humbug. Smartly striped in red and white satin: sensible shape, no arms to nudge your knitting. £8 10s., from Fortnum and Mason

Brave attempts were made to provide and maintain pleasant home surroundings throughout the austerity period, but in comparison with many American homes of the same time they were inevitably rather plain and shabby looking. During the war years, America appeared to be a Utopia filled with affluent houses stocked with the most modern appliances. European cinema audiences watched the portrayal of American homes and home life with longing and admiration. Large refrigerators were shown full of eggs, meat and butter; rich-looking iced cakes or jumbo-sized ice creams were served as quite ordinary family desserts and large bowls of fruit stood on side tables. Varying types of radios were available in many rooms, and confident, well-dressed teenagers (usually called 'bobby soxers' in the forties, because they frequently wore pushed-down socks and gym shoes) jitter-bugged to brassy swing music played on the latest style gramophones fitted with long-lasting needles and several pre-selected records which were put into position for playing in turn by the new, automatic record changers.

During the first year of the war glamorous fashion conscious furniture was still obtainable in Britain

In Europe food was one of the main preoccupations in the home. In the occupied countries rations were so meagre and their availability so unreliable that families suffered from the effects of

"DRIED EGGS are my eggs — my whole eggs and nothing but my eggs"

Dried eggs are the complete hen's eggs, both the white and the yolk, dried to a powder. Nothing is added. Nothing but moisture and the shell taken away, leaving the eggs themselves as wholesome, as digestible and as full of nourishment and health-protecting value as if you had just taken the eggs new laid from the nest. So put the eggs back into your breakfast menus. And what about a big, creamy omelette for supper? You can have it savoury; or sweet, now that you get extra jam.

DRIED EGGS build you up!

In war-time, the most difficult foods for us to get are the body-builders. Dried eggs build muscle and repair tissue in just the same way as do chops and steaks; and are better for health-protection. So we are particularly lucky to be able to get dried eggs to make up for any shortage of other body-builders such as meat, fish, cheese, milk.

Your allowance of DRIED EGG is equal to 3 eggs a week

You can now get one 12-egg packet (price 1 3) per 4-week rationing period — three fine fresh eggs a week, at the astonishingly low price of 1¼d. each. Children (holders of green ration books) get two packets each rationing period. You buy your dried eggs at the shop where you are registered for shell eggs; poultry keepers can buy anywhere. Don't hoard your dried eggs: use them up —there are plenty more coming!

Note. *Don't make up dried eggs until you are ready to use them; they should not be allowed to stand after they've been mixed with water or other liquid. Use dry when making cakes and so on, and add a little more moisture when mixing.*

FREE — DRIED EGG LEAFLET containing many interesting recipes will be sent on receipt of a postcard addressed to Dept. 629U, Food Advice Service, Ministry of Food, London, W.1

ISSUED BY THE MINISTRY OF FOOD

Most older Britons remember the way dried eggs helped to supplement the small ration of fresh eggs during the war

malnutrition unless they supplemented their diet from the exorbitantly priced black market. In Britain, people had enough to eat but the diet was generally dull and stodgy, relying to a large extent on bread and potatoes. Apart from the limited amount of local fruits available, only when they were in season – and a few oranges at Christmas time – other fruits such as bananas, melons, peaches, grapefruits and lemons were not imported into Britain for general consumption; shipping space was needed for more essential supplies. When fruit reappeared in the shops after the war 8- or 9-year-old children had never seen a fresh banana or pineapple before and looked at them with great interest and excitement. Their experience of tropical fruits had been confined to an occasional small helping of tinned fruit usually opened as a special treat for a birthday party or at Christmas time.

The allowances of basic foods were always small and subject to periodical reductions if certain types were in very short supply. Examples of the varying weekly rations per person were as follows and were usually at the lower end of the scale: from 4 to 8 ounces of bacon, 1 to 8 ounces of cheese, 2 to 4 ounces of tea, 8 ounces to 1 pound of sugar, 1 egg, 6 ounces of butter and margarine. Housewives sometimes mixed butter and margarine together with a little tinned milk to make a more palatable, slightly creamy spread. Some families were willing to forgo their egg ration to be allowed to keep a few chickens. Areas in gardens previously used as decorative flowerbeds were turned into chicken runs with wooden hen houses; the family usually benefited from the conversion with a larger supply of eggs than would have been possible from the ration quotas. Families, and particularly children, often became fond of their small group of chickens; they were known by name and the suggestion of killing any of them for food brought forth howls of protest and floods of tears from their young protectors.

Powdered dried egg imported from America proved to be a popular and useful substitute for real eggs. Ministry of Food advertisements showed a drawing of a rather plump self-satisfied looking chicken proclaiming 'Dried Eggs are *my* eggs – my *whole* eggs and *nothing but* my eggs'. The advertisement went on to explain the property of dried eggs and gave details of the permitted allocation; adults were entitled to one twelve-egg packet, price 1/6 (7½p) a month, and children were allowed two.

Children were also eligible for orange juice and extra milk. The British wartime diet, although dreary and monotonous by later standards, was considered in retrospect to have been a healthy diet, low in sugar and fats and higher in roughage content. Children born and brought up in the austerity years are often thought to have been stronger and healthier than the ones whose formative years were spent in the early decades of the century.

Because of the problems of food shortages and the difficulties in stretching rations to feed visitors, a new form of social politeness and manners developed between guests and their hosts. Visitors arriving at the home, instead of bringing flowers and chocolates as they might have done before the war, brought instead rather mundane but very welcome gifts of butter, sugar or tea. This lessened the chance that

The ITMA comedy team rehearsing one of Britain's most popular radio programmes. From left to right, Jack Train, Carleton Hobbs, Mary O'Farrell, Michele De Lys, Tommy Handley, Clarence Wright, Lind Joyce, Fred Yule, Jean Capra, Hugh Morton and Charles Shadwell

Patriotic advertisements like this one were used by the Ministry of Food

their hosts might have had to sacrifice their own small basic rations in order to provide the hospitality of a meal for their guests.

The prospect of a father's or a son's leave usually brought great excitement and anticipation into the home. The house was cleaned and smartened up, fuel stocks were checked, and considerable efforts were made to get the best food available. Men returning briefly to the home environment enjoyed seeing their growing children, the company of their wives and the comforts they had once taken for granted. Because time was short and the future uncertain, families tended to make the most of leaves and the enjoyment of each other's company was heightened. When husbands had to return to the Services, their wives, cheered by the reunion, resumed their quiet lives with their young families. Home entertainment was often limited to listening to the radio: the news bulletins, favourite comedy shows like Tommy Handley's ITMA (*It's That Man Again*) and softly sentimental late evening dance music which helped to provide many wartime wives with a soothing end to a day filled with domestic chores and familiar routine.

Women in the forties spent more time out of their homes than they had done in the earlier decades. Young unmarried women were conscripted into the Services or directed to work in armament factories. Houses and flats with bedroom curtains drawn during daylight hours usually indicated that a member of the household was involved in night-shift work and was catching up on some sleep during the day. Women with children under the age of 14 were not compelled to do war work, but many felt they wanted to be involved in the war effort and volunteered for part-time employment. To enable them to do this children were often looked after by friends on a rota basis.

Homes and home life during the Second World War were more disrupted than at any other time in the century. There were very few households that remained totally unaffected throughout the period; even remote farms and cottages had evacuated families or the conscripted women farm workers, the Land Army, frequently billeted in them for at least part of the time. Civil servants and

Service personnel were also frequently directed into homes as compulsory lodgers. The British, with their well-known reserve, sometimes had the quiet privacy of their neat suburban homes disturbed by lively young British and American servicemen and women.

One of the best-remembered characteristics of the war years was the improved friendliness of people towards one another inside and outside the home. The threat to the freedom and independence of Britain and the shared hardships of rationing, bombing and bereavement united the country as never before and produced a cheerful good humoured comradeship which older people still think of with nostalgia today over 40 years later.

By 1944, although the duration of the war with Japan remained uncertain, the end of the war in Europe appeared to be in sight and eventual victory for America and the Allies seemed assured. In Britain, thoughts and plans started to take shape for the post-war era: democratic schemes for social security, schooling and the provision of new mass housing were all under way.

At last the public began to feel they could relax a little and make some personal plans for their future after the war. The heavy bombing of the early 40s had eased off and become more and more

Young couples reunited for a few precious days greatly enjoyed the pleasure of being together again in their own home

intermittent. Many people lulled into a false sense of security had gradually drifted back to their city homes. Unfortunately, they were just in time for a new bombing terror in southern England, the flying bombs or 'doodlebugs'. The sound of the droning engine sometimes brought almost frozen horror to the waiting civilians below – particularly the moment when the engine cut out and which immediately preceded the bomb dropping. Between June and September 1944 at least nine thousand flying bombs fell on Britain. Despite the Allies' advance across Europe some of the most devastating bombing attacks, from the more advanced missiles, the V2 rocket bombs, took place on civilians late in the war and homes were still being destroyed in the early months of 1945.

The acute housing shortage in the early post-war years was widely expected. The accumulated effects of the complete stop in domestic building and the bombing of thousands of houses had reduced considerably the number of houses available to well below the levels of 1939. The problem of housing was clearly formidable. But there was, however, a more basic and realistic attitude to the situation than the rather patronising views held by some in 1918 of rewarding 'our gallant lads' with a better home for their efforts in the war. Governments were in no doubt that action on providing homes would be demanded by the tougher generation which had grown up during the 1939-45 war. The rather fanciful idea popular at the end of the First World War of building pretty workers' houses designed in the traditional cottage styles of Britain was completely out of tune with the down-to-earth realism of the 1940s. The provision of a basic home which was well insulated, which made the best use of a small compact space, which let in the maximum daylight and which was simply but adequately equipped, was the main priority.

The quickest and most economical way to construct new houses was also of great importance; easy-to-assemble prefabricated homes, although lacking in style and often looking like a rash of matchbox shapes on some of the newly cleared bomb sites, did provide acceptable homes in a reasonably short space of time. Model 'prefabs' were put on show to the general public in city centres during the last year of the war. They were usually single storey buildings with one moderate-sized living room, two smallish bedrooms and a kitchen and bathroom and for display purposes they were sparingly furnished with utility furniture. In retrospect they appear very basic and utilitarian but to many people in the mid-40s, used to a home life in dreary rented rooms and air-raid shelters, the new prefabricated bungalows looked bright and modern.

Prefabs were built to last between 7 and 10 years and were expected to serve as temporary homes while permanent houses and flats were built in more traditional materials. Some prefabs still exist as homes today 40 years later. Many families, expecting to live in their temporary homes for just a few years, stayed for several decades bringing up families from their babyhood to their adult years. Young men and women who had been brought to their supposedly transitory homes as newly-born children left them to get married and move into their own houses a generation later.

The idea of prefabricated houses was not new to the middle 1940s. Early designs had been worked out in the thirties and American architectural journals featured schemes for prefabricated homes regularly in the early forties. Some forward thinkers expected to see the general acceptance of rather transitory, quickly-assembled homes within a decade. It was thought they would be produced on an assembly-line basis and sold under well-known trade marks like cars. Although second homes in caravans and boats became far more widespread in the post-war decades most people remained wedded to the traditional ideal of a static, permanent house built from a combination of new and conventional materials as their main home.

By the autumn of 1946 a great deal of domestic building was under way in Britain. Over 40 000 prefabs had already been built and many thousands of more conventional houses in brick or concrete – sometimes incorporating prefabricated sections – were under

Early postwar houses with their simple lines and larger windows had a frank more open look than the fussy mock period styles popular in the twenties and thirties

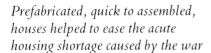

Prefabricated, quick to assembled, houses helped to ease the acute housing shortage caused by the war

construction and there were countless older buildings which had been, or were being, repaired. Although considerable activity was taking place, it was too little to alleviate the serious housing shortage. Two million men and women had been demobilised from the armed forces and many others were being released every day. Marriages and births soared and young families living in temporary lodgings or staying with relations often felt very frustrated by the seemingly endless wait for a basic home of their own. Unoccupied houses and flats that landlords were reluctant to let because of rent restrictions and legislation protecting tenants proved a source of much irritation to the homeless. The Government took steps to allow the requisition of any unoccupied accommodation that was brought to the Authorities' attention. Owners of empty properties were sometimes horrified to find an official requisition notice fixed to the door of one of their houses or flats.

With the steady depletion of the armed forces many military camps became deserted; families desperate for a home took over the empty camps in 1946 and received widespread publicity as 'squatters'. It was estimated that as many as 20 000 people had moved into military huts with mattresses, pieces of furniture and cooking utensils. Life was fairly uncomfortable for the families of squatters in Britain but they were at least together as a family unit and the publicity over their action drew further attention to the acute housing problem.

The end of the Second World War did not bring any noticeable improvement in living standards for much of the world's population. Shortages, restrictions and rationing continued for several years – in Britain food rationing lasted well into the 1950s and fuel was restricted to a set allocation until 1955. Britain's cheerful wartime spirit evaporated in the grey post-war years of austerity. The early months of 1947 produced some of the most severe winter weather of the century. It could not have happened at a worse time; fuel was in very short supply; and the added strain on reserves resulted in long power cuts and severe restrictions. Food rations had to be reduced below wartime levels and bread and potatoes which had never been restricted during the war joined the range of rations. Housewives had to add yet more papers to the family's large collection of ration books: sweet coupons, clothing coupons and identity cards.

Bad as the situation was in Britain, in parts of Germany and Eastern Europe it was very much worse. Thousands had to endure the depressing conditions of life in an officially-run displaced persons camp; through no fault of their own people once used to an ordered day-to-day life and a comfortable standard of living, lost within a few years, their families, their homes and in some cases, owing to the realignment of countries and border divisions, their nationality. Many towns and cities had been almost totally devastated and countless families still lived in partially destroyed buildings or cellars. Many people had no laid-on power or water supply and huddled round wood burning stoves trying to keep warm. Some of the weaker members of the population, young children, the sick and the elderly, died from hypothermia between January and April 1947.

America emerged from the Second World War as the most powerful nation in the world with an increasingly affluent population ready for improved and style-conscious homes. American magazines and books devoted to the home were thick and glossy with many colour pictures of glamorous, rich looking home settings and detailed advice on the most up-to-date equipment for kitchens and bathrooms.

There were several popular styles for home interiors. In the *House and Gardens Complete Guide to Interior Decoration* published in 1947, a section on period styles pointed out the bewilderingly wide range of fashionable trends, showing clearly the prosperous home market in America and the surprisingly frivolous attitude which already existed towards ultra fashion-conscious homes. 'Today scarcely a season passes but from Grand Rapids we are swept by the publicity for a new style – Victorian, Swedish Modern, Pennsylvania Dutch. Our serenity is broken by threats of a Queen Anne revival and a West Coast movement that makes us nostalgic for the old Craftsmen's styles. Those who had just recovered from Classic Modernism were left a little breathless when Regency came over the horizon or stood aghast before what was solemnly called Louis XV Modern. French Provincial had two comebacks and Biedermeier one, in as many decades. Regency enjoyed polite support, Saltbox and Shaker furniture brought their tribute to our sterner ancestry . . . and now, the wheel spinning merrily on, we are threatened with furniture based on Babylonian motifs.'

The preoccupation with the finer points of stylishness so soon after the end of a devastating war showed the tremendous contrast between America, which was already a land of plenty, and most of Europe still in the grips of rationing and austerity, where many households would have welcomed some furniture of any period and most homes were too concerned with basic necessities to consider fashion.

The most widely popular styles for interior décor in America were developments of the advanced design trends of the late 1930s. The elegant Georgian and Regency period which Americans sometimes interpreted as their Colonial style, with late 18th and early 19th century antique or reproduction furniture, striped wallpapers and

FIND THE *Problem Child*

"Mother, don't we just love breakfast now!"

Peggy *used* to be a "problem child."
Skimpy breakfasts, then scooting
off to school . . . no wonder she got
poor grades! But it's different now,
with this fascinating *Toastmaster*
Toast 'n Jam Set making breakfast
fun. How children love the way the
automatic *Toastmaster* toaster
ticks away, timing the slices to a
T, then popping them up, piping
hot and perfect! No watching,
turning, or burning . . . *You'll* be
delighted too—with everything
about this handsome set. Stunning

toaster, walnut tray, colorful Fran-
ciscan Ware jam and marmalade
jars and toast plate, all for $17.95.
See it, wherever fine appliances are
sold. And write McGraw Electric
Co., Dept. L, Elgin, Ill., for 16-
page booklet, "Entertaining Hints
on How to Entertain."

JUST THE THING for pantry raids
after school. Turn the youngsters
loose! They can't burn fingers or
leave the current on.

TOASTMASTER *Toast 'n Jam Set* DE LUXE

"TOASTMASTER" is a registered trademark of McGraw Electric Company, Toastmaster
Products Division, Elgin, Illinois • Copyright 1941, McGraw Electric Company.

This American advertisement showing how children can be enticed to eat with novelty gadgets was in marked contrast to the food shortages in many parts of the world

appropriate mirrors and curtaining was considered the safe and accepted good-taste style of the time by many.

British family cars like this 1948 'Humber Hawk' showed a strong influence from the streamlined designs already popular in America

Rather more daring and dashing was the Victorian revival which had been gaining in popularity throughout the forties particularly amongst the fashion conscious who preferred a richer more obvious show of affluence. The Victorian style was really more of an influence from the previous century than an accurate re-creation of it: the heavy darkness of most late 19th century homes was never revived in its original form and many of the rooms of the late 1940s were a mixture of Regency and Victorian influences. Regency striped upholstery was put on Victorian dining chairs and late 19th century chaise longues; mid-Victorian gilt mirrors were placed over late Georgian tables, and 1800 corner cupboards were sometimes fixed to burgundy-red Victorian walls near clusters of pictures in ornate frames.

Very different from the plushiness of the neo-Victorian interiors was the lighter, fresher look of the modern Scandinavian style. This made use of light wood in simple functional shapes which were cleverly complemented with colourful upholstery, usually a plain surface interest fabric, a heavily slubbed tweed or a linen weave effect, in bright yellows, orange or turquoise blue. To show off the simple lines of the light-wood furniture and the brightly coloured chair coverings and curtains, one wall was often painted a rich intense colour such as chocolate brown or olive green; in some very advanced rooms all the walls were coloured in a single dark shade but this idea became more generally popular in the following decade.

American kitchens were the envy of the world in the late 1940's. Comparatively spacious, well-lit rooms were brightly painted in strong blues, clear yellows, or fire engine red; windows were often fitted with venetian blinds in white, or colours chosen to tone with the wall decorations. Well-planned ranges of storage units, working tops, pull-out ironing boards, ready-placed electric mixers and cleverly positioned eating areas which were sometimes arranged as a bar with high stools or built-in small sections of corner seats were all designed to take up the minimum floor space. Washing machines had also become standard equipment in these prosperous homes, and to complete the unity of design very extensive ranges of enamelled cooking pans were available in the bright shades so popular in the fashionable kitchens of the time. Cheerfully coloured, well-planned

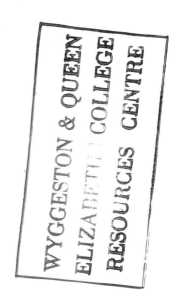

*In austerity Britain, even the basic
household irons were difficult to
obtain in the early postwar years*

and equipped kitchens, so common in later decades, were rare outside North America 35 years ago; when more progressive ones began to appear in Europe at the end of the forties they were often described as 'American kitchens'.

Austerity, although severe until the end of the decade in Britain, did show some tentative signs of lifting slightly during the last year or two. Finding a home of their own was still a great problem for many people who had to put up with temporary home sharing and rented rooms in someone else's house. Some progress, however, was gradually being made to improve the housing shortage. By 1948 new houses were being built at the rate of 200000 annually and some of the first planned 'new towns' were beginning to take shape.

Many late Victorian and Edwardian family houses with six or seven bedrooms were turned into two or three self-contained flats. The conversions were sometimes rather crude by later standards, with ugly external staircases leading to the entrances of the upper-storey flats, and unsuitably proportioned rooms were converted into very basic kitchens and bathrooms. Central heating was very rarely installed and buckets of coal frequently had to be carried up several flights of stairs. Because many of the houses had been built by turn-of-the-century speculative builders and were never intended to be used as flats, sound insulation was often poor. The noise of radios and people moving about, particularly boisterous children, or crying babies at night were sometimes a cause of irritation and disputes between tenants in the same converted building.

Despite the disadvantages of living in a conversion, many young couples were delighted to get one and to be alone in their own self-contained home often for the first time and, within the limitations of post-war austerity, have the freedom, without interference, to decorate and furnish their small flat in the style which most appealed to them. Enterprising couples enjoyed bringing to life dull, old fashioned rooms with brighter decorations and their own personal collection of new and secondhand furnishings.

Two-colour effects were liked by the younger generation; a lemon yellow ceiling and one matching yellow wall were often used for living rooms where the other walls were painted white or pale grey; and a predominantly white bedroom would have a single pink wall with toning shades of pink used in the patternings of the curtains and bed covers. Utility furniture continued to be teamed with renovated older pieces, and light cheerful touches were given with a selection of brightly coloured cushions, groups of framed flower prints and stands or hanging baskets filled with flowering plants.

Most kinds of basic home equipment remained in very short supply; advertisements for electric kettles and sets of saucepans pointed out tantalisingly in the copy that the manufacturer hoped supplies of the goods featured would soon be available. Pictures of cutlery and china tea and dinner sets were usually captioned with a note pointing out that for the moment they were for export only. Most china for the home market continued to have a rather thick texture, and it was mainly available in a slightly grainy off-white colour.

Conventional carpeting was difficult to obtain, but felting in a limited range of colours was more readily available and often made a surprisingly good looking and hard-wearing substitute. Other seemingly unlikely fabrics such as mattress ticking, duster materials and parachute silk were acquired by clever women, were carefully dyed and well made up into attractive curtains. Because of continuing shortages and the painfully slow rate of improvement in the range of consumer goods, initiative in finding unusual and unlikely items and the ability to renovate and repair was almost as useful as a large budget to the homemakers of the early post-war years. The satisfaction in presenting the home completed with great personal effort to friends and relations was in a way greater than it was in other periods when the choice of every kind of easily obtainable home equipment at well-known prices was so extensive.

The new estates of semi-detached houses followed the basic lay-out and size evolved just after the First World War, but with some notable changes to the style of the exterior and with minor rearrangements to the inside plan. Mock period effects were finally abandoned in favour of plain lines. These sometimes featured mid-toned natural wood, or white painted boarding, on the upper half of the building and pleasantly large casement windows particularly for downstairs front rooms, some fitted with window boxes which added to the brighter, open look of the newer houses. The lighter quality was further emphasised with simple porches held by narrow wooden pillars and with front doors featuring long glass panels. The inside plan often did away with the older idea of two distinctively different small living rooms, a modest sized kitchen and tiny back kitchen. This it did in favour of one good sized living room with a section set up with a dining table and one better planned working kitchen, or alternatively a fair sized living room and a larger

American interior of the late forties featuring Scandinavian style wood furniture, bright colours and textured fabrics, all trends that were to become internationally popular in the 1950s

combined kitchen/dining room. Upstairs the floor space – usually divided in pre-war houses into two moderate sized bedrooms and a very small third bedroom or box room and bathroom – was usually planned in the new houses as three bedrooms of a more equal size plus bathroom.

The pretentiousness of many small semi-detached houses built in the twenties and thirties where living rooms approximately 12 to 14 feet square were described as 'drawing rooms' and kitchens about 8 feet by 10 feet were called 'morning rooms' had become outdated by the more realistic and casual approach to homes and home life.

Attitudes towards gardens also altered amongst the more liberally minded. The rows of almost identical suburban homes each with their firmly closed off small plots of lovingly cared for gardens, so characteristic of the inter-war years in Britain, were less rigidly followed after the war. Some of the new housing developments copied the American suburban idea of communal front areas of grassed-over lawns, trees and shrubs which usually gave a more open, better laid-out appearance – providing, of course, the maintenance of the garden spaces was properly organised. Back gardens were still left to individual interpretation.

Blocks of flats built round communal gardens had been growing in popularity since the 1920s and became even more general after the Second World War. Although tenants enjoyed the convenience of centrally administered garden areas, some people wanted the personal interest and satisfaction of cultivating their own piece of

Striped wallpaper often described as 'Regency' stripes were popular throughout the forties

garden, however small. Balconies with colourful well–tended tubs and window boxes became increasingly popular and helped to soften the rather plain, functional looking lines of many blocks of flats.

The initial approach to gardens around prefabricated houses, which were only expected to last for a few years and were sometimes erected on difficult to cultivate bomb sites, was for easy–to–grow, quickly maturing flowers and shrubs; it was not thought worth cultivating hedges and trees for such supposedly impermanent homes. However, as the lifetime of many prefabs gradually extended, some attractive gardens were cultivated and matured pleasantly round the buildings' dull, boxy silhouette.

Home life in Britain after the Second World War did not see dramatic changes take place as rapidly as those that had followed the 1914-18 war. The basic problems of assembling a home took several years for some families, and nearly everyone young or old had to deal with mundane day-to-day chores; shopping, cooking, cleaning, gardening and the general running of the home were all shared more fairly amongst the family in all classes than had been usual 25 years earlier. Apart from elderly retainers and loyal part-time help, domestic staff had practically ceased with the war and was never resumed on the pre-1940 level.

Parents and children spent more time together and there was a continual drift towards casualness and informality in the home. The radio remained the centre of home entertainment until the end of the 40s. Hardworking housewives often rested after lunch and listened

After the war more homes adopted the idea of a kitchen and dining room combined

Cheerful looking indoor plants, hanging baskets and window boxes became increasingly popular

EVERY HOME'S IDEAL

with the BENDIX
Automatic Home Laundry

Rapidly becoming a household word, the Bendix Automatic Home Laundry is the greatest labour-saving device ever invented. Washdays become a joy when you have a complete laundry service in your home. The Bendix is easy to install, quick, clean and gentle with your clothes, easy on your precious coupons—and always yours to command

You just put in the clothes, add soap, set the dial—and the Bendix takes over. Once you've clicked the switch you're off duty and can walk out on the laundry. Your hands need never touch water

WHAT THE BENDIX DOES

● Fills itself	● Changes water for each rinse
● Washes the clothes	● Damp dries
● Drains away dirty wash water	● Cleans itself
● Rinses three times	● Shuts itself off

ALL AUTOMATICALLY

Although washing machines were far from general in Britain in the late forties, a receptive market was growing for labour saving appliances

to *Woman's Hour*, followed later in the afternoon by *Mrs Dale's Diary*, one of the most popular and long-running serials the BBC ever produced. At five o'clock children home from school tuned in to *Children's Hour* and early in the evening slightly older children habitually followed the exciting adventures of *Dick Barton, Special Agent*, despite frequent protests from parents pointing out the homework which still had to be completed. One of the highlights of Saturday evening broadcasting was *Saturday Night Theatre*, when a really gripping play performed by the very competent BBC Repertory Theatre was listened to intently by the whole family sitting round a coal fire on a cold dark winter evening.

Although the radio and the gramophone were an established influence on children and teenagers, conventional toys and games were still popular and reading continued to be an important interest. Catering for special teenage tastes and cults had not really begun in Britain, although precocious American teenage behaviour in the home was already being shown in films and the younger generation in general were written about in the press. In an article on *Books for Teenagers* written in 1948 the emergence of the new section in society was not greeted with enthusiasm: 'the cult of the teenager, which originated in America where they have teenage clubs, teenage dresses, hats, ties, shops and endless teenage magazines and books, has not yet made itself felt to any great extent in this country, and it is hoped that it will not, for many aspects of it can only be regarded as deplorable.'

A great novelty and point of interest in the home in the late 1940s was a television set. In Britain regular television broadcasting had been in operation as early as 1936; it was however available only in the London area and was suspended for the duration of the war. When it was resumed again it was at first limited to a 50 mile radius of central London but from 1949 onwards a much wider area of the country, although still not all of Britain, came into the broadcasting range. Early post-war TV sets were expensive in relation to current earnings; prices for table model sets with 8- to 10-inch screens started at about £50 with an additional cost of at least £10 for an external aerial.

Cabinet models on wheels with 10- or 12-inch screens in the £100 to £200 price range plus the charge for an aerial were considered luxury items by most people. The television set was housed in a veneered wood piece of furniture and the screen could be closed-in with doors when not in use; door handles were made in fancy-shaped wood or ornate metal; many cabinet models of the late forties looked like a 1930s cocktail cabinet and were proudly shown off to admiring friends and relations.

For a few years television was quite an important status symbol in many suburban homes just as the early radio sets had been in the twenties. Children on family walks pointed out with interest the new H-shaped aerials fixed to chimney stacks but the novelty interest of a TV vanished within a decade. Rooftops all over the country had sprouted a forest of TV masts, which by then had become unremarkable except for their ugliness.

Television began to keep people in the home again, particularly the middle-aged and the elderly. Although the early post-war sets had small screens and black and white pictures only, the convenience of having varied entertainment available in the home had an instant appeal which it has never lost. Watching a children's programme was often the high spot of Christmas or birthday parties in 1949, and news bulletins, variety shows and plays watched in a comfortable living room proved to be a strong discouragement to going out of the home particularly during the long dreary winters of the Northern Hemisphere. Cinema and theatre audiences began their long and seemingly irreversible decline. By the end of the decade Hollywood had become seriously worried by growing competition from television and on the principle of 'if you can't beat them join them' started to put considerable efforts into building up special programmes and stars especially for the new quickly expanding media.

The family car of the twenties which had become the family cars of the forties in many American homes was still a pipe dream for most people in Britain. Households with a car had grown steadily in the 1930s but were still not general; during the war private motoring was severely curtailed and new cars were practically unobtainable. After the war petrol was still restricted, and new cars although produced were mainly for export; the small allocation for the home market often meant a wait of several years for prospective buyers who usually had their name on the waiting lists of several manufacturers. Families lucky enough to get a new car in the late forties found they were amongst the first customers to have the new streamlined British models which were strongly influenced by the American designs of the time. The latest Standard Vanguard or Morris Oxford, although not popular with more traditional tastes, were impressive to most younger people; status conscious schoolboys were delighted to be collected from school by their parents driving one of the well publicised new car models.

The Second World War and the austere years which followed it dominated the entire decade: survival had been the main preoccupation in the early forties; basic priorities such as food and shelter took precedence over the more frivolous and decorative aspects of life such as developments in fashionable homes. Creative designing came to a halt. This was particularly so in the style centres of Western Europe where no raw materials or manufacturing facilities were available with the exception of the very small amount of Government supervised production. The atmosphere was completely unreceptive to novel design ideas. When the provision of new homes was revived in the later years of the decade, styles for domestic architecture, furniture and interior décor had remained frozen in the mould of the late thirties; trends picked up where they had left off in 1939 and were simplified to fit in with the limited resources available.

Post-war homes were more democratic in concept; class divisions which had softened after the First World War became even less clearly defined during the 1940s. The many levels of class consciousness, each aspiring to the way of life enjoyed by the one immediately above, became less important after the years of shared hardships experienced by a large cross-section at home, in the

In 1949 Television in the home was still an admired status symbol; within 10 years a TV set had become almost as unremarkable as a radio and watching television had become the major form of home entertainment for many people

services and factories. One general living room and dining room combined, a well planned working kitchen, three bedrooms and a bathroom became the basic accommodation sought by most homemakers in State or private housing.

American homes and home life had never been subject to the deprivations suffered in other parts of the world. For most of the decade America's progress in home developments had been fairly unhampered. Many attractive and comfortable new houses and apartment buildings were constructed, with the most up-to-date equipment and with a wide variety of colourful styles of furnishing and décor. Although considerable refinements and innovations were made in all areas to do with the home, which were later adapted by other countries, no really significant and dominating new style emerged which compared with the authority of art nouveau, art deco or the modernistic movement of the late twenties. A clearly defined strong new design direction had to wait for the arrival of the international 'contemporary style' of the 1950s.

The world situation at the end of the 1940s brought renewed anxieties into many homes and reminded people uncomfortably of the developments of the later 1930s. Amongst the struggling efforts to recover from the effects of the war came the fear of a new, even more destructive world war in which thousands of homes would be wiped out by atomic bombs. Rearmament began, civil defence forces were revived, and in America and in parts of Europe new public shelters were constructed and air-raid warnings practised.

In many parts of the world the unpleasantly combined problems of home austerity with the fears and preparations for war dampened out any possibility of the abandoned, wild behaviour experienced in the 'good time' jazz age of the 1920s. Four years after the end of the Second World War parents found most of the young generation quite serious and purposeful. Instead of practising tennis strokes and the latest dance steps, post-war sons left their homes, as similar young men had done 10 years before, for their first short back and sides military haircut and this time, for the start of their 2 years' compulsory national service. Although no longer regimented, neatly dressed daughters were expected to take life responsibly and were often engaged in some form of further education.

Mothers at home in Britain worried about stretching the rations and the gloomy outlook for the new decade. Rationing and restrictions were eased slightly during 1949; bread had become unrationed again and sweets and chocolates were taken off coupons although only temporarily at first. A slightly larger allocation of petrol was allowed, building licences for home improvements were increased and clothes rationing ended.

By 1950 good homes and affluent living standards for a wide section of the population had already become a reality in America; Germany was making a miraculous recovery from the devastation of the war and, to the amazement and dismay of many austerity weary British households, declared the end of rationing apart from sugar. Fortunately the post-war gloom in Britain was dispelled within a few years and life got decidedly better as the fifties advanced; improved homes for the majority were less than a decade away.

The 1950s

In 1950, at the mid-point of the 20th century, the generation reaching their fifties had gone from birth to middle age and had already witnessed one of the most revolutionary and fast-changing periods in history. The social pattern developed over successive generations, and the comparatively stable world of many Edwardian childhoods had been shattered beyond repair by the First World War. The brief post-war years of optimism and the brittle modern ideals of the 1920s coloured the young adult years of the generation born at the turn of the century; this was followed all too quickly in the 1930s by disillusionment and the economic depression. The approach of middle age had coincided uncomfortably with the beginning of the Second World War. The war, however, and its hardships, had proved to be a rallying point in the century for all age groups and classes, particularly in Britain where it was followed by the prolonged years of drab post-war austerity which were generally borne with a resigned acceptance by the entire population.

The quick succession of turbulent events during the first five decades of the century inevitably affected and changed significantly homes and home life throughout society. Living standards altered, the gulf between the classes narrowed, and the general level of homes became more democratic than anything which could have been envisaged in 1900.

By 1950 there were practically no households still living in the old long-established 'grand style', with palatial accommodation and unlimited numbers of servants which had been usual for many upper class families until 1914 and revised in a modified form between 1919 and 1939. Crippling taxes, the sale and requisition of land, spiralling costs for maintenance, and the demise of the servant population had put an end to the earlier impressive scale of top people's houses and their elegantly leisured way of life for the foreseeable future.

Most middle class homes had also become smaller and less pretentious over the years, with growing importance attached to updating household equipment – particularly labour saving appliances. Working class homes showed by far the most encouraging and noticeable improvement of the half century, and the differences between middle class and lower class housing became much less distinct. Types of architecture, the number of rooms, furniture, kitchen and bathroom fittings, and the size of gardens – although still recognisably different in style and quality – had lessened in each decade, particularly in the early post-Second World War years of the late forties and early fifties when special emphasis was often placed on fostering social equality.

Many young, newly married, middle class couples in 1950, looking anxiously for their first home, would have been happy to find a flat or small house to the standards used in the new, more enlightened State-sponsored housing, with their architect designs and professionally approved specifications, which were gradually becoming available for some of the more fortunate working class families of the time.

The social pattern in Europe in the first 6 or 7 years after the war was very different to the lively one which quickly followed the First World War. The blurring of class divisions, and the move towards a

A British living room of the early fifties, furnished in a quiet version of the new contemporary style

more equal level for homes, taking place against a background of continuing austerity further aggravated by the onset of the Cold War, all created an atmosphere which was not receptive to the introduction of light-hearted or frivolous new ideas for the home. The confident lead once given by European architects and sophisticated interior decorators in the twenties and thirties and the ultra style-conscious clientele with the time and money to receive the stylists' transitory design crazes were definitely in eclipse in the new post-war decade. At the beginning of the fifties a sensible and functional approach towards progressive ideas for the home predominated in most countries, including, sadly, Western Europe with its long tradition for design innovation.

Many believed the initiative for launching new styles had passed permanently from weary Europe to the stronger and more dynamic United States which had the financial and manufacturing resources to produce experimental and forward looking ideas and which had an increasingly affluent population to take them up. In 1950 prosperous American homes were more luxurious than ever; many Americans were enjoying the benefits of the early years of post-war expansion and naturally spent money on improved homes. Pleasant looking architect-designed houses and bungalows in a gently modern style, had attractively spacious living areas – colourfully decorated, richly curtained, and well arranged with new-looking furniture including the most up-to-date television sets and record players. Very modern kitchens and bathrooms were standard in these homes and many houses featured terraces and patios set out with glamorous looking garden furniture, which sometimes, in traditional Hollywood style, overlooked the family swimming pool.

Affluent American homes represented to many Europeans an almost fantasy world of unobtainably high living standards. Homes in America remained at a higher level than in most countries during the following decades, particularly for the middle section of society;

Young people's first independent home was often rather a basic bed-sitting room; the room above with its good quality of modern furniture would have been of a higher standard than was general at the time

Modest semi-detached house showing definite characteristics of the fifties with the use of wood boarding and bright colours

but gradually after the difficult years in the middle of the century, Europe and other parts of the world began to recover and rebuild and expand their industries. The 1950s became a period of slow but steady progress for the majority. By the end of the decade the gap in living standards between America and Europe had closed far more than most people would have thought possible 10 years earlier, and European designs for a mass market in architecture and interior decoration had become once again major trend setters and an important world influence. Scandinavian, Italian and British designing all contributed to the new international style; France and Germany took part in the progressive developments but were not as prominent as they had been in the modernistic design movement of the 1920s.

In England the 1951 Festival of Britain staged in London and cleverly timed to take place on the centenary of the Great Exhibition of 1851 acted as a catalyst for the revival of design consciousness and the emergence of more clearly defined post-war style for exteriors and interiors in Britain. It also helped to give a strong boost internationally to the prestige of British goods, which it was hoped would create the extra impetus needed to expand further the important export trade as an earner of hard currencies, particularly American dollars.

Restrictions on building and furniture production had lingered on in Britain into the fifties and had held back the development of a strong new character for the style of post-war homes until the Festival year, when the value of promoting designers and their new ideas had at last been realised. Well-respected manufacturers of furniture and household goods produced ranges of forward looking styles especially for the Exhibition. Art schools and art colleges, such as the well-known Royal College of Art in London, which emphasised designing for industry and, with the interest generated by the Festival of Britain very much in mind, also actively encouraged their 1951 students to produce lively and imaginative ideas for textiles and pottery. There was a growing and exciting feeling that designers were on the verge of a kind of renaissance in industrial and decorative styling, albeit a rather controlled one at first.

Few important design developments take place suddenly and their origins can usually be traced back for at least a decade. The new 'Contemporary Style' which was to become so typical of the 1950s, and is often thought of as unique to the 10 year span, was no exception; it had its beginnings in the modern Scandinavian furniture and textile designs of the late thirties and the progressive American ideas for open plan homes in the forties.

The arrival of a new style at quite a commercial level was noted in the *Daily Mail Ideal Home Book for 1951-52*. 'This has been a satisfactory year for designers of contemporary furniture. Modern furniture has had to battle in a world which has fallen deeply in love with Regency and Victorian styles, but now there is a change. Contemporary furniture is seen everywhere and is attracting new admirers every day. And now its general character has crystallised into a recognisable form. Its woods are always sleek and light. It has

Opposite
Colour was one of the most important features of the new designs for furnishings and textiles

an air of simpleness, almost rusticity, which is deceptive in such graceful and sophisticated stuff. The chairs and tables all stand on outspread tapered legs like a ballet dancer on her points. This off-the-floor feeling prevails in all the new furniture. Even pieces of such weight as wardrobes are poised on little legs. The idea is to give a feeling of wider floor space in small rooms – floating, the designers call it.'

Some of the contemporary furniture of the fifties tends in retrospect to look rather top-heavy and precariously balanced on their unsubstantial splayed legs; broken furniture legs, like broken stiletto heels on fashionable women's shoes, tended to be a rather characteristic feature of the time. Slim legs were also emphasised in another section on new designs for varying sized coffee tables which were becoming increasingly popular in the fifties. 'Tables are all slim, pale, glossy, and – of course – on tiptoe. Small coffee tables are made in imaginative shapes called after clouds, boomerangs, palettes, or just down-to-earth kidneys. Many of these are planned to fit round the side of armchairs, where they look just like shy tots cleaving to a well-upholstered Mum.'

These rather fanciful descriptions of what today seems rather ordinary and unimpressive furniture perhaps need to be viewed in the context of their time. In the early fifties Britain and most of Europe had been starved of new developments in interior design for over 10 years and were naturally joyful over the beginnings of a more imaginative era. Looking back on the recent past of 25 to 30 years ago, the styles of the period are still too near and familiar to have acquired the nostalgic charm of the more distant decades such as the twenties and thirties, which in the fifties were generally considered far more unattractive than the designs of a generation ago are today. Time distance usually adds enchantment to earlier styles of interior decoration or past fashions in clothes.

The basic designs and shapes of the contemporary furniture of the 1950s, particularly in the first half of the decade, were fairly straightforward and simple with very little ornamentation and surface decoration. Easy chairs and couches were frequently based on the traditional lines of a high-backed upholstered library chair, with curved sides and comfortably rounded arm rests, or alternatively wooden arms similar to the ones used on country style Windsor chairs. Two-colour effects were sometimes featured in these soft furnishings; a dark shade, particularly black, was often used for the back and sides and the contrast was further emphasised in some cases by the application of another fabric such as leather. For people who preferred straighter, space-saving lines for couches, convertible bed settees which looked like conventional divan beds on raised legs, with firm flatly upholstered backs, were very popular especially in small flats or bed sitting rooms. Neatly proportioned, understated-looking dining-room furniture with long narrow sideboards often with plain undecorated sliding doors were a popular choice in many newly furnished homes. Room dividing units which consisted of varying spaced and adjustable shelves together with high and low placed cupboards, mounted on a framework of metal or wood, were becoming increasingly popular for useful additional shelf and storage

Fashion conscious homes often mixed plain and patterned walls in the same room

space and to act as partitions to separate living rooms from dining-rooms or dining-rooms from working kitchen areas. Bed-room suites, although declining in popularity, were still liked in many middle class homes; the newer designs followed the quiet lines of the modern style with plain or panelled doors and long slim shapes, for dressing tables, chests of drawers and narrow matching wooden bed-heads.

Apart from the obligatory widely angled leg shapes in metal or wood, so admired at the time, the character of the new contemporary style relied rather less on design innovation and more on the use of colour than the other important design movements of the 20th century. Strong colour burst on the fashion scene in the early 1950s and gave the new developments in interior design some powerful additional impact; the emphasis on plenty of colour was possibly a natural reaction from the grey years of rationing and restrictions. In the *Homes and Gardens 1952 Design Review* the unadulterated primary shades of red, yellow and blue were extensively used for wall decorations, furnishing fabrics and light-fittings.

A design for a 'Harlequin' dining-room 9 feet by 12 feet leading into a working kitchen space 8 feet by 6 feet featured cerulean blue, lemon peel, and cherry; one wall in the dining area was white, another bright yellow; the cupboard unit with a framework of white had alternately coloured doors in red and black, and the narrow dining-table top was divided into two equal halves, one white and one brown. Matching thin legged stools each had a different coloured seating top: red, white, yellow and brown. The floor in both rooms was covered in a harlequin patterned linoleum in red, white, blue and yellow, and the kitchen wall facing the wide opening from the dining area was painted in strong cherry red. The room was a more extreme example of the trend for very bright colour, but it emphasised the conviction already held by leading magazines on interior decoration for uninhibited colour schemes.

To soften the use of clear primary shades, colours such as flame red or lemon peel yellow were sometimes contrasted with sludgy tones; dull greens, rather appropriately called Thames green, inky blues and deep grey browns. To lighten the overall effect of mixing powerful bright and deep intense colours for walls, ceilings and furnishings, white was often used for paintwork, one wall, a ceiling, and possibly a lampshade or some picture frames. Some of the more sophisticated colour schemes featured colour-clashing bright shades, such as red, orange and purple which were used separately for the upholstery of individual plain-coloured couches and chairs. The hot colours of the furnishings were calmed by the use of cool, pale tints for walls and ceilings. Walls were painted in silver grey, and the ceiling in pale lilac. To tie up the planned colour scheme, one wall or room dividing screen was painted in one of the hot bright colours and the carpet toned to the lighter coloured walls or ceiling.

For people who were unsure about decorating their home in a very strong colour spectrum, mid-tones provided a fashionable alternative range. Citrus colourings, such as lime green and acid yellow were popular with many new home-makers and were very characteristic of the early 1950s, especially when teamed with pale or dark greys, lightish blues, particularly soft turquoise, terracotta, and reddy-brown plum shades.

Patterned wallpapers which had been out of favour for several decades made a confident return to style-conscious homes in the early fifties as an additional part of the much more extrovert trend in wall decorations and furnishings which were quickly gaining acceptance with the younger generation. Designs for wallpapers ranged from tiny neatly drawn dots, stars and classic Regency style stripes to large trellis patterns, huge motifs and great medallions. Big designs were usually used for one wall or the alcoves on each side of a fireplace and were often available with a matching coloured paper drawn in a small unobtrusive but complementary pattern for use on the other walls. Instead of the rather busy look of mixing various sized patterns together, some rooms featured either a small or large designed paper with two or three walls painted in a matching or toning plain colour.

New design trends in furnishing fabrics were also enjoying great popularity, particularly the wide range of prints for curtainings. Although subtle, modern designs for woven fabrics were well established and traditional printed floral designs remained successful and commercial with a large section of the conservatively minded general public. The newer ideas of the early fifties were usually in the form of abstracts. Motifs such as medallions, sun faces, and stylised flower or leaf shapes, drawn with considerable artistic licence, were all widely used themes; the most inventive and characteristic designs of the time were, however, the smallish all-over variety of shapes

Opposite
A Harlequin dining room with an uninhibited use of bold primary colours

142

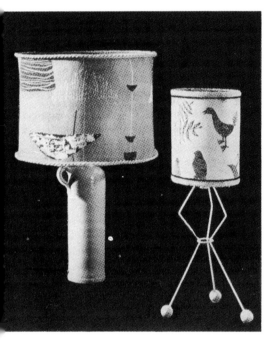

The influence of contemporary styling extended strongly into light fitting designs; new ideas for table lamps, centre lights and standard lamps were unashamedly 1950s with their insect-like legs

and lines, which were quite different in style from the severe abstracts of the late twenties and early thirties. Designs of the fifties were less hard and clearly defined and tended towards a rather whimsical approach. Squares were never quite square and varied in size and shape in the same pattern. Oval or lozenge shapes were used instead of true circles, and both rounded and squarish motifs were often featured together on a background of fine stripes or were arranged to form banks or blocks of irregular stripes which were sometimes interspersed with scratchy looking lines, usually spikey hat-pin or knitting needle shapes, or unrelated triangular or harlequin motifs. Colourings in these busy patternings followed the fashionable bright and mid shades, often combining the two, and because of the moderate scale of most of the designs rarely looked as dominant as the wider expanse of colour available for plain and patterned wall decorations.

Many well-known stores promoted their ranges of contemporary household fabrics to give a total look to the new style in interior décor. Liberty's department store in London, always noted for exciting textiles, advertised their 'Young Liberty' range regularly, pointing out the variety of designs 'so moderately priced! 48 inches wide, a yard 11/9 (59p)'. David Whitehead textiles were also very well known in the fifties; they were closely associated with the new style movement and were respected for their commercial interpretation and marketing of progressive designs. Types of fabrics were still limited in selection, particularly during the first half of the decade; simple cotton twills and poplins or linens with slub or hopsack weaves were the base fabrics mainly used for printing on and were in fact more suited to the designs of the time than the wide ranges of lusher materials which became available in the later post-war years.

The influence of contemporary styling also extended strongly into light-fitting designs. Novel ideas for table lamps, centre lights and standard lamps were unashamedly 1950s modern. The simple drum, pumpkin or pendant shapes in white or parchment coloured plastic, glass, linen or raffia, became everyday basic fittings in many homes and often remained unchanged and unnoticed for years. More distinctive styles sometimes replaced conventional standard lamps and featured a metal stand with two or three movable arms each fitted with individual lights. New ideas for table lamps had either long curved stems or an insect-like leg with a centre joint. Plain brightly coloured metal shades usually completed the various styles and were specially designed to be easily angled up or down. Some of the simple better proportioned light-fittings blended in well and helped to complete the look of rooms furnished and decorated in the new style. A few of the most successful, easy to adjust, table lamps became firmly established classic designs which are still manufactured today.

The more extreme and aggressive examples of 1950s styling, with overdone and exaggerated angles and curves, and the multi-lamped centre-ceiling fittings, described as 'cascades', with six or nine brass or steel highly-arched brackets finishing in black and red enamelled lampshade holders, represented the harsher side of contemporary designing which, although chosen for some homes, were more

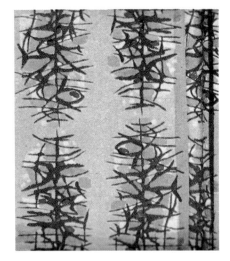

generally used in commercial buildings such as hotels, bars and restaurants.

Homes furnished and decorated in the newly modern style of the fifties showed the most complete change since the late twenties. The outside design of houses built a generation ago can also usually be dated to the style of the early post-Second World War era. The exterior changes, however, although considerable, had not arrived as quickly or with the same impact as the colourful developments for interiors. The trend which became so widespread in the fifties for gently modern homes with plenty of open-looking windows and porches, built in brick or stone and partly weatherboarded, had been a clearly emerging style for over 10 years, and some advanced European and American houses built as early as the late thirties could easily be wrongly dated to the early fifties. The contemporary design for interiors had also started tentatively before the war but the strongly recognisable character of the style belongs much more definitely to the 1950s.

The lay-out and design of houses, bungalows and blocks of flats in the 1950s and early 1960s saw the full development of the important new mid-20th century style in domestic architecture for the mass market. Plenty of natural light, improved comfort, and the use of open plan ideas in the distribution of floor space, arranged for a casual and informal way of life, were the cheerful characteristics aimed at in the new homes. The modern style was most successfully interpreted in bungalows and semi-bungalows with simple, unpretentious lines which usually incorporated slightly sloped or angled end or centre walls built in natural brick or stone. Windows were nearly always made the most noticeable feature in these frank looking homes. Living areas sometimes had floor-to-ceiling windows at each end with the main garden end-windows made as sliding doors, opening a large proportion of the room directly on to the garden and giving the benefit of a pleasantly outdoor feeling to life in the summer months. To emphasise the idea of linking the house and the garden more closely, varying sized house plants providing areas of flowers and greenery became popular throughout the living areas. The fashionable big window theme was also frequently used next to, or around, the front door revealing clearly the hall, staircase and landing. Some of the conservatively minded, particularly the older generation, used to a more private look to their homes, were very unsure about houses where the internal contents and day-to-day family life were so publicly on view. *Punch*, with its flair for social comment, showed many drawings on the subject, usually pointing out the lack of privacy accepted without concern by families living contentedly and unself-consciously in their contemporary style homes.

Although not all the modern houses built in the fifties featured wall-size windows, large areas of glass were very much a part of the space conscious open-plan designs which were quickly gaining acceptance with younger home-makers. Most of the new homes were at last built with efficient central heating and better insulation; open solid-fuel fires were either dispensed with altogether or kept to one centrally placed fire in the living room, usually in the form of a

Textile designers in the first half of the decade usually favoured rather busy looking abstract patterns

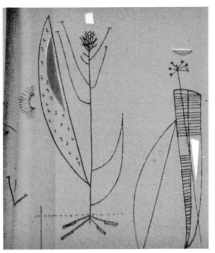

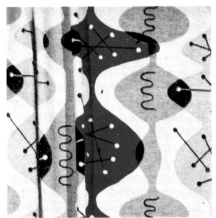

Liberty

of London

simple square opening in the wall where the fire was lit for its cheerful effect rather than as an essential form of heating. The establishment of good insulation and easy-to-run forms of central heating made the use of big windows and of open, intercommunicating living and working areas practical in a way that would not have been possible for homes earlier in the century.

Ground floor room space in many new houses was often planned as one overall family living area. Conventional ideas on rooms were merged into one another; entrance halls were formed at the end of the general living/dining areas and were partially separated by permanent or movable screens or room-dividing sections of shelves and cupboards. Working kitchens or a combined kitchen and eating area were partly screened off, were sometimes placed round the corner of an L-shaped main room or opened directly from the sitting room area through a wide entrance space.

The main advantages of open-plan homes were that they gave even modest sized accommodation a feeling of spaciousness and unity; family living became closer, busy housewives were nearer to their children and husbands and felt less isolated by the time inevitably spent in the kitchen, which in earlier homes had always been quite separated from the living room or dining-room. The disadvantage of opening up the family living space was the loss of some privacy through the amalgamation of rooms and the more communal way of life understandably led at times to strain and irritability in many households. The more extreme concept of open-plan homes did not prove to be as universally popular or as enduring a trend as had been expected by forward-looking architects and interior designers in the fifties, but it did help to establish the importance of making the best use of limited floor space, with fewer unnecessary small rooms, good natural lighting, and working kitchens adjacent to the living areas. All of these have remained basic and accepted ideas for house and flat plans up to the present day.

The style and lay-out of gardens around the contemporary houses of the fifties changed to suit the architectural lines of the new homes. The neat varying-shaped flower beds, and the artificially created divisions with hedges, fences and complex arrangements of pathways, so popular in the earlier decades, looked too fussy for the simple uncomplicated lines of the newer houses. A sweeping landscaped approach, even for the comparatively small garden, with the maximum use of easy-to-maintain lawns, paved terraces and patios edged with casually arranged flowers, shrubs and trees, provided a much more complimentary and flattering setting. It also gave the modern developments of houses and flats the benefit of longer and wider views – even if the scope of the outlook was limited to other houses and gardens, there was at least a less boxed-in feeling which suited the more informal approach to neighbours and every-day life generally adopted by young families of the time.

Between the late thirties and the mid-fifties many house prices trebled; the price increases were usually higher than advances in earnings over the same period and were viewed with growing concern by many people particularly first-time home-seekers. Although the rate of inflation in property values was still modest in comparison with the hyper-inflation of later decades, it was already seen as a disturbing trend. Buying a home as an important investment grew in popularity with a larger section of the population more than ever before and the age of mass home ownership began in earnest. By the second half of the fifties typical, modest semi-detached houses with three bedrooms, and two-bedroomed bungalows which were being built all over Britain, were in the £2000 to £3000 price bracket; larger individually designed detached houses and bungalows were generally from £3000 to £5000. Then, as today, a high proportion of houses, particularly new houses, were bought with Building Society mortgages. Interest rates varied slightly but were not as volatile as the worrying see-saw of rates endured later in the century. In the 1950s interest was usually around 5 per cent or 6 per cent and normally repayable over a slightly shorter period than the much heavier mortgages so common today.

Until the 1950s flats were usually rented. This began to change with the post-war housing shortage and the steep rise in the value of domestic property. Finding a flat or apartment to rent, especially unfurnished, was very difficult in many countries particularly where rent-restricting legislation – originally designed to stop profiteering

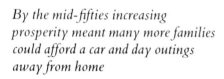

By the mid-fifties increasing prosperity meant many more families could afford a car and day outings away from home

Specially designed patio areas were added to many more homes

by freezing rents at their pre-war level – had eventually resulted in an aggravation of the market scarcity. Tenants on fixed rents were naturally reluctant to move and landlords with available accommodation were not prepared to re-let at an uneconomic rent. A way round the situation was often found by asking prospective new tenants for what was known as 'key money': totally unrealistic sums of money were charged for fixtures and fittings – usually fairly unremarkable carpets, curtains and kitchen equipment. If a substantial sum was agreed for the so-called fixtures, arrangements were then made to reassign leases at their low controlled rents. In view of the difficulties in renting, and the growing investment value of home ownership, people began to consider the idea of buying a flat on a long lease or if possible freehold, particularly in the cities.

Newly converted flats in large Victorian houses and apartments in new purpose-built blocks soon found a receptive market. Some of the more highly priced conversions, however, which took place in London's fashionable districts were at first considered very expensive by people still unused to the idea of buying a flat. Two- and three-bedroomed apartments in elegant houses in Knightsbridge's Ennismore Gardens, for example, were offered on long leases in the later fifties for around £3000 to £5000; many people expressed doubts about finding buyers willing to pay such prices.

The 1950s undoubtedly saw great changes in homes. Many of the new concepts: the better use of space, improved comforts and equipment, a more casual style of living and the tremendous increase in home ownership, all came to fruition during the decade and have remained as an established part of later 20th century attitudes towards homes. The changes of the fifties like the earlier innovations of the century were not immediately adopted in all homes or even the majority of them, and particularly in Europe where the more universal updating came in the following decade when general prosperity reached its peak. Although the acceptance of new ideas was not as widespread as it was to become a few years later, the contemporary style in architecture and interior decoration during the fifties was certainly a more extensive and commercial movement taken up by a larger section of the population than the earlier fashionable styles of the 20th century. This was owing to expanding economies with almost full employment and rising earnings on a much larger scale than anything experienced in the previous decades. A mass consumer society was taking shape and the bright new designs for homes appealed to the growing range of customers.

Increasing prosperity also produced changes to life inside the home and to family relationships. Parents and children were no longer obliged to spend so much time together in the home because of the lack of money for outside activities. Teenagers were made much more generous allowances and young people starting in their first jobs usually received far higher earnings than their counterparts in any of the earlier decades. The young in all classes had more spending money than ever before which they disposed of readily on clothes, entertainment, and for a growing number, their own transport. Car ownership was still not usual for people in their late

A softer interpretation of a planned contemporary living room; less vibrant colour and the 1950s modern furniture teamed with traditional style, dining chairs

Whole living room walls of windows opening directly into the garden were a popular feature of many of the more expensive new houses

teens and early twenties in Europe but motorbikes and motor scooters parked at the side of the steadily increasing number of family cars were becoming a familiar sight in many streets.

Tearing around on motorbikes, meeting friends in the new coffee bars, and playing loud pop music in their rooms was all part of the new teenage cult which had spread to Europe from America. The early pop singers, Elvis Presley, rock-and-rolling Bill Haley and his Comets, and the skiffle groups were the new heroes of the mid-fifties teenagers. Many young people formed groups imitating their favourite professional performers and practised their loud music in one another's homes. Laboured piano playing was less frequently heard from neat suburban houses but exuberant if somewhat amateurish rock-and-roll resounded from family homes and sent a stream of complaining older-generation neighbours to many front doors; the complaints, passed on to their children by weary mothers and fathers, were usually received curtly with comments, in the teenage jargon of the fifties, of not being 'with it' or of being 'square'.

Firm parental control and dominating home influences which had been lessening since the beginning of the century declined even more sharply during the fifties. Many parents felt they were unable to compete for their children's attention with the strong external influences on the behaviour patterns of the young. This was especially true in America where prosperous homes and liberally minded uninterfering parents had become an established way of life. The American media began to debate the lack of closeness between the generations in some families which was often described as the 'generation gap'.

A more placid acceptance of the social changes was usual in Britain; the middle aged were enjoying their more comfortable homes and felt less inclined to worry about their children's differing attitudes and tastes. Television viewing provided at least one focal point in the home for all generations; most families were still experiencing the novelty of watching their first television set.

Children followed the adventures of Muffin the Mule regularly, and teenagers' feet tapped and hands and arms sometimes hand-jived to the sound of the introductory music to the *Six Five Special* and *Juke Box Jury*, both of which were habitually seen to keep up-to-date with the progress of the latest 'disc' in the 'charts' which were already published weekly and had become the established barometers of popular music. Later in the evening mothers and fathers settled comfortably to watch Eamonn Andrews present *What's My Line* with its well-known panel of celebrities which usually included the unpredictable Gilbert Harding; John Freeman's searching interviews with the famous in *Face to Face* were also often considered compulsive viewing. The power of television to hold many people's interest in the home during the limited number of broadcasting hours each evening, to the exclusion of all other activities, frequently resulted in pre-prepared evening meals being eaten round the television set in the dim glow of the black and white picture from a small screen. Enterprising suppliers of frozen foods produced a selection of special TV dinners, rather like, and of a similar standard to, the average aeroplane meal. The TV dinners came in sealed foil containers which were easily heated up in the oven and reduced the time spent away from television viewing to the minimum.

Convenience foods in general began to gain worldwide popularity; frozen vegetables, meat and fish were used on an ever-growing scale. Many more married women went out to work in the new era of high employment and consequently had less time to spend in the preparation of meals. Living styles changed amongst younger married couples; less importance was attached to the old housewifely virtues of thrifty housekeeping which had been practised by mothers and grandmothers with careful shopping, with preparing time-consuming but cleverly economic meals, with jam making and fruit preserving. The higher joint incomes of the time were spent on home improvements, with their growing investment value, new cars, and continental holidays.

Europeans visited one another's countries in far greater numbers and more frequently than ever before. The conservatively minded British, influenced by many more holidays taken abroad, began to become more internationally minded; French and Italian ideas on food and drink began to alter the traditional British diet. Coffee and wine drinking increased substantially, foreign cheeses grew in popularity, and pasta dishes established themselves as basic favourites with many families.

Further education with the tremendous increase in Government-sponsored grants and scholarships was another cause of changes in family life. Many more young men and women from modest backgrounds benefited from University, art, and design training and left their home environment in their late teens or early twenties to take up a place at a college in another part of the country where they experienced the freedom of living away from parental supervision in their own bed-sitting room or in flats shared with other students. This generation born between 1935 and 1940, to parents who had been fearful for their future, turned out to be one of the most fortunate of the century. They were too young to be seriously affected by the war and its aftermath; as they were growing up most of the world's economies were beginning a period of unparalleled expansion, career choice and opportunities were available to the majority on a scale previously unknown, and 20 years still lay ahead free from world wars and economic disasters.

A less inhibited, more democratic way of life with wider horizons and a strong preference for a home in the contemporary style was becoming established on an international scale with the bright new generation reaching their adult years. The slightly older, well-established, and affluent section of society in the thirties to fifties age groups were less enthusiastic about homes in the modern style; many were still influenced by the richer, plushier houses of the well off in the pre-war years. With the end of austerity and the return of a consumers' market there was, amongst some of the prosperous and mature, a definite revival of the earlier grander way of life and a more obviously affluent style of interior decoration.

Victorian and Regency influences which had been so popular in fashion-conscious circles in the late 1930s and during the 1940s became even more lavishly interpreted in some of the richly fashionable homes of the 1950s. Strongly coloured walls in ruby reds, yellow golds and emerald greens were painted, or papered with textured flock-type wallpapers which sometimes had the tone-on-tone effect of a darker shade used on a slightly lighter version of the same colour. Pictures and mirrors covered the walls in almost the same profusion as they had at the beginning of the century and were often framed in ornate gilt. Expensive over-elaborate and heavily gilded mirrors edged with neo-classic columns, twisted vine leaves, clusters of flowers, and sometimes topped with a couple of angled horn-blowing cherubs were greatly admired features in some living rooms or entrance halls. At least one fancily framed gilt mirror per household usually set over a Victorian marble fireplace, had become almost obligatory in these pseudo-19th century interiors.

Rooms were busily furnished with a variety of not always very complementary styles, which ranged from the formal elegance of the 18th century to the solid heaviness of the late Victorian years. Early

"*You can't go wrong with G.E.C.*"

says Eamonn Andrews

Televisions like the cabinet model on the opposite page and this less expensive table set found their way into more and more homes as the decade progressed and television personalities such as Eamonn Andrews became household names

153

19th century French Empire chairs in black and gilt were upholstered in bold Regency stripes and set next to turn-of-the-century chesterfield couches in deeply buttoned squeaky leather. Simple English country style corner cupboards in well-matured polished wood were placed near marble topped tables which were supported by crouching turbaned black slaves or a complicated network of elaborately decorated legs painted in gold. Cabinets, desks and sideboards in differing types of wood and styles of design were often found in the same room, and round side tables in the typical Victorian style, were covered in silk or velour cloths and their tops were cluttered with a selection of old family photographs, books, ornaments, and matching cigarette lighters and ashtrays in simulated marble with decorative gilt tippings. Styles for table lamps also followed period influences and were often designed as gilded classic columns or copied the look of old-fashioned oil lamps with specially designed bases in glass or china. Centre light-fittings literally topped all the theatrical richness and show with huge gilt lanterns or cut-glass crystal chandeliers.

The early 20th century architects and interior designers who had pioneered so passionately for an end to Victorian clutter and the adoption of cleaner simpler lines, more suited to what they saw as the beginning of a new century of scientific progress and social reform would no doubt have been disappointed to see the showy clutter of many of the ultra-chic homes of the 1950s. They would have been astounded to know how some fashionable homes had changed from the despised fussiness of the early 1900s to the almost monastic simplicity of the late twenties in a generation only to be quickly followed in less than a decade by a reactionary trend, culminating in the space of another generation in a popular neo-Victorian revival. Fashion had turned a full circle in under 50 years.

By the late fifties many countries were becoming accustomed to more affluent times, and trends in interior design began to quieten again after their rather exuberant phase. The two predominant trends, of 19th century revivalism and the contemporary self-consciousness of the 1950s, both softened and in many cases merged into a pleasantly human style where old and new ideas mixed quite harmoniously. Vibrant colour was less popular for wall decorations; plain white walls were liked again together with hessian shades and soft tobacco browns. Individual walls in strongly contrasting colours, although still used, were becoming less fashionable; when a strong shade was featured it was usually painted on all the walls of a hall or dining-room; chocolate browns and dark greens were especially popular and provided a flattering and sophisticated background for pictures and furniture.

Many of the young style-conscious home-makers began to mix quite dramatically different types of furniture successfully in the same room and were less concerned with presenting a total unity of style than had been usual in the earlier part of the decade. Expensive modern leather armchairs and matching stools, so sought after by the young, were often put with items as varied as a Victorian bentwood rocking chair and a simple basket shaped seating unit in wicker set on

Opposite
Rich looking 19th century influences in interior decoration which had been fashionable since the late thirties continued to be popular in many affluent homes

metal legs or suspended by cords from the ceiling. Simply constructed light-looking storage units with easily adjusted wooden shelves placed on a framework of black painted metal sometimes acted as a combined sideboard, bookcase, and display section. Nearby dining tables were either in a similar complementary style with a wood top and slim black metal legs, or to add an interesting period touch to the room, Edwardian pub tables with marble tops and curved wrought iron legs were sometimes used with black or brightly coloured bentwood dining chairs, originating from the same period.

Modern coffee tables had become standard furnishings in these rooms. They were usually in wood, oblong shaped with a lower shelf for magazines and newspapers and set on the familiar thin, angled legs. Table tops were in matching wood, glass or fancy tiles, usually in darkish blues or browns. Coffee tables became a focal point in most modern rooms, particularly with the decline in the use of open fires. Table tops were often used to display items of personal taste and interest such as unusual ashtrays, pottery, and large glossy books on art, travel or the theatre. These books began to be described as 'coffee table books' and were easy for visitors to glance through while busy hosts in the servantless post-war age prepared drinks or a meal.

The use of wall space in the modern homes of the late 1950s was quite relaxed and varied considerably according to the preferences of the occupiers. Prints of well-known pictures by fashionable painters, such as the rather haunting works of Bernard Buffet, often shared a wall with a primitive style oil of a colourful still-life group painted by a less well-known artist. In the same room novel items as differing as a Russian style ikon, a late Victorian mahogany wall clock, and a Hussar's helmet or sword, probably found in London's Portobello Road or the Paris flea market, shared space with line and wash drawings of a pale and interesting looking girl with long straight hair, or a moody young man with a Marlon Brando inspired Roman haircut. Paintings, drawings and photographs were hung singly or in groups and although not as crowded together as in the plushy Victorian inspired homes, they were always important features, chosen carefully, and usually proved to be a talking point with new guests to the home.

The style of entertaining had changed to suit the new attitudes and newly designed homes of the young sophisticates. The anti-establishment behaviour of the much publicised Beatniks proved to be an influence on some of the young. Girls in tapered trousers and over-sized sweaters, or schoolgirl style flannel pinafore dresses designed by the clever new young designer, Mary Quant, and worn with black stockings, lounged on couches and chairs talking to bored looking young men in dark trousers, polo neck sweaters and leather jackets. A studied 'cool' manner was cultivated and the world's problems were often debated over many glasses of wine and to the background of an Ella Fitzgerald or Frank Sinatra LP.

Floor coverings were given special attention and importance in the more prosperous homes of the 1950s. Patterned lino or squares of patterned carpet with a surround of stained floorboards, so usual in

Veneer, although less widely used was sometimes adapted to contemporary design themes like the harlequin effect on the above sideboard

the early decades, was often considered old-fashioned and unsuited to the new trends in interior décor. Plain coloured, good quality wall-to-wall carpet became the admired ideal. Many people who had been used to the un-centrally heated cold floored homes of their childhood revelled in the comfort of warm houses and close carpeting; carpeted bathrooms were considered especially luxurious. Less expensive but serviceable fitted carpets for more budget-minded homes were made in strong haircord and were usually in practical colours such as grey, brown or dark green. Although all-over carpeting was aimed at by many home-makers, some of the new open-plan houses with their expanses of window and sliding doors opening directly on to patios and gardens required more basic easy-to-maintain floor coverings. Polished wood, cork squares or tiles were often favoured in these homes with two or three rugs used to break the colder effect of uncarpeted surfaces.

Patterned carpeting and rugs were sometimes used in style-conscious homes but the predominating trend was for plain colours, possibly because of the extensive use of multi-colour designs for curtainings and wall decorations, especially in the earlier part of the decade. Plain tufty cream wool or bleached fur rugs became very fashionable in the late fifties for use on either fitted carpets or plain surfaced floors and looked attractive and flattering with the modern or period furniture popular at the time.

Until the 1950s the ideal for a bathroom had been fairly standardised; modern fitments were in white or a limited range of colour tints; wall tiles were in a toning shade and sometimes had a neat border in contrasting dark blue or black. Large unframed mirrors, heated towel rails and plain functional cupboards completed the uncluttered rather clinical appearance which had been considered the ultimate in progressive 20th century bathrooms. Enthusiastic

The leather club style chair has become a classic design still produced today

estate agents often described these plainly modern bathrooms in their advertisements with pride, going into great detail over all the fittings.

In the later 1950s a reactionary trend away from austere bathrooms began to develop. The new more lighthearted and varied approach to decorating a bathroom as a more interesting room, ranged from the boldly colourful to the prettily feminine. Small rooms with basic white fitments were livened up by the use of a strong colour scheme such as red, white and black. The walls were painted fire engine red and hung with white framed mirrors and pictures; white paint was used for the ceiling and woodwork; the side panel of the bath was usually in black and the floor was covered in a black and white square design either in the form of tiles or lino. To echo the patterned flooring and complete the colour scheme, curtains were made in a smaller sized black and white check gingham; simple cotton gingham was very popular in the fifties both for household fabrics and dress materials.

The wider use of patterned wallpaper also helped to give character to some bathrooms although the effect was sometimes too overpowering. Contemporary style abstracts, particularly harlequin designs in strong primary shades, were memorably striking, and unexpected, but sometimes found to be dizzily distracting when

Typical kitchens of the period with units and working tops in several different colours

Chequers

A design by Terence Conran

A selection from the range of patterns in Midwinter Modern **STYLECRAFT** tableware. You can buy it piece by piece from open stocks and replacements will be available for years to come.

W. R. Midwinter Ltd., Burslem, Staffordshire

viewed for the first time in the early morning. Small flowery Victorian designs in pastel colourings gave a far more gentle look, and the countrified influence was often followed through with the use of fancily framed mirrors and small groups of pictures. Lace curtaining or softly draped semi-sheer fabrics hung from old-fashioned brass or wooden curtain rails and hooks added to the feeling of femininity. One or two pieces of turn-of-the-century furniture, such as a small glass-fronted cabinet or a marble topped washstand complete with bowl and jug all helped to give emphasis to the quaint old-world effect which was becoming a growing trend and one that would develop even more strongly in the later decades when nostalgic styles of décor became so commercially successful.

Some of the kitchens in fashion-conscious homes also began to lose the starkly functional appearance which had been associated with modern kitchens from the thirties onwards. Stainless steel sinks and draining boards set into a group of planned wall units which usually included the cooker and fridge, once so admired by Europeans as ultra-modern American kitchens, had become much more commonplace all over the world and were built into most new houses and flats as a standard range of fittings. These mass produced units with metal or wood cupboards, some fronted with frosted glass sliding doors and teamed up with Formica shelves and working tops, usually formed a pattern of strong contrasting colour. The basic framework of the units was painted white and the non-glass doors, open shelves and surface tops were in bright red, yellow or blue and in some cases equal amounts of two of the colours such as alternate doors in red and blue with shelving space in either red or blue; or in another scheme all the cupboard fronts were in one shade and the

Very 1950s-style tableware designed by Terence Conran later to become famous for the Habitat shops with their new concepts in home equipment and furnishings

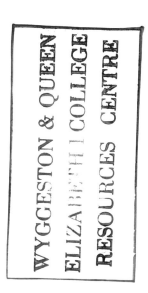

Next page
Many inner city families in the later fifties moved from small houses into new blocks of high-rise flats

working tops in another. These boldly extrovert kitchen designs began to look rather garish and tinny in the more understated quieter homes of the late fifties.

Fashionably minded young people began to include both the kitchen and the bathroom in the general character of the home and arranged them as pleasantly inviting rooms. Although the calmer use of coloured Formica remained a standard style for many kitchens, natural-toned wood began to be a newly admired feature in the rather more countrified style of others. Pine doors were popular for cupboard units and matching wood seating sections were sometimes built-in to a corner to save space and had high wood strip backs rather like traditional wall seats in English country pubs.

Other larger kitchens adopted an old-fashioned farmhouse style with the revived use of dressers displaying fancy china on open shelves and a sturdy wood table surrounded by a selection of natural wood or cheerfully painted late Victorian or Edwardian chairs. Over the table a converted brass oil lamp was often hung, and a red and white check tablecloth and matching check curtains together with pottery storage jars on open shelves, and hanging bunches of fresh herbs all added to the informal charm of these cottagey kitchens.

Convenient kitchen equipment; refrigerators, modern cookers and washing machines which had been available since before the Second World War, were mass produced in far larger quantities during the 1950s at competitive prices that were within the reach of many more families with modest incomes. By the end of the decade up-to-date electric or gas cookers and moderate sized fridges had become general in most homes and were considered necessities rather than luxuries. Other less essential kitchen appliances – improved cooking pans, electric mixers, and scales – although not as usual as in the homes of the sixties and seventies, were steadily increasing in popularity.

The growth in consumer spending encouraged manufacturers of every type of home furnishing and home equipment to improve the design and selection of their products; competition increased and a buyers' market developed on an ever-growing scale. Manufacturers in Britain had at last shaken off any of the lingering effects of post-war restrictions and were quickly gaining a good reputation for styling and quality.

Conran furniture, which was to become so well known in the following years in the now world famous Conran and Habitat shops, was already building its name for advanced styling at modest prices. A set consisting of dining table, four chairs and side table from Conran was available complete in 1957 for £53 19s 0d (£53.95). The slightly more conservatively modern G-plan ranges of co-ordinating furnishings was one of the best-known names of the fifties, extensively promoted and popular in many of the newer middle level homes. Style features such as the use of wood, shape of legs, types of door handles and knobs, and the colours and textures of upholstery were all designed to be interchangeable without losing the unity and character of the range. They were also budget priced; armchairs were from £15 to £19 and matching couches £28. Dining-room furniture, designed to go with the couches and easy chairs, were in a similar

price bracket, dining chairs were about £4 15s 0d (£4.75) each, sideboards £24 12s 0d (£24.60) and dining tables £16.

Many items bought for the home 25 years ago before inflation began to gather pace at such a frightening rate seem wonderfully cheap in retrospect; earnings, however, although not always at an equally low level, were generally very much smaller than today. A dinner set for six people at £14 6s 6d (£14.32½) and six glasses for 10/- (50p) with whisky or gin to put in them for 35/- (£1.75) a bottle, all considered expensive enough less than a generation ago seem today to represent a scale of living costs which by the inflation-hardened standards of the 1980s is as remote as the prices in the pre-1939 or 1914 years so often remembered and quoted nostalgically by parents and grandparents.

A better life for the working classes with modern well-equipped homes, which had been pioneered for since the beginning of the century by social reformers became a reality in the 1950s. State sponsored houses and flats were built at an ever-increasing rate and in the later part of the decade, American inspired, high-rise blocks of apartments began to alter the skyline of many European cities and the character of inner town districts as streets of small low-level houses and shops, with their close neighbourly way of life, were demolished to make room for the new tall, impersonal looking, buildings.

The material standard of the new homes with their modern kitchens and bathrooms, central heating and television sets was at a higher level than anything which could have been hoped for by some of their older first occupants when they were young, and many people were happy with the convenience and comfort of their new high-level homes. Others were less content with the new style of living; they missed the homeliness and cosiness of small houses with open fires and back yards or gardens, and sometimes felt a sense of isolation in their homes on the upper floors of a new tower block.

Married women who did not go out to work and were on their own or were confined with small children for many hours each day were particularly susceptible to a feeling of restriction; and despite the growing prosperity and more affluent living standards of the time, anxiety and depression became an increasing problem in the home, and many more bathroom cabinets contained bottles of sleeping pills, pep pills and tranquillisers than in the early part of the century when life had been a much harder struggle for the majority of the population.

City life in general was becoming far more stressful. Car ownership was growing at an ever-increasing rate and traffic congestion, particularly in the morning and evening rush hours, had become a frustrating and established feature of everyday life in major towns and cities. With expanding economies in many parts of the world competitiveness in commercial and business life inevitably increased; a growing number of people reached positions of responsibility at earlier ages than before and often felt some degree of strain. The prospect of getting away from it all at regular intervals became an attractive ideal for most executives and their families living in the cities.

161

Second homes by the sea or in the countryside, although enjoyed by the well off for many generations and growing in general popularity between the world wars, became far more usual in the late fifties and throughout the sixties and seventies. Characterful country or seaside cottages had been increasingly sought after for several decades and, apart from those in remote districts or in need of considerable restoration or modernisation, had become much more difficult to find at a reasonable price by the middle of the century. New holiday flats with open-plan designs and sun balconies began to be built in ever-growing numbers to cater for the demand for middle level second homes. Sadly, some of the new developments were put up with little consideration for the natural beauty of the local area or the character and charm of the existing town or village. For those who wanted to vary their holiday destinations, caravans proved to be an attractive mobile home for many families. The small driveways of many suburban homes where the sight of one family car 25 years before would have been very impressive, now sometimes included two cars, a motorbike and a caravan; some front lawns had to be sacrificed and paved over to provide extra parking space for the family's selection of vehicles.

Despite persistent worries for the continuation of a peaceful existence between the world powers, optimism and confidence in the future grew and a much more receptive atmosphere for design innovation was established. American homes became even more progressive with the continual updating of labour saving and automated equipment. Some of the more fanciful designs for new houses, no doubt influenced by the tremendous interest in space exploration, were built in a round shape with rows of oblong or porthole-like windows. These experimental homes which looked rather like illustrations of flying saucers in the popular science fiction stories of the time, perhaps fortunately remained very much a fringe movement in design.

Italy, with its long tradition for architecture and inventive designing, made a remarkably quick recovery from the effects of the war and enjoyed an important revival in design innovation. Within a few years Italian ideas were admired and sought after all over the world. The lead in new styling ranged from shoes and motor scooters to some of the more elegant contemporary designs for new buildings and furnishings. 'Designed and made in Italy' became an important selling feature for modern furniture and household fitments from the mid-fifties onwards.

At the close of the decade a new generation had grown up, too young to remember the pre-war world and with only hazy childhood memories of the war itself. Many of them were very style conscious and sometimes rather materialistic; most were forming very definite ideas about the style of home and the type of home life they wanted to achieve in the new decade ahead. Fortunately, the buoyant atmosphere of the sixties, the most prosperous period of the century, provided many people with unique opportunities to fulfil their ambitions, in some cases, beyond their wildest dreams.

The 1960s

The 1960s, although still a comparatively recent decade, are already viewed by many people with affection and nostalgia. The 1960s and the 1920s were the brighter spells in the century, happily characterised by a good deal of optimism and many progressive and creative ideas. Today, fairly youthful middle-aged men and women are sometimes unexpectedly reminded of their advancing years by interested enquiries from the under thirties age groups as to what life was like in the now legendary period immortalised as the 'swinging sixties'.

Despite several worrying international crises, localised wars, particularly the conflict in Vietnam, and the desperately poor housing conditions borne by millions of the world's deprived population, better homes were enjoyed during the sixties by more people than ever before. American living standards continued to lead, but Western Europe, Japan, Australia and a number of other countries were catching up.

In Britain, Harold Macmillan's famous remark, reputed to have been made in the late fifties, about the British never having had it so good, although sometimes quoted rather cynically, was by the early sixties a fairly accurate description of the more prosperous way of life which had been attained by many people. The progressive ideas of the later fifties pioneered the comfortable more affluent style for homes which became firmly and widely established during the 1960s and continued with developments and variations throughout the 1970s and into the 1980s.

Old ideas on middle and lower level houses modelled as smaller versions of the upper class, multi-roomed homes of the beginning of the century, still lingered on into the early 1960s in a modified form with some of the older generations. Most younger people, however, had accepted the quite different concept of a modern mid-century home; the best use of floor space, good natural and artificial light, sound insulation, efficient central heating, well-equipped bathrooms and special attention to the planning and contents of the kitchen, all gaining in importance during the previous 10 years, became the most highly valued priorities in the composition of most of the new homes of the sixties. Impressive gardens and richly furnished rooms were usually considered less important than in the early decades.

Domestic building which had been increasing steadily since the end of the Second World War accelerated even more quickly in the 1960s and the third boom period of the century for new housing was noticeably under way. Once again the character of many towns and cities changed as new and extended suburbs spread still further into the countryside.

Nearly all the new housing was built in a version of the contemporary open-plan style which had evolved so distinctively in the 1950s. The characteristic designs of the middle part of the century, with the generous use of windows, and simply styled well-proportioned porches and balconies, were adopted even more widely and commercially for the numerous large scale building projects of detached, semi-detached and terrace houses under construction all over the country by nationally known companies. These sizeable organisations had by the sixties generally replaced the

The sixties were boom years for domestic building; new blocks of flats were often rather stereotyped in design but many, like the ones on the left, had good sized living-room windows and balconies

many smaller local family businesses of speculative builders who had been responsible for so much of the earlier 20th century housing.

Large scale, quickly constructed buildings inevitably led to more standardised homes, particularly new flats and apartments. Until the late fifties, high-rise blocks of flats had been unusual in most countries, although some Americans, particularly New Yorkers, had been used to life in tall apartment buildings since the late twenties. During the sixties the rehousing of families in many parts of the world into tower blocks on a mass scale became one of the most fundamental changes since the industrial revolution had brought countless peasants from country cottages into city tenements.

The ever increasing number of new multi-level homes, all very similar in style, began to give the appearance of cities from South-East Asia to Northern Europe, despite their widely differing cultures, a degree of uniformity unknown before in recorded history.

As well as the redevelopment, sometimes beyond recognition of many city centres, new so-called satellite towns of sky-scraper blocks were often built on the outskirts of major cities. Local communities used to a quiet semi-rural life frequently had their environment changed dramatically within a few years into a very different, greatly urbanised district of high-rise flats, new schools, shopping centres and factories.

Because of the great demand for small modestly priced houses, cheaper to construct terrace homes were revived

Many people welcomed the new housing schemes of the sixties and were unperturbed by the growing move towards a more stereotyped style of home unit. Other sections of the population reacted away from the large scale centralised planning of private and public domestic buildings; they felt these to be too impersonal and closely populated for those who preferred some individuality in the style and situation of their home.

Many alternative ideas for homes began to be developed. A wide variety of old buildings in the cities and the countryside were renovated and in some cases almost totally reconstructed, often imaginatively, to form attractive and uniquely individual homes.

Mews buildings, coach houses, warehouses and cottages, although sometimes converted in earlier decades, were redeveloped on a far more extensive scale in the sixties. Modern ideas on open-plan living areas and well arranged and equipped kitchens were usually incorporated into the renovation plans, either with a complementary new large windowed exterior, or were cleverly positioned behind the original facade of the building. Developments of this kind were usually expensive and confined to homes for the better off, but the idea of updating older houses soon began to grow in general popularity, particularly amongst the younger generations.

Less obviously interesting and appealing properties such as 19th century artisans' terrace houses and turn-of-the-century Edwardian villas, which 10 years before would have been dismissed as old-fashioned and ugly, were looked at with new interest and their potential for renovation assessed. As the decade progressed, streets of older, often rather shabby and faded looking houses, began to take

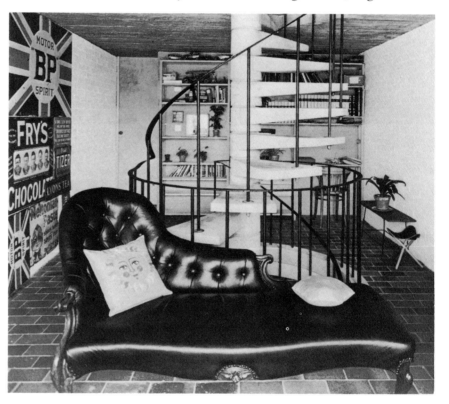

An early sixties interior mixing modern furniture and a space saving spiral staircase with a Victorian chaise-longue covered in new leather

on a new lease of life as some of the houses were sympathetically modernised by enthusiastic young couples, many of whom did a considerable amount of the alterations themselves; this trend grew even more strongly during the following decade.

The simpler modernisation of detached and semi-detached houses built in the twenties and thirties – with improved kitchens, the installation of central heating, and with the replacement of the original small-paned windows by plain larger windows and front doors with fancily patterned glass panels, by undecorated glass or wood front doors – although providing practical and comfortable homes, were generally less visually attractive and appealing than the warmer more homely charm of many of the older converted properties.

An optimistic and increasingly receptive mood for new designs had been established by 1960. The lively youthful character of the new decade was, however, not at first very evident; it was a few years before the 'swing' went into the pace of the sixties and the

Renovating and adding new extensions to old buildings became increasingly popular; the small cottage on the left was cleverly joined to a new section in the modern style of the time

styles and fads now considered so typical of the decade were popularised in the middle and late years. In the early sixties, interiors in most style-conscious homes continued to develop the pattern, which had emerged in the late fifties, of mixing quietly contemporary designs with old characterful items.

Light-coloured wood units, which were still often used as room dividers, and housed books, ornaments, television sets and record players, were placed near a late Victorian chesterfield or chaise longue covered in leather, and a modern dining table and chairs. Natural wood, or painted louvred effects were popular for cupboard doors, and rather nautical looking desks or chests of drawers called 'military chests', with inset brass handles, all formed part of the fashionable ideas of the time, which were put together in various permutations – in living rooms painted in browns, ranging from tobacco to dark chocolate, corn colours, or the safe good taste of the period, plain white walls and ceilings.

These rooms were often pleasant and easy to live in but they lacked the stronger conviction and character of earlier and later styles of décor. The young generation growing up in the early sixties were already adopting new controversial styles of dress and were ready for an equally radical approach to interior decoration.

Large windows, above, were still a feature of many new and renovated homes and, left, is a typical family house of the early sixties with the use of natural wood boarding and a balcony

The Conran organisation, headed by Terence Conran, had been building a good reputation for modern styling in furniture at moderate prices since the late fifties and were one of the first companies to realise the potential of the younger market which had become a much larger and less class-conscious section of the population in the post-war era of high employment and rising living standards.

In May 1964 the first Habitat shop was opened in London's Chelsea. The shop stocked an almost total collection of complementary goods for the home, ranging from pepper mills and egg baskets to important pieces of furniture. Other shops and stores of the period offered a wide selection of differing styles and price ranges, hoping to have something for everyone. Habitat, however, boldly presented an uncompromisingly young modern style in the same way as the young dress designers of the time confidently launched a clearly defined and co-ordinated look for hair styles, make-up, clothes, tights and footwear.

In a write-up in the *Sunday Times* on the launching of Habitat entitled 'What the smart chicks are buying', the attitudes of the sixties were well expressed; '"The bright young chicks have got to have a red Magistretti chair the way they've got to have a Sally Tuffin and Marion Foale dress" says Terence Conran with a blissfully happy smile. Say "Sally Tuffin and Marion Foale" to the average furniture man and he'll say "Who?" But to furniture designer and manufacturer Terence Conran, who makes and sells Magistretti chairs, the world of fashion and furnishing do equate. He has a happy knack of knowing what the "smart chicks" and the simply smart, want next in furniture and is doing his best to make sure his firm is selling it.

> 'Furnishing is becoming more and more fashion conscious; there is a growing feeling, particularly amongst young shoppers, that they want to make shopping for the home an impulsive, gay affair. It is difficult for the furnishing world to cope with the built-in obsolescence price tags of the fashion world, but today people are not ready to invest their all in one good piece and have it round their necks for ever more. Habitat mirrors the beginning of this trend; "we see ourselves as the Mary Quant of the furnishing world" says Conran, and the vocabulary of the fashion world and a tremendous awareness of its trends and moods are reflected in the conversation of the founders of this new shop.'

Since its beginning at the height of the young designer cult of the sixties, Habitat has developed and adapted to the changing circumstances of the decades, but the original concept of simple well-designed modern merchandise at moderate prices for a youngish clientele, particularly first time home-makers, has remained constant and today there are 43 Habitat shops in Britain, 9 in the United States, 21 in France and 2 in Belgium, together with an extensive mail order business.

By the mid-sixties as well as the widening range of well-designed rather functional modern furniture for the growing middle level market, many advanced and creative new ideas were changing the

Many mass-selling types of furniture like the ones above continued to follow the quiet contemporary lines of the late fifties

look of the very fashion-conscious homes. Most of the designs had an element of fun about them; they were often made from synthetic materials such as plastic, fibreglass and foam rubber, which frequently did away with the need for traditional springing and upholstery, and allowed plenty of scope for imaginative new chair and couch shapes.

Chair styles were amongst the most characteristic types of furniture of the period. Some of the more fanciful ideas ranged from designs that looked like huge scooped-out egg shells on swivel stands, mobile globes in fibreglass, and sculptured shapes made on a tubular steel frame with polyether upholstery and removable nylon jersey covering, to the ultimate in casual disposable looking seating, inflatable PVC chairs and shiny, squashy bags made in skinflex and filled with polystyrene granules, which looked unfortunately like a plastic rubbish bag.

The sixties was the most notable decade so far for intensive space exploration. The imagination of the general public was stimulated by the historic developments – particularly the unforgettable scenes as the first men walked on the surface of the moon, watched by millions of people all over the world on television sets, some already with colour pictures, in the comfort of their own living rooms. The dawning of the space age had a considerable influence on fashions in clothing and interiors.

Exciting, futuristic looking rooms in gleaming shiny white were furnished with inventively shaped furniture, also in white, or strong clear colours such as red, yellow or orange. New designs for chairs were put with starkly modern coffee and dining tables made in clear Perspex, coloured plastic, or polished tubular steel with glass tops. The walls in these ultra-modern rooms were often hung with huge unframed abstract paintings in vibrant shades or dark moody looking tones. Steel framed lithographs in precise geometric patterns were also popular; they featured unusual and sophisticated colour schemes which mixed reds with purples and blues, or grey with black and browns.

The forward looking character of interior decoration in the mid and late 1960s was in many ways a close parallel to the modernistic developments of the late 1920s, although the sixties style was a rather more lighthearted and less purist movement. The exciting ideas started in the two periods were, however, quickly followed by reactionary trends.

The modern pop styles of the sixties were often considered too brash and impermanent looking for fashion-conscious people who preferred a warmer more gently enveloping style for their homes. Patternings, colourings and furnishings from the art nouveau and arts and crafts designs, fashionable at the beginning of the century, were revived and admired again.

The well-known designer Bernard Neville, and Liberty's store in London helped to popularise furnishing fabrics inspired by the earlier period, particularly the designs of William Morris, often bringing them up-to-date with a 1960s slant on colourings which tended to be more subtle and understated, or more clearly positive than the originals. The new versions favoured soft greys, beiges and browns mixed together and pale sea colours, teaming blues with greens; in contrast, other designs used much stronger shades such as mauves and pinks with purple or emerald green.

The Edwardian influence was also popular for furnishings. Bamboo, and particularly bentwood were keenly collected; dining chairs, rockers, and hall stands were all liked by young home-makers who scanned antique and junk shops for original pieces. Manufacturers, anxious to take advantage of the growing demand, reproduced adaptations of early 1900s bentwood designs, some of which were successful enough to become standard lines run for many years.

London's well-known fashion shop of the sixties, Biba, famous for beguilingly feminine young clothes, and a mecca for trendy shoppers, made a special feature of its pretty neo-Edwardian décor, with painted clothes stands, potted palms, and vases filled with coloured ostrich feathers. The shop interior provided inspiration for women who wanted a softer more romantic look for their homes as well as their clothes.

The turn of the century influence extended strongly into the bedroom; old style brass bedsteads became the fashionable features of many rooms and were often covered with country style patchwork or delicate flower printed quilts. Sturdy looking chests of

Opposite
By the mid-sixties some high fashion interiors had a rather futuristic space-age look possibly influenced by the exciting events of the time

drawers, sometimes in stripped pine, small tubby looking upholstered easy chairs, window seats, and bedside lamps copied from
19th century oil lamps all added to the updated and romanticised
interpretation of the bedroom styles which had been familiar in
many grandparents' homes when they were young children.

A strongly reactionary trend away from the brashness and
materialism of the sixties was also expressed in the later part of the
decade by the international hippie movement with its mystical and
spiritual influences from the East; in an extreme form these
sometimes sadly led to damaging drug-taking and a withdrawal
from everyday life.

Hippie attitudes of a more moderate kind were often gentle and
fairly unalarming providing inspiration for the style of some young
people's home décor, which in some cases began to resemble a cross
between an Afghan market stall and a Bedouin's tent. Eastern rugs
were pinned to walls or scattered on wood or tiled floors, fabrics
were draped on three sides of some rooms to give a tenting effect,
and normal height chairs and couches were abandoned in favour of
floor-level day beds and a variety of large cushions covered in Indian
style printed or embroidered cottons. To complete the exotic
influences from the East, incense was often burnt and the occasional
whiff of marijuana smoking was sometimes smelt in these very
different style homes. Complete room decorations and furnishings in
hippie designs were not usual but parts of the style, Eastern rugs, and
large cushions as an alternative kind of seating, found their way into
many of the younger generation's homes.

The fashionable design crazes of the sixties were undoubtedly
taken up by a far larger cross-section of the population than ever
before, but there was a more varying range of styles than in the early
decades of the century and more relaxed attitudes about the degree
with which they were adopted.

Some trends, however, became respected and enduring. Well
designed, classically modern furniture of a high standard, in wood,
metal and leather, made in many countries found an increasingly
receptive market, particularly furniture from the Italian designers
with their special flair for inventive styling. Firms such as Albrizzi

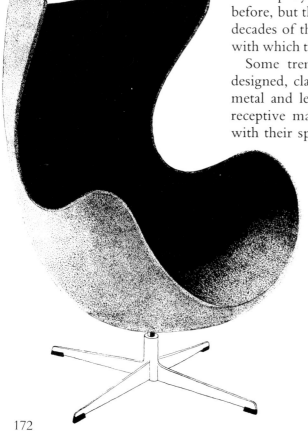

*New styles of chairs were amongst
some of the most inventive designs of
the time and included scooped out
egg-shell shapes, squashy bags filled
with polystyrene granules and a
simple moulded design on slim metal
legs*

produced many good examples of dateless modern furniture some of which is still made almost unchanged today. Designs of a rather similar style, originating in the late twenties, particularly steel and leather couches and chairs were revived in the later sixties and have become 20th century classic styles, internationally popular and manufactured continually throughout the seventies and into the present decade.

In the sixties, despite the extensive awareness of stylish ideas for the decoration and furnishing of the home, many people still did not adopt any of the new designs and remained firmly committed to earlier types of décor. Well-off, older generation homes were frequently furnished with antique or good quality reproduction furniture, deeply swathed curtains, and plushily covered couches and chairs in velvets, slubbed silks or brocades.

Many middle level homes belonging to the over-thirty age groups, with growing families, continued to be furnished in the comfortable style of the quieter contemporary designs which most young couples had adopted when they were married in the 1950s. These families often preferred to spend money on the growing investment value of home improvements such as room extensions, added porches, modern kitchens, and central heating systems, rather than replacing their adequate furnishings with new designs in one of the fashionable style crazes of the decade.

Changes, and new additions to the homes of the less affluent sections of the population during the prosperous 1960s usually

Floor and wall tiles became more fashion conscious and manufacturers offered a much wider selection

In contrast to the ultra-modern interior designs of the sixties Edwardian influences were revived particularly for wallpapers and simple country style furniture

concentrated on acquiring what are now thought of as quite basic kinds of fittings and equipment. Wall-to-wall carpeting, refrigerators, washing machines, television sets and record players, so usual in the homes of the eighties, and available in their earlier forms even before the Second World War, only became general in modest homes all over the world from the sixties onwards. For working class families a generation ago, the convenience of their first refrigerator, or the fun of buying the latest pop record to play at home on an impressive looking record player, represented satisfying and obvious examples of progress and rising living standards, rarely experienced by their parents' generation. Fortunately, expanding world economies geared to the manufacturing of consumer goods continued throughout the decade and expectations for an ever increasing standard of living with improving homes remained an achievable aim for many people.

The buoyant economic conditions of the sixties were accompanied by many far reaching social changes which inevitably affected homes and home life. The growing prominence of the young which had been noticeable since the mid-fifties developed even more strongly in the lively sixties making it one of the most youth-oriented periods ever known. Opportunities for the young were widespread and many men and women achieved acclaim and material success in their chosen careers before they were 30. Even the larger sections of the population employed in more basic occupations reached higher rates of pay far earlier than before and free spending became an established characteristic of this lucky generation. Manufacturers, realising the spending power of the young market, concentrated on designs which would appeal to youthful tastes.

The new generation was very mobile and diversion seeking; new cars, particularly fast sports cars like the famous E-type Jaguar and

Turn of the century dressers and knick-knacks were popular again for homes decorated in a soft feminine style

the most modern motorbikes were much admired status symbols; great pride and pleasure was taken by those affluent enough to afford them in seeing the gleaming new models parked prominently in front of their homes.

Holidays were taken more frequently and further afield. A second home in a sunny climate, even a simple one-roomed studio flat became a much more achievable ambition enabling a growing number of people to have an impressive all-the-year-round sun tan associated with the glamorous cosmopolitan way of life familiar to famous personalities of the time such as film and pop stars. They frequently had a collection of homes dotted about the world and were described by the press as the 'jet set'.

Although sometimes disapproved of by worrying parents, many more unmarried young couples lived together openly and their rather transitory and less permanent attitudes towards relationships and everyday life began to be reflected in some of their homes. Unusual drawings or posters were pinned to plain white walls and an interesting selection of modern paintings and lithographs, framed and unframed, were often casually propped up instead of being hung. Windows were frequently left curtainless or had simple blinds haphazardly pulled down to various levels; plain wood floors lightly stained were often preferred to the plushier look of carpeting, and were scattered randomly with rugs, cushions, and untidy piles of books, magazines and long-playing records. Portable television and radio sets were carried from room to room and the latest Rolling Stones record was played throughout the home.

A large bed was the main feature in the sparsely furnished bedroom and traditional top sheets and blankets were replaced by an easy-to-arrange padded duvet quilt. Sports equipment, surf boards, skis, squash raquets and a selection of boots were dumped in halls ready for regular use, or left unnoticed for months. Uncommitted home attitudes were also reflected in the preparation of meals, cooking was undertaken much more according to mood rather than as a part of an everyday disciplined routine, many meals were bought from take-away bars and restaurants or ordered direct by telephone from dial-a-meal services.

A neat and methodical approach to homely chores which had been accepted in a conformist way by earlier generations, never occurred to many of the free living young of the 1960s, who would have regarded older conventions such as trousers pressed with knife-edge creases, and gleamingly polished shoes placed ready for the next day, as a quaintly amusing quirk, bordering on the eccentric.

The most up-to-date, efficient, and impressive looking music playing equipment was an important if not essential feature of many prosperous young homes and was often given a much higher priority than more conventional items such as unnecessary pieces of furniture and carpeting.

The merits of various kinds of hi-fi and stereo equipment available were often debated at length by young men while their girlfriends discussed the latest designs for clothes. The great importance attached to selecting the most suitable hi-fi for the home was well expressed in a write-up of the mid-sixties headed 'Strictly for hi-fi maniac'. First, remember there's no best hi-fi set up. No two

The most up-to-date stereo equipment was often an important status symbol for 'trendy' young men

enthusiasts could ever agree on that. Loudspeakers are all different. So too are pick-up cartridges and amplifiers. No two pairs of ears hear alike. And the same equipment sounds different in different rooms.

Sales of consumer goods including items to provide more entertainment in the home boomed during the prosperous sixties

'A friendly dealer who will actually lend you equipment to try in your own room, flat or house, is the one to look out for and to be cherished. He won't be all that friendly if all you really crave is a thirteen-quid pop player, but the serious prospect of a large sale may well make it worth his while lugging heavy and costly gear half way across London.

'To choose units that are compatible with well designed modern furniture is difficult. Less flair has been applied to hi-fi styling. To the untrained eye all amplifiers are apt to look alike, as speakers certainly do. A dozen manufacturers produce a dozen near identical products. A sad uniformity.

'Some producers of hi-fi are seeking to escape from the dull norm. The Sunshine Sounds unit is available in many combinations, including a modular centre standing unit based on a central square. The Perspex covers come in many colours. Way-out ovoid speakers are on the stocks. The Transcriptors turntable and fluid arm must fit with the most in trendsville. The big

loudspeakers in glowing colours, cannot yet avoid the box shape and give the good sounds. Bang and Olufsen have made a splendid technical slide rule job, but why the teak?'

In contrast to the high value put on material possessions and a trendy style of home by some of the sixties generation, other young people of the time rejected any kind of conventional way of life and adopted a quite different attitude towards homes.

Some of the anti-establishment young felt a fixed home with its inevitable running costs to be unnecessary and squatted in unoccupied houses and flats, particularly in the major cities. Many of the squatters of the sixties, unlike the early post-war home seekers (who had moved into unused property, especially empty military camps with their furnishings, and had tried to make a reasonably comfortable home), were not looking for permanent housing, but merely a temporary base and reasonable shelter. Their possessions were usually limited to some clothes, a few household items, sleeping bags and possibly a mattress. Normal facilities, lighting, heating and water were frequently cut off and conditions in these temporary homes sometimes became squalid. There was considerable publicity over the problem of young squatters and television news bulletins often showed heated scenes when groups of young people, some with children, were forcibly evicted from the

The widely publicised hippie movement with its influences from the East began to be reflected in interior décor. On the right is a high fashion interpretation of the trend

properties they had taken over. Some of the genuine cases of the homeless, particularly distressed young unmarried mothers with small children, desperately in need of a home, were dealt with sympathetically by social workers and were found some form of adequate accommodation.

A more cheerful type of alternative home environment was adopted by young people who left the cities to start a new life in the countryside and formed themselves into communes. The rejection of an urbanised way of life was taken up by a cross-section of classes who were talked of as having dropped out of the 'rat race'. These newly formed groups of people looked for a large size property with some farming land. Rambling old rectories or dilapidated manor houses, often inconveniently situated, were available at comparatively low prices in rural parts of the country; when a suitable one was found it was bought collectively by the group with their pooled resources and the restoration of the new home was then undertaken by everyone involved in the venture. The decorations and furnishings in these communal homes were usually simple and natural looking, both through the lack of finance and a preference for a quietly unadorned home background.

Life in the communes was organised for the benefit of all its members, and if possible, made the best use of individual talents; some people enjoyed cooking, others were happier looking after the children. Many of the men preferred gardening or trying their hand at farming, growing crops and keeping a limited number of animals. The commune tried to be as self-sufficient as possible providing most of its food and selling any surplus produce to pay for other essential commodities.

Eastern influences of a more moderate kind; patterned cushions like these were popular additions to many young people's rooms

Although many communes started with high hopes for a better and more healthy way of life, they often had a limited time span in their original form. A way of life geared to the needs and well-being of a group of men, women and children, and devoid of selfishness and self-seeking was hard to sustain over a number of years; disagreements and personal dislikes inevitably developed; other members simply became bored with the style of living and returned to a more conventional and comfortable home life in the city. Communes remained very much a fringe movement of the 1960s and 1970s but they helped to start the drift towards more natural home styles which became an important trend for the later decades of the century.

Women's role in the home, which had changed throughout the decades of the century, altered significantly during the 1960s as part of the more liberated way of life many women were adopting, and 'women's lib' became a rather over-used catch-phrase of the time. Women were certainly less prepared to be housebound and often considered a job or career to be an important part of their life. The pursuit of outside activities and a more generally independently minded attitude were greatly encouraged by the introduction of the revolutionary contraceptive pill; for the first time women could more easily control the timing and size of their families.

Young couples shared home responsibilities more equally than before; men quite frequently cooked the family meals, dealt with the laundry in the washing machine or at the local launderette and were more involved in looking after their children. Outside facilities helped; mobile nappy services were available, and pre-school-age small children between the ages of 3 and 5 were often away from the home in the mornings at playschool.

New estates of budget priced semi-detached and terrace houses were built in increasing numbers between 1960 and 1970 for a very receptive market

The well-designed and equipped bathroom as shown below became one of the most important features of affluent homes

Unsatisfactory marriages were less readily tolerated in the sixties and divorce followed by second marriages became commonplace. Many children had to adapt to a disrupted family life, alternating between two homes and two sets of parents. Home life for most children was more sophisticated and related to the adult world. Open-plan living areas, television watching, and pop music playing in the background, together with barbecue parties in the garden during the summer, were shared by all age groups from babies to grandparents.

Nurseries and bedrooms were no longer furnished and coloured in a soft babyish way with pale blue or pale pink furniture and walls decorated with delicate animal motifs. Later 20th century children's rooms were cheerful and functional with natural wood bunk beds, work tables and stools. Walls in clear primary shades, reds, yellows and greens, were in practical washable paint and equally colourful curtains in plain or patterned fabrics were usually made from easy-care materials.

Despite the familiarity of television as an established part of everyday life in the home, some parents were worried by its power to influence and tried to limit their children's viewing time. However, mothers wearied by arguments and boisterous behaviour eventually gave in to demands to have 'the telly on' and were often secretly relieved at the quieter atmosphere which descended over the house once their young family's interest was focussed on the television screen.

Most sixties children, as part of their more adult style of life, were brought up to enjoy a diet which was much more similar to a grown up's. Savoury foods were often preferred to older style sugary dishes and the food favoured at children's parties was usually quite different from the ideas of the previous generation; particularly in Britain where the emphasis was changed from fancily iced cakes, trifles and jellies, to hamburgers, sausages, cheese snacks and pasta.

Although there were many changes in children's lives their interest in toys remained as strong as ever. Traditional favourites – pretty dolls, farm animals, soldiers, train sets and cars updated to the sixties in style – were all still popular and were joined by new ideas. 'Lego' construction sets, which could be assembled in numerous ways and added to with further pieces as later presents, became a great success, and 'Action Man' sets – male dolls with a variety of tough looking uniforms for small boys to dress them in – were one of the equally successful new ideas and proved that despite the interest in scientific progress and space travel, many small boys, like their counterparts in earlier generations, were still fascinated by uniforms and military paraphernalia.

Cuddly toys continued to find a warm place in the affections of many children. The popularity of teddy bears, an all-time favourite, was strongly reinforced by the Paddington Bear stories; books about Paddington were followed by television programmes and thousands of Paddington Bear toys. Countless children fell asleep wrapped round *their* Paddington and it became one of the most famous and widespread children's cults of the century which has continued to the present day.

The social changes of the sixties affected the homes and the home life of the old as well as of the young. In the earlier part of the century parents and grandparents had often lived with their children in the later years of their lives. Middle class houses were usually large enough for the family to have individual rooms and there was enough domestic help to prevent the elderly from becoming a burden to the younger generations. Older people often led a rather sedate life and other members of the family usually tolerated fixed attitudes and behaviour patterns; grandma's place at the dining table, her special fireside chair with its comforting collection of cushions, and an over-sensitivity to draughts and noise were all an accepted part of family life in many homes.

The position of the elderly was very different by the 1960s: people were living longer, remaining in better health, and were far more active than in the early decades of the century; they were also much more likely to live alone. Family closeness had faded over the years; it had become more usual for adults to have their own small homes even if they remained unmarried and few families had spare accommodation for ageing parents. One of the most satisfactory solutions to the provision of homes for the old was the 'granny flat' or annexe. Families who could afford it, converted a part of their

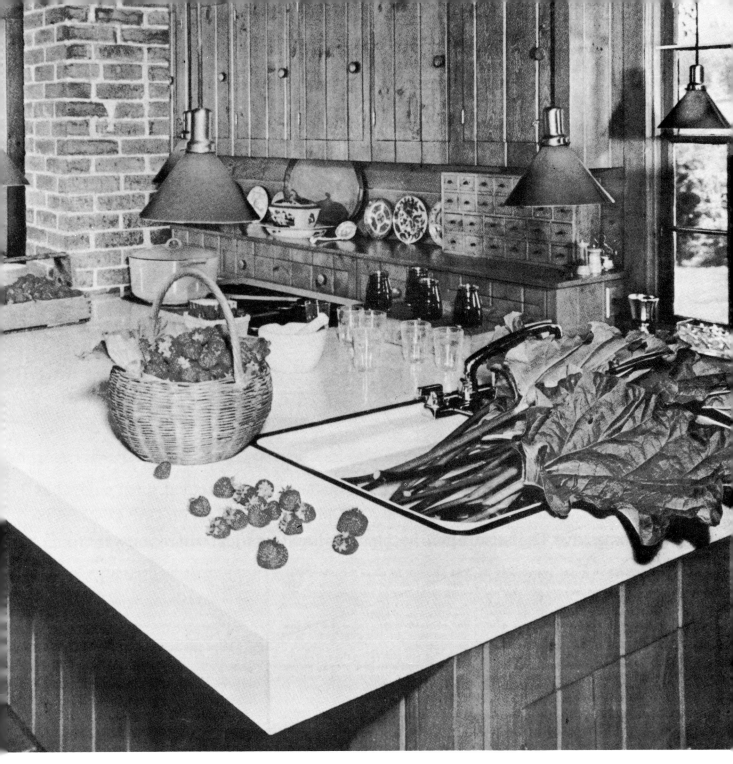

house into a self-contained flat, built additional accommodation over the garage, or added a back extension to their home. The arrangement helped families and parents to be separate and independent but near to one another if they were needed.

Specially constructed homes, adjacent to grown-up sons' and daughters' houses, were not always possible either because of the expense or through the unsuitability of an existing home for conversion or redevelopment. The idea of special old people's homes began to gain quickly in popularity at all levels. Compact and easy to run flats and bungalows were built in increasing numbers, both by the State and private property developers. For old people who found the running of their own individual home too much to cope with, residential homes, State run or privately owned, provided a growing number of elderly men and women with a reasonably comfortable

A very advanced kitchen using natural brick walls, wood units and a centrally placed working area

and secure home. The new homes were a far cry from the old Dickensian ideas of an institutionalised way of life. Many of the homes were purpose built low-level buildings set in pleasant well-maintained gardens. Individual well-equipped rooms were often available and some were furnished with the tenants' own furniture. Meals were provided and communal lounges and television rooms set up for general use. Staff and a residential warden were employed to look after the old people and a different, much more cheerful image began to emerge for these new style residential homes. Accommodation of this kind, so usual today in many parts of the world, has been established comparatively recently; even a generation ago many of the elderly were still frightened by the idea of being 'put in a home'.

By the 1960s the role and the importance attached to rooms and their furnishings in the home had been revised and altered completely from the ideas which had been so firmly established at the beginning of the century. A new pattern for the interior of most homes, which has remained up to the present day, had emerged clearly. In the earlier decades the principal living room – the 'drawing room' in middle and upper class homes, and the 'front parlour' in modest terrace houses – had been given first priority in decoration and furnishing, followed in importance by dining-rooms and bedrooms; kitchens and bathrooms were granted the least attention and were often very dreary and basic even in spacious and affluent homes. These ideas changed gradually during the century and in the sixties the kitchen and bathrooms had often become the most impressive rooms in the house.

Young women took great pride in the style, planning and equipment of the kitchen; it was considered a great compliment if friends and acquaintances visiting a new home for the first time were heard to have reported that it had got 'a really super kitchen'.

There were two predominant designs for fashionable kitchens: the clinically modern, and an updated country style. Severely modern kitchens were fitted out with an impressively wide range of Formica units in white or in a strong colour such as olive green or tan. Bright reds and yellows were also featured but were not as popular as in the previous decade and the use of two or three strongly contrasting shades or of a harlequin effect were far less fashionable. Formica units, as well as containing plenty of cupboards and drawers, also had sections for sinks – which now often came in pairs and contained a waste-disposal gadget – fridges with special deep-freeze compartments, dishwashers, food mixers and cookers. Some of the new cookers were of split-level design; the oven part, which often had a glassed front or an internal glass door, was usually set into the wall units; the separated hobs were placed in a more open area with a special hood fixed over them to extract fumes and cooking smells. One of the most advanced ideas for kitchens in the sixties was the island unit which either extended into the main part of the room from the wall units or was separately constructed in the centre of the room. Sinks and cooker hobs were frequently installed in the centrally-placed area, which had the advantage of being accessible on three sides.

The 'deep freeze' was a new and progressive addition for the home but became more general in the following decade

Some people preferred a less clinical space-age look to their kitchens and favoured the equally popular country style. The appliances and equipment in these were just as modern and extensive as the ones used in the futuristic-style rooms but they were housed in more traditional looking wooden cupboards. Wood panels were also used for some of the wall areas, usually combined with other walls in natural brick and centre-room working-tops built on a brick base. Complementary looking tiles in natural earth colours, particularly quarry or chateau styles, were often used to complete the pseudo-rustic appearance aimed at in these softer, warmer looking rooms.

Many kitchens contained the main eating area. Special dining-rooms had declined in popularity and were dispensed with altogether in many homes; any reticence about eating and entertaining in the kitchen had disappeared and most young couples were only too pleased to show off their well-planned, cheerfully decorated and expensively fitted kitchens which had become unquestionably the best room in many new homes.

Bathrooms were also given special attention in the more progressive homes of the 1960s and were sometimes highlighted as especially glamorous features. Until the 1950s good-sized family houses in Britain were usually built with only one bathroom and lavatory. A downstairs cloakroom with a washbasin and lavatory was available in some but not all houses; and flats in continental Europe frequently had the lavatory and bathroom tucked away from the main rooms of the apartment at the end of a long passage.

Prosperous families who could have afforded to install second or even third bathrooms often accepted, without any thought of change, the inconvenience of a one bathroom home, with rationed

A leather and steel chair designed in the twenties, revivied in the sixties and manufactured continually up to the present day as a 20th century classic

time for all members of the family during the morning and evening rush. A second bathroom, particularly the *en suite* bathroom leading from the main bedroom, was pioneered, like so many of the new ideas of the century, in America. By the sixties most higher level houses and flats were built with two bathrooms; showers, mixer taps, and electric shaving points were all standard equipment in these homes and specially designed plain and patterned wall and floor tiles were usually installed.

Some homes had additional luxury features. Long-piled carpets, which had become fashionable for living rooms and bedrooms, were extended into the bathroom, and conventional wall cabinets were sometimes replaced by large flatteringly lit mirrors and a washbasin dropped into a specially constructed cabinet with plenty of storage space and a large surface area around the basin; sunken baths were sometimes installed, and to give a really glamorous film star look to some homes, a sunken bath was fitted into the floor of the principal bedroom.

Other more basic items for the bathroom followed the trend for a richer style. Towels and bath mats became plushier with the wider range of fabric qualities which had become available; several kinds of towelling were produced, some with a smooth velvety texture and an extensive colour range. It became much easier to tone towel colours to wall decorations and carpeting shades. Well-known dress designers took advantage of the increased importance attached to stylish looking towels and became associated with designer named ranges; a group of varying sized towels in elegant stripes or patternings with a Dior or St Laurent label became popular presents for people who appreciated fashionably-named merchandise.

As well as the changed importance attached to rooms and their contents, and the high value placed on technical home equipment such as hi-fi systems, tape recorders, and television sets – particularly the arrival of colour which became one of the status symbols of the late sixties – there were many small changes which altered the look of homes during the decade.

With the spread of comparatively inexpensive, easy-to-run central heating into homes at all levels, traditional solid fuel burning fires declined even more sharply in popularity and unused fireplaces were removed from many houses; this trend was sometimes regretted in the seventies when fuel costs began to accelerate alarmingly and there was a general return to a more homely style of living.

Ways of lighting the home began to alter. Standard, central light-fittings were no longer such a universal style; many living areas did away with them altogether and relied on an interesting collection of table lamps or cleverly positioned spot lights. These were angled onto pictures and ornaments or, in some homes, threw a flatteringly soft light from the floor level onto groups of household plants and foliage which in turn became even more fashionable in the sixties and added a much-needed bright and cheerful note to some of the more sparsely furnished modern rooms of the period. Spot lights were also well-used in kitchens to focus light onto working areas and in bathrooms to illuminate mirrors over washbasins.

The growing enthusiasm for outdoor living and entertaining in the

garden during the summer months led to many families revising and replacing their rather basic collection of unfashionable wooden garden furniture with up-to-date designs in plastic and metal. Visiting friends were sometimes surprised by the transformation; new circular tables with colourful, centrally-placed parasols and a collection of light-looking, fold-away metal chairs and sunbeds covered in boldly striped or patterned canvas had often replaced old style, well-used deck chairs and rickety wood or wicker garden tables. Barbecue parties, which had been popular in America for several decades, were taken up by many more European families in the 1960s and barbecuing equipment joined the growing range of garden furniture and garden appliances which was finding its way into many of the homes of the freer-spending families.

There was generally more disposable income for most people 20 years ago than in the earlier or later parts of the century. Household bills were far less of a burden to most budgets a generation ago before inflation became a serious world problem; food prices, rates, heating costs, were all much more manageable. Food, which became so expensive in the seventies – especially meat, fish and dairy produce – formed a larger part of many family diets and was often used quite extravagantly by the younger generation. Parents brought up in more difficult times sometimes felt their children's use of food to be unnecessarily wasteful. The possible health hazards from an over-rich diet which are pointed out so regularly today were rarely worried over in the sixties; most people had comparatively recent memories of rationing and austerity and revelled in the abundance of food in the more affluent countries of the world.

The designs of Britain's David Hicks became a well known inspiration for this kind of chic living room with its daring use of colour and patternings

The arrival of heating bills, or demands for local rates, dreaded in so many homes in the financially difficult eighties, particularly by the elderly living on fixed incomes, usually received scant attention two decades ago. Heating, which is now often used sparingly or carefully conserved, was run far more freely in the prosperous sixties; complaints were frequently made that many public buildings and some homes were uncomfortably over-heated.

Because of the comparatively low running costs of the home and the benefit of steadily increasing earnings, surplus income was often available for more new cars, clothes, entertaining, holidays, and second homes.

Second homes for the middle levels of society had been increasing steadily since the late fifties; they reached their peak of popularity from the mid-sixties to the mid-seventies. In the richer countries, particularly America and Western Europe, as well as the growth of second homes within the country, prosperous businessmen and their families in countries with uncertain climates such as West Germany and Britain bought alternative homes more extensively than ever in the sunnier parts of continental Europe and the Mediterranean islands.

Ibiza, Majorca, the Algarve and Spain were all popular, but Spain with its easy access by plane and modest costs became the most popular of all. Numerous quiet fishing villages, which had hardly altered over the centuries, were transformed in a few dust-filled years into hard looking modern resorts, full of new supermarkets, restaurants, bars, and many villas and apartments usually owned by foreigners. The local population generally accepted good naturedly their large alien population. During the summer months unfamiliar car number plates, fair-haired blue-eyed looks, and the sound of English and German became a familiar part of everyday life; 10 years later with its weakened currency, Britain, and particularly London, experienced the increase of affluent foreigners buying second homes.

In the closing years of the sixties a rather less exuberant mood began to develop. Some of the brash self-confidence of the young softened a little and there was a growing feeling that the wilder more experimental phase in home designing was coming to an end and that a less obviously extrovert and more sophisticated approach was succeeding it. Some of the newer designs for blocks of flats and houses were breaking away from the frank-looking designs with their large windows and generous use of balconies and porches which had been the predominant style for so long, in favour of rather more serious-looking buildings with less revealing windows and deeper, more discreetly placed balconies. Red brick and long sweeping gables were revived for some of the new, quieter designs, and although they were obviously a modern form of styling they had a rather less open look about them. As well as the return to slightly more traditional designs for some of the most fashion-conscious new homes, obvious revivalism was also quickly gaining in popularity for the large middle-level market. Georgian designs which had been a recurring and successful style throughout the decades of the century enjoyed a considerable boost in popularity in the late sixties, and many neo-Georgian detached, semi-detached, and terrace houses

The character of many quiet towns, fishing villages and stretches of coast line in Spain, Majorca and the Algarve were transformed in a few dust-filled years into modern resorts of high-rise flats and hotels

were built for a widening market and were often described as 'town houses'.

In addition to complete houses in this very commercial style, Georgian features were often added to homes originating from other less-admired periods. Georgian style bay windows and panelled wood front doors with fan shaped windows over them were added to late 19th century terrace houses, Edwardian villas, and 'Metroland'-style semi-detached houses built between 1920 and 1940. This trend has remained enduringly popular with many people and Georgian features, particularly windows and doors, are mass produced in larger quantities than ever today for a well-established market of new and renovated homes in all price ranges.

By the end of the 1960s fashionable styles for interior decoration had been generally consolidated into three main groups: Modern, neo-Edwardian, and the rustic country style.

Modern design had become more elegant and mature looking. Rooms were often decorated in creamy beiges, and instead of being painted they were sometimes covered in a silk or linen type of fabric or wallpaper; other fashion-conscious rooms were coloured a deep chocolate brown or a browny-red Chinese lacquer shade. Popular furnishings in these rooms usually included one or two floor-to-ceiling wall units made in polished steel with glass shelves, on which expensive looking books, interesting ornaments and modern sculptures were often rather self-consciously displayed. Chairs were used less frequently in some of the newer room arrangements and were replaced by the more opulent look of large couches, usually in pairs, or a comprehensive range of seat units which could be positioned into various groupings. Both kinds of seating were covered in soft expensive leather or suede or alternatively in a cream coloured slub silk. To act as a focal point for the soft furnishings, a large glass-topped coffee table, set on polished steel legs, was usually placed in front, or in the middle, of the group of seats; and to complete the ultra-stylish look of these very urbanised rooms the most fashionable style of wall-to-wall carpeting was a neat geometric pattern in brown and cream designed by the internationally known interior decorator, David Hicks.

The neo-Edwardian style of décor was a much softer and less obviously expensive style, very popular in women's homes. Art nouveau colourings, particularly light turquoise blue, soft golds, and mauvey pinks were used for plain coloured walls or patterned wallpapers which were strongly influenced by the designs of the early 1900s. Matching printed cotton curtains or plain velvets in flatteringly toning colours were often featured. Curtains in these very feminine homes were usually floor length and were held back at windowsill level with matching fabric ties or fancy cords in a complementary design and colour.

Furniture followed the turn-of-the-century influence with button-backed easy chairs and couches, covered in velvet, silk or cotton, and a collection of bentwood and bamboo pieces. Stripped pine dressers, chests of drawers, and wardrobes were also sometimes used in these homes; they were certainly usual features in houses which followed the more cottagey, country style. The neo-Edwardian and the natural rustic trends in décor sometimes overlapped and some homes were a pleasant mixture of the two. Houses which strongly favoured the deeper country influences, usually included walls in simple colour washes or delicately flower-printed wallpapers, wood and tiled floors, and a collection of old pieces of furniture usually stripped to a natural wood colour, or new light wood pieces made in traditional country styles.

The sixties was undoubtedly one of the most home-conscious decades of the century. General world prosperity meant many more people could enjoy furnishing and equipping their homes in an up-to-date style rather than regarding them, as in earlier periods, as barely adequate and which they had often found a struggle to maintain.

Home ownership increased steadily, and so too did the value of houses and flats. Many homes once again doubled in price over the decade and the investment value of property became evident to everyone. Young people, who in the earlier part of the century would have rented their first homes, were often persuaded by parents in the 1960s to use part of their higher earnings for buying rather than renting.

Some businessmen, realising the potential money to be made quickly from property development, renovated old houses and flats and resold them easily and profitably. Property developing was an ever-growing industry in the 1960s, which became even more lucrative in the first half of the 1970s.

At the end of 1969 many people had experienced their first full decade of uninterrupted affluence and a more liberated way of life, and looked forward to a continuation of these fortunate trends for the foreseeable future. As yet, there were no signs of the more difficult times ahead; mass unemployment and prolonged recessions were associated with the past rather than the future. Sadly, the 1970s returned to some of the old problems and worries which had been so recurring and hard to resolve in the 1920s and 1930s.

The later decades of the 20th century saw the continuation of many of the newer ideas for home development and the introduction of several new directions; the pace, however, was slower and the atmosphere less receptive than in the years of greater opportunity which stretched from the late fifties to the early seventies.

The 1970s and on into the 80s

ADD VALUE AND ELEGANCE TO YOUR HOME

With a little bit of imagination — and these elegant glass fibre mouldings — you can transform your home into one of the most desirable properties around. We'll even install them for you if you like. Simply write or phone stating the features that interest you.
① Louvre shutters
② Moulded fascias
③ Garage doors
④ Columns
⑤ Porticos
⑥ Door surrounds
⑦ Moulded cornices
⑧ Niches
⑨ Fire surrounds

Popular neo-Georgian design features were sometimes added to existing houses

Mid-20th century expansion and prosperity, which had grown throughout the 1950s and 1960s, peaked in the early 1970s, and by the beginning of the last quarter of the century a less favourable period had begun to emerge. In some ways the 1970s followed a course which was a reversal of the developments of the 1950s, when standards of living in many parts of the world, after an austere start, had improved steadily and ended the decade happily enjoying a much more progressive and optimistic phase than would have generally been thought possible 10 years earlier. The seventies, in contrast, began with an all-time high in living standards and expectations, but sadly ended with a growing world recession which was unfortunately combined with world inflation. Stagnation and contraction in international trade, with its inevitable effects on earnings and styles of life for many people within 10 years, were rarely envisaged in the confident atmosphere of 1970.

The decade started with no apparent signs of a change from the established pattern of the later sixties, and high standards of living were well maintained at first in the richer countries of the world. Inflation, however, began to accelerate far more rapidly; money was noticeably losing its value, and higher and higher earnings were continually needed to be able to enjoy the free-spending consumer society to which many people had grown so accustomed.

The self-defeating spiral of wages chasing prices was soon set; industrial unrest grew, and the safest and least vulnerable havens for investment away from the problems of the manufacturing industries were more frequently sought out.

Property proved to be one of the best forms of investment at all levels throughout the decade. Many house and flat prices doubled and trebled in the early seventies, paused briefly in the middle of the decade, and then went on to double and treble again in the following few years. Homes from tiny workmen's cottages to spacious mansions were all carefully assessed and their market value approximated. Fortunes were quickly made through clever property speculation, especially in many major cities. In the fashionable residential districts of central London some house and flat values increased by staggering amounts between 1970 and 1980. Appreciations of over 1000 per cent were achieved in many cases. Britain's devaluing currency contributed to this inflationary trend and some of the highest prices attained for London homes were from sales to affluent foreigners with funds in strong currencies.

Most people in Britain and in many other countries became increasingly conscious of their home as an important, if not the most important, investment of the time. In consequence more money than ever was spent on home developments and renovations. Middle-level home-makers discussed and debated at length with their friends and relatives the additional value to the family home of a new kitchen, installation of good central heating, or an extension to the house; the costs of the improvement schemes were gone into in detail and the potential profit to be reaped from a future sale of the home was pointed out with great satisfaction. Impressive and sometimes astounding stories about the money to be made from the buying and selling of homes became one of the most popular topics at social gatherings. Most people had their own special story or incident to relate. Discussions of this kind would have been considered 'bad form' by many of the middle classes at the beginning of the century, who would have thought such blatantly mercenary attitudes relating to the home as a highly commercial commodity, to be very vulgar indeed.

In the seventies many astute middle-class couples in their thirties and forties naturally wanted to take advantage of the boom in house and flat prices, often acquired the most valuable homes they could afford and so the general approach to the family house altered because of the important economic considerations of the time. Financial resources were strained to buy a home that would prove to be a good investment. Home priorities concentrated on aspects such as buying in a favoured district, the size and amenities of a property, and its overall value as a steadily growing asset, rather than costly new furniture, curtains and décor, which unless of an exceptionally high standard, had a far lower and less assured chance of proving to be a sound investment. It became far more usual for houses of an impressive commercial value to be pleasantly but modestly furnished, clearly indicating that most of the finance available had been put into the property itself rather than its interior decorations.

Hyperinflation in property prices meant many people had to revise their attitude towards what they considered to be an acceptable kind of home. In London's fashionable residential districts such as St John's Wood, Kensington, and Chelsea, family-type flats and houses became almost prohibitively expensive for most people with middle-level incomes who soon found they had to accept the idea of living in a less prestigious area if they wanted a reasonably-sized home, particularly one with a garden. Previously underrated inner city suburbs such as Clapham, Wandsworth, and Fulham which had often been considered shabbily old-fashioned until the late sixties, began to go up in the world rapidly during the seventies. Youngish couples completely renovated and smartened up late Victorian terrace houses and semi-detached villas; many were excitingly transformed from the dreary and neglected, to the attractive and ultra-fashion conscious. Some streets showed interesting contrasts in styles of living existing side by side. Trendy looking houses occupied by smart young families with upper-class attitudes and voices, often lived next door to a solidly working-class household, who usually accepted, without prejudice, the new influx of affluent neighbours who had migrated from their more traditional homelands of Chelsea and Kensington.

The spiralling value of homes was good news for most property owners at all levels; but for some first-time home-makers with limited finance, getting into the property game was often a worrying problem. Enterprising young people stretched their resources to buy some kind of home, however modest; they then gradually did it up themselves until it reached an acceptable commercial standard for re-selling at a profit, enabling them then to buy a slightly larger home and so begin to move up the property ladder towards even better homes and higher levels of investment.

Home improvements and extensions became more popular than ever; especially to front and back porches

HAMMERSMITH

FLAT PURCHASED IN AUGUST 1970
£8,000

SOLD NOVEMBER 1971
£12,000

£4000 ON DEAL 1

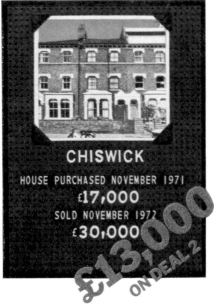

CHISWICK

HOUSE PURCHASED NOVEMBER 1971
£17,000

SOLD NOVEMBER 1972
£30,000

£13,000 ON DEAL 2

Inflation quickly gathered pace in the early seventies, and house and flat prices often rose steeply in a matter of months

The boom in home improvements led to a marked increase in suppliers catering for the enthusiastic amateur renovator and decorator. Special 'do it yourself' (DIY) shops opened in many towns and cities, offering to the general public practically all the materials available to the professional building contractor and decorator.

Home renovating, both amateur and professional, became one of the fastest growth areas in many countries during the 1970s and 1980s. Most youngish people felt they could save money by undertaking some form of home improvement work even if it only extended to painting the kitchen or a bedroom. Others became extremely competent and undertook ambitious projects such as installing new doors, windows, kitchen units, and in some cases new bathrooms and complete home extensions and garages. Materials improved to cater for this busy market and to help make the work as easy as possible for the untrained home renovator. Central heating systems, double glazing, and pre-constructed carpentry, such as cupboards and units, although not new to the period, became much more generally available and were less complicated to install. Detailed catalogues covering a wide range of home requirements were produced for the general public as well as the building trade. Basic items such as domestic paint were improved; they became easy

to apply, had a better surface appearance, smelt less strongly, dried more quickly and were produced in a far more extensive colour range. Many shops installed colour-making services with special machines which quickly mixed from a stipulated formula any shade chosen from the displayed colour charts.

As well as the obvious satisfaction of adding considerable value to the home for the lowest possible cost by doing the renovations and improvements themselves, many people enjoyed the work. It often had creative appeal and quite a lot of men and women, particularly those working in routine occupations, found that the contrast between their business life and their efforts and achievements in improving the home had an almost therapeutic effect on their general well being.

The strong incentive in the seventies and eighties to improve and develop the home extended into the best presentation of the garden or patio. A pleasant garden area, however small, was considered an important asset to any home. More money was spent on outdoor features and garden centres catered for every kind of requirement – from trees and shrubs, numerous varieties of flowers, plants, and bulbs, to different sorts of fencing, a large selection of garden furniture and miniature statues – all available at very competitive prices. Speciality garden centres became as popular and successful as DIY shops; they were usually well laid out and often provided a pleasant outing for the whole family. Some centres included miniature playgrounds for the children, small shops selling country-style foods and imaginatively stocked self-service restaurants.

Retail outlets, selling some kind of home equipment, multiplied in most towns and cities from the mid-seventies to the mid-eighties.

Previously underrated turn of the century semi-detached villas in some of London's inner suburbs, like the one opposite (interior shown above) were attractively refurbished and districts such as Fulham became newly fashionable

195

Apart from practical items such as building and decorating materials and garden requirements, other shops specialised in old furniture, wall and floor tiles, and soft furnishings including curtaining, chair and couch covers, and upholstery. Because of the increased scope for general expenditure on the home, many people became extremely price conscious and shopped around for good value in home furnishings and tried to make the best use of the limited budget left for the fashion-conscious side of furniture and décor.

Careful considerations over the use of money for the home may well have been one of the reasons why the approach to fashionable styles of furniture and decorations began to change. Many people felt less compelled to follow set styles and had a generally more relaxed attitude to the presentation of their home. Apart from the high cost of adopting new trends, many people were becoming more confident about compiling their own mixture of styles for the home and for their clothes. The younger generation, although very fashion conscious, were less intimidated by design trends which were declared to be 'correct', or 'in'; the power to dictate fashion had waned considerably and designers and merchandisers presented a widening variety of styles for the home and for clothes – far more as suggestions than as directives.

Design trends in the seventies generally fell into groups of styles, many of them developed from the popular ideas of the sixties; new directions also started but they evolved more slowly and gently than many of the more forceful styles popularised earlier in the century.

A soft enveloping style became popular for some fashion conscious bedrooms with the use of cream and pale gold colourings, a fur bedspread and draped curtains

The smart ultra-modern trend of the later sixties, with the use of mirrored walls, polished steel and lacquered wood or shiny plastic, and the prominence of large silk or leather covered couches, carried on into the next decade. Rooms in this style were dominated by their seating arrangements which, in some of the more affluent looking living rooms, were sometimes built into a sunken area in the centre. Bedrooms in these homes also followed the idea of impressive built-in features; large beds were often placed on a slightly raised platform which was approachable on three sides by a carpeted step. The area around the top of the bed was boxed in at a low table level with another carpet area into which light switches, radios, a telephone, and hi-fi equipment were sometimes set and, in some cases, controls for television. To add a further touch of luxury to the rather pampered and indulgent character of these bedrooms, bed covers in soft fur were sometimes placed over the 'king size' bed.

Glamorous, plushy home interiors of this kind were often featured in the sets of the slick modern films of the period and frequently provided the background style used for houses and flats in the popular James Bond adventures. Sleek homes, beautiful young women, the latest fast sports car, were all part of the fantasy world promoted by the media in the early seventies and often aspired to by youthful men pushing ahead in their careers, who talked about having 'the right image', and adopting a modern 'lifestyle'.

Complete interiors in the modern style of the 1970s sometimes looked rather hard and masculine and although often admired

Expensive groups of leather seat units, dropped into a lower level area, like the ones above were an opulent looking feature used by some interior decorators of the seventies

objectively by fashion-conscious women, they were rarely chosen by them for their own homes. Part of the style, a steel and glass coffee or dining table, or a group of leather or silk seat units were sometimes used to mix in with older pieces of furniture and soft-coloured curtains and decorations. Many women preferred a gentle feminine look to their homes with very few influences from the modern designs of the sixties and seventies. The growing range of romanticised turn-of-the-century styles, which had been gaining in popularity for over a decade, appealed to their tastes and an even more receptive and highly commercial market for pretty country types of designs became firmly established.

The famous Laura Ashley shops with their attractive collections of cleverly co-ordinated prints, for wallpapers, fabrics and tiles, epitomised the much loved cottagey style at a level that appealed to a very wide cross-section of people; and like Britain's other very successful and expanding group, Habitat, Laura Ashley presented a total look at reasonable prices which could be adopted either extensively or in small areas. By the end of the decade countless homes in Britain and many other countries had at least some examples of her designs, usually in the form of curtainings and wallpapers.

Pretty prints for walls and furnishing fabrics were very complementary to the growing craze for old pieces of unpretentious furniture originating from the late 19th and early 20th century. Collecting old-fashioned, homely looking furniture had gained in popularity during the sixties and by the seventies it had become one of the most important and enduring trends of the later part of the century and has continued strongly right up to the present day. The demand for items such as pine dressers, kitchen tables, dining chairs, chests of drawers, small tables, hall stands and wing chairs has far exceeded their availability, and higher and higher prices have been paid for these newly admired pieces which a generation ago would have often been dismissed as almost worthless junk. Grandparents are sometimes surprised to see furniture which in their youth would have been used as basic items in kitchens and workmen's cottages, elevated to prize possessions in the new homes of some of the younger generation.

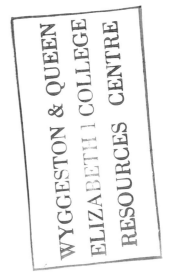

Less optimistic and more worrying prospects for the future often seem to encourage nostalgia for the recent past. The threatening outlook in the late 1930s fostered nostalgia for the more settled world of the later 19th century and a neo-Victorian revival in dress and interior decoration grew in popularity. In a similar way, the gloomier developments of the 1970s made the stylishness of the 1920s and early 1930s appear light-hearted and attractive in retrospect. Films and television helped to spread and commercialise the nostalgic feeling for the inter-World War years and many enjoyable productions were set in these popular decades.

Influences from the twenties and thirties soon became one of the most fashionable new trends in interior decoration. After the clear bright colours which had been so successful in the fifties and sixties, plain cream walls with a subtle peach tint were re-introduced. Couch and chair shapes clearly based on the designs of earlier periods were

Opposite
An impressively modern room of the seventies furnished in polished steel, black leather, glass and Perspex

199

revived, usually with boxy lines or for the more avant-garde and glamorous looking homes, designs with shell-shaped backs and curved arms were sometimes featured. Original pieces of furniture from the twenties and thirties, which would have been considered unattractively old-fashioned in 1960, were admired and collected by the fashion-conscious young of the seventies – particularly modest sized items such as low tables and small cabinets. Also greatly sought after were art deco style ornaments, figurines, and bronze Olympic style statues holding discs and globes. By the middle of the decade these kinds of pieces, especially good quality objects, had become increasingly valuable collectors' items.

Homes showing a strong influence from the art deco period remained a fairly limited trend which was confined mainly to the ultra-fashion-conscious and sophisticated. But the more subtle adaptations – the growing popularity of cream coloured walls, modern furniture with a slight look of the twenties, the use of geometric designs in soft shades for curtainings, chair and couch covers, together with art deco style patterned lampshades – all found their way into many middle-level homes as the decade progressed.

The prominence of industry and the power and strength of organised labour in many countries, with its accompanying pressures for an even more egalitarian society, was one of the strong characteristics of the 1970s which was soon reflected in fashion. Jeans and overalls were worn as fashion garments as well as work wear, and one of the new trends for advanced homes, which owed nothing to revivalism or nostalgia but was obviously influenced by factory interiors, was 'high tech'.

The term 'high tech' was used to describe industrial-style rooms where technical equipment such as music centres, television, videos, and computers were prominently displayed. Metal dominated in these rooms and the basic use of bolts and screws were unashamedly shown. A scaffolding effect of metal poles fixed into the floor and ceiling, and divided into display sections, storage space, and hanging areas for clothes, was usually featured on several walls. Metal was also often used for ceiling supports, spiral staircases, and most of the furniture; the metal was occasionally painted bright red or green but was more generally coated in a dull matt black which added emphasis to the very functional appearance of these new style interiors. Furniture was equally sombre and industrial looking; it often had a heavy duty quality. Metal wire mesh was sometimes placed under thick glass table tops and was also used for chair backs and seats. Other popular forms of worker-type seating included sturdy metal stools with a moulded tractor style top, and steel and leather wing chairs. Part of the high tech style was quite readily adopted, a wall unit, a chair or a table; but entire homes or even complete rooms in the new designs were rare.

The industrial style was at its most successful when used for commercial interiors, particularly of young men and women's fashion shops. The simple unadorned scaffolding or framework type of wall fixtures were ideal for showing off exciting ranges of colourful co-ordinated clothes and accessories. High tech, like the other very futuristic and modern trends of the 20th century, was felt

by many people to be too severe and cold looking for home interiors.

A reactionary trend for interior décor completely alien to the hard and modern, and one which offered a soft and luxurious retreat from the grim realities of urban life in the later part of the century, began to evolve for many of the homes of the affluent generations in the thirties to fifties age groups. The style was in some ways a richer, more urban version of the neo-Edwardian country cottage trend which had become so firmly established for many middle-level homes. Softness was the predominant feature of the new grander style; colours were always mid-tones and gentle tints, peachy creams, coral, pale gold, lemon yellow, light greens, powdered turquoise and bluey grey/green eggshell tones, were all popular for wall decorations and furnishing fabrics in both plains and prints. Patternings were never too strongly stated and ranged from

A romanticised nostalgia for the twenties and thirties led to a revival of art deco styles of furnishings for ultra fashion conscious rooms

traditional flower, leaf, and trellis motifs, to delicate abstracts which formed swirling cloud shapes or large blurred stripes and chevrons in soft rainbow effects. Walls and curtaining, particularly in bedrooms, were often in matching colours and designs and the curtains in most of the principal rooms were draped up at the tops of the windows as festooned blinds, which could be let down to various levels on the window and were sometimes made even more feminine looking with frilled edges and rosette trimmings. As the decade advanced curtaining of this kind became almost obligatory in these pretty, womanly homes.

Furniture was never obviously modern or too distinctively period in character; a pleasing conglomeration of pieces was usually preferred. Couches and chairs were often new but slightly influenced by the art deco period in shape; French 18th century style winged chairs and small tables or desks were frequently stripped down to the natural wood to soften their outlines, and china lamp bases slightly influenced by Chinese designs were topped with lampshades in light coloured linen or slubbed silk. Floor coverings were kept fairly low key in character and were either lightly stained natural wood with pale toned rugs, or they were covered with coconut matting or close pile wall-to-wall carpeting in fondant shades. Kitchens and bathrooms in these homes continued the overall theme of softness and had ranges of natural or painted wood fitments with traditional panelled doors and brass or china door knobs and handles.

The trend for a gentle but luxurious and rich type of home décor gained steadily in popularity during the seventies and early eighties. In London, well-known firms such as Designers' Guild and Colefax and Fowler were often associated with their versions of the new status-conscious style. The high level attained by homes that were clearly decorated in one of the most successful and fashionable trends of the period was obviously impressive in an era of world recession, and the style itself in its best forms was pleasant to look at and often had a quietly seductive and enveloping quality. Less successful interpretations were usually too sugary in colouring and generally over-decorated and over-prettied to the point of sometimes being in rather questionable taste.

Kitchens and bathrooms which had been gaining in status throughout the century, and had become one of the most important features of progressive homes by 1970, were given even more attention in the seventies and eighties; good kitchens and bathrooms unquestionably became one of the first priorities in the home and were subject to changing fashions and a variety of styles in a way which would once have been reserved for drawing rooms and principal bedrooms. Many younger home-makers in recent years have put the composition of their kitchen and bathroom before the living room and have frequently spent more money on their equipment and decoration.

Stark rather clinical style kitchens with a comprehensive range of Formica type units and work surfaces, although well established and widely used, were challenged in the seventies by the growing popularity of the warmer and more traditional appearance of wood fitments. They varied from the use of pale coloured lightweight

Opposite
The appeal and charm of pretty country style living room-kitchens has continued up to the present day

wood for complete or part sections of cupboards, shelving and drawers, to the more solid and impressive character of entire kitchens fitted with mid-toned woods, custom-made into country-dresser style panelled and glass fronted cupboards, together with numerous well planned drawers and shelves in varying shapes and sizes. Kitchens fitted out with good quality wood units became one of the most admired features in homes during the seventies and early eighties; they were considered a great asset and usually cost several thousand pounds to install, often more than the total cost of a medium size family house a dozen or so years earlier. Mothers visiting the homes of affluent sons or daughters were nearly always impressed by the style and scope of the kitchen which compared so favourably with the much more modest and basically equipped kitchens of their early married years.

Bathrooms also advanced considerably and became at least as style conscious as the modern kitchens of the time, and a dreary or poorly equipped bathroom was often thought of as a serious let-down to the general standard of the home. Bathroom departments received special attention in stores, and shops catering exclusively for the bathroom were opened in many towns and cities. All types of bathroom fitments were available in these shops from complete rooms offering every kind of known luxury feature to a simple soap dish. Colour ranges were very extensive and it was possible to match and co-ordinate plain and patterned wall tiles with wallpapers and coloured bathroom suites far more widely than ever before. Washbasins were made in several designs and were sometimes arranged in sets of two; lavatories were usually styled into neat unobtrusive shapes and bath designs included corner and circular models. Showers had become almost standard in most modern bathrooms and were available at many price levels which ranged from inexpensive hand-operated attachments incorporated into the bath taps to luxuriously fitted shower cubicles. Apart from the exciting selection of modern designs for the bathrooms of the late seventies and early eighties, revivalism which had become such a

The variety of designs, colours, layouts and fitments for bathrooms expanded throughout the seventies and into the eighties. Old fashioned looking baths copied from early 20th century designs, as shown bottom right, were reproduced to fit in with the general revival in Edwardian styles of décor

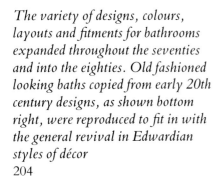

recurring feature in other forms of interior decoration, began to be extended into the décor of bathrooms. Edwardian or 1920s and 1930s style fitments copied and adapted to appeal to later 20th century tastes were manufactured for the homes of some of the very fashion conscious. Although the scope for stylish bathrooms had increased considerably, rooms fitted out with the more unusual and luxurious designs were confined to the homes of the well off. The more modest adoptions of the trend, with well-chosen colour schemes, attractive tiles, and colourful curtains, possibly combined with a superior range of taps and towel rails, did become widespread and welcome developments in many homes.

Changes in the style of domestic architecture inevitably slowed down in the recession years of the 1970s and 1980s. Far less State and private building projects were undertaken in the countries adversely affected by the economic difficulties of the time. When property developments were constructed, the design of the new houses and flats tended to be quieter and less adventurous in character than in the

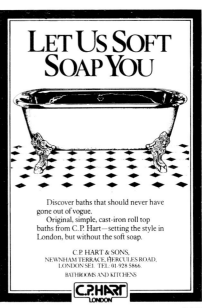

boom years in the middle of the century. Neo-Georgian styles with their fairly assured commercial appeal were frequently used for speculative building aimed at the middle-level market of executives and their families.

Modern designs both for private and State houses concentrated on understated styling with the more discreet use of windowed areas and balconies. High-rise blocks of apartments which had been so confidently erected in the late fifties and sixties as the predominant form of mass housing for the foreseeable future, began to lose favour in some countries during the seventies. This was particularly so in the continent of Europe where there was a return to alternative lower style blocks of flats and more traditional groups of small houses where conscious efforts were made to vary the design details in the developments and re-establish more human and less stereotyped ranges of homes. England, with its deep rooted liking for houses and gardens, welcomed the different direction for home planning, and the acceptability of life in a flat in tall blocks declined quickly.

Home attitudes and life in the home began to change during the seventies; improving standards for the majority, which had been accepted as an ongoing trend for two decades, were no longer possible on such a wide scale in the less stable conditions of the time. Signs of change were becoming noticeable quite early in the decade, demands for higher earnings led to an almost continual succession of strikes and industrial disputes. Britain in particular became locked in many bitter confrontations between 1971 and 1975 and power and fuel disruptions were endured by a long-suffering general public during several successive winters. The withdrawal of services was, however, efficiently organised to spread the inconvenience fairly amongst the entire population. To conserve fuel stocks, the disruption of power supplies was planned on a system of high and low risk days; the week was divided into alternate days for this purpose. Power was nearly always switched off for several hours in the mornings, afternoons, and evenings on high risk days and as a warning of the approach of the disconnection supply was sometimes cut for a moment a few minutes before the longer withdrawal of services began. In large towns and cities zones were worked out and the disruption was arranged on a rota basis; it was quite usual for one side of a street to be blacked out while the opposite side had power and vice versa. Candlelit suppers and sitting rooms darkened except for a glow from the fire were no longer chosen just to give a romantic atmosphere for special evenings but were forced on thousands of homes through emergency Government regulations. Paraffin and candles were scarce in a way that reminded older people of the austerity years of the 1940s and expensively dressed women with chauffeur driven cars were sometimes seen trying to charm an extra supply of candles from their local shopkeepers.

Frustration and antagonism between sections of the population in the seventies did not help the more difficult economic conditions of the time and the gulf in living standards which had narrowed from the 1940s to the 1970s began to widen again by the 1980s. The differences between the 'haves' and the 'have nots' in society had once again become more noticeable.

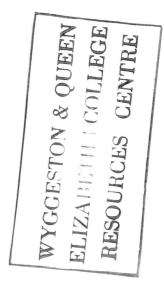

Gentle looking prints were very popular for many of the feminine style rooms of the early eighties

For those who can afford them, new and improved items and equipment for the home, benefiting from progressive technology, have become continually available and have helped to make life in affluent homes easier and more interesting for the whole family.

Modernisation and lower fuel consumption have become important features of newer developments for the home. Some forward looking houses and blocks of flats have been built with, or had installed specially, glassed solar panels in the roof to store energy from the sun. Washing machines are often designed to use less power, and non-stick pans, self-cleaning ovens, single sheet tops to ovens with indicated hot-plate areas marked in a circle rather than with harder-to-clean individual hobs, automatic defrosting fridges, together with microwave ovens enabling food taken from the deep-freeze to be made ready for immediate use and food processors (developed from the automatic mixer) which shreds, chops and grinds food, have all become quite general in progressive homes in recent years.

Other less widely adopted developments include waste-disposal units which consume items such as tin cans and wine bottles, and to help with home management, futuristic home computers have been installed. Home computers became a growing talking point in the late seventies and early eighties; from 1982 there was an enormous increase in ownership of them. The age when they can simplify housekeeping by checking accounts at banks and stores, order food and household items, make direct contact with doctors, schools and offices, so often discussed, and the arrival of cable television is growing steadily closer.

Video recorders have grown steadily in popularity during the last decade and have enlarged considerably the scope for home entertainments. Programmes of interest can be recorded for later viewing and the range of video films to buy or rent has continued to expand excitingly. Video games played on televisions have proved to be a very useful way of occupying children, who are often excited by the new kind of play and thoroughly enjoy operating their screen controls; grandparents with memories of the very different children's pastimes when they were young are also frequently enthralled by today's videos and sometimes enjoy playing video games with their young grandchildren. Computer games small enough to hold in their hands have also gained a wide following with today's children and have often proved to be a very effective way of preventing boredom and irritability during long journeys.

Teenagers of the 1980s, like their counterparts in all the decades of the century, relate strongly to current popular music which somehow always seems to capture the mood of the moment. Today's young might be surprised to think of Granny with her arthritic hip and Grandpa with his circulation problems as the exuberant teenagers of the twenties, irritating their parents by repeated playings of the latest charleston record and by overturning small pieces of furniture as they launched into their high-kicking dance steps. The thought of middle-aged parents as accomplished rock-and-rollers in the late fifties might also amuse their children growing up in the more sophisticated pop world of the eighties.

Today's young, lucky enough to belong to prosperous households, often have their own individual music systems, televisions and videos, and present-day parents are often wearied by competitive blasts of different hit recordings coming from several rooms at the same time which are also sometimes accompanied by the sight and sound of a practice 'bop session'.

'Walkman' sets with their earphone attachments which can be played anywhere, indoors or outside, have been welcomed into many households as a quieter and more private way of listening to music, although attracting the listener's attention with a shout when there is a telephone call or when meals are ready is not always possible, and some mothers are often worried by the sight of their son or daughter roller skating or cycling down the street with the Walkman earphones firmly in place.

As many of the well-off homes of the last decade have become steadily more progressive and better equipped, others affected by the adverse economic trends of the period have struggled to maintain their accustomed standards. Expensive improvements and added financial commitments have been out of the question for these

Video recorders, which were a great novelty in the early seventies, found their way into countless homes by the mid-eighties

Although stark futuristic kitchens have remained popular, alternative, more traditional designs like the one on the left have been preferred by some people

homes; running costs have increased continually and bills for repairs, taxes, and heating have become worrying burdens. Many households have had to cut back on expenditure and lower their general standard of living, particularly those who have to live on incomes and pensions which cannot keep pace with inflation, or who are among the growing numbers of unemployed.

During the last few years unemployment in many countries has begun to approach the proportions of the Depression years of the 1930s and although unemployment benefits are very much better than in the earlier period, many families have had to make painful adjustments to a more basic style of life devoid of the attractive consumer goods which fill the shops so tantalisingly. The young and the middle aged are often the most seriously affected members of the population. Young people often through no fault of their own have drifted into their twenties without ever having known the self-respect associated with holding down a job, and many men thrown out of work in their late forties and fifties have understandably found it difficult to get alternative work when in competition with younger age groups holding similar qualifications. Fathers and sons in the same home have become unemployed more and more frequently in the eighties and a certain amount of resentment, tension and despair has inevitably grown in many of the more deprived homes of the present decade.

The problems of a prolonged world recession and the widened gulf in living standards may well have contributed to the alarming growth in urban crime during the last 10 years. Burglaries, robbery and incidents of mugging have all increased rapidly in many countries and home security has become an important consideration for most families. Homes from quite a modest middle level upwards now have a far more elaborate number of anti-burglar precautions than the majority of people would have dreamed of a generation ago. Complicated ranges of door and window locks, chains, spy holes and alarm systems have all become familiar and unremarkable features in many homes and are usually insisted on by companies offering home insurance cover. Entry phones have been well established in homes and flats for over a decade, particularly in the cities, and miniature television screens are becoming additional standard features in most new developments, enabling the identity of callers to be checked in the home before allowing entry into the building.

In marked contrast to the exciting and the sometimes sombre developments affecting homes in the last quarter of the century, other aspects have shown a surprising and unexpected revival of earlier styles of living and ways of life.

The cheerful look of open solid fuel burning fires with their hereditary appeal to many people has become very popular again. Grates closed in the years of comparatively cheap central heating in the fifties and sixties have often been re-opened, and disappointment and regret is frequently expressed that so many modern houses and flats have been built without working fireplaces and chimneys.

Warmer looking, more homely styles of décor and furnishings, with the greater use of wood and natural brick or stone continue to grow in popularity. Gardens, or at least a small patio, which less than 20 years ago, people were expected to give up cheerfully for the supposed convenience of life in a high-rise block of flats, have become greatly valued assets in the later part of the century and are often listed high on the range of priorities aspired to by today's home-makers. There has also been a revival in home produced vegetables and fruit which are often thought to have more flavour and goodness than the ones cultivated on a mass commercial scale. The quality of freshly grown vegetables has become part of the general revival of interest in more natural types of food and simpler styles of cooking.

The general public has become far more informed on the properties of food and the value of dietary balance; the media continually points out the dangers of obesity and an over-rich diet and their probable link with many health disorders. The high consumption of meat, sugary foods, the over-use of salt and a substantial intake of dairy produce, particularly butter and cream – all of which had been so favoured by successive earlier generations in the richer countries of the world, and thoroughly enjoyed in the

Gas fires with logs have made a very effective and easy-to-use substitute for solid fuel burning fires with the inevitable work they entail

post-austerity Europe of the later fifties and during the sixties – were strongly discouraged in the seventies and eighties. Discussions on diet and the content of foods, like views and information on property, have become very characteristic talking points in present-day homes.

A preventive approach to health dangers has been accepted by many more people; high cholestorol levels are watched in daily diets, particularly by the middle aged working in stressful occupations; health food shops flourish and the benefits of roughage in a balanced diet are now widely known. There has been a marked increase in the sale of wholemeal bread and some households prefer to bake their own health style bread and guests are often informed proudly that they are eating special home-produced bread.

Health consciousness, alternative medicines, and a striving for a better, general feeling of energy and well being have all grown in recent years and are no longer considered cranky or eccentric. Many young and old people often practise some form of relaxing technique or meditation, a programme of exercises or some individual range of all three regularly as part of their life in the home. The middle aged make greater efforts than in earlier periods to stay reasonably slim and fit with moderate sized meals and an active participation in some form of sports. Tracksuits and running shoes for parents as well as children have become familiar in many homes and mothers and fathers are sometimes seen leaving the family house in the early morning or evening for a toning-up jog. Many find jogging a good

Homely comforts, an open fire natural wood, warm colours and inviting looking couches plus some modern equipment, music centres and video's have all become part of a firmly established home ideal for many people

counterbalance to hours spent in offices, driving through heavy traffic, or sitting watching television screens.

General aids to help revive jaded spirits and foster good health have been adopted in some homes. Jacuzzi baths with their swirling jets of water, and cleansing and refreshing sauna cubicles are installed in some homes and various kinds of sun lamp equipment sometimes help to relieve aches and pains and can also be used carefully to give a slight suntan or preserve a fading one. Suntanning aids are especially popular in the countries of the northern hemisphere which are deprived of real sunshine for such long periods during the grey winter months.

The range and scope of cosmetics in many homes has continued to grow in recent years, although a dressing table as the centre for the application and display of make-up and perfume is far less popular today than in some of the earlier decades. In the twenties and thirties dressing table tops in most fashion-conscious women's bedrooms had become a very noticeable feature where all kinds of beauty aids were laid out ready for use. Special dressing table sets were usual; they were often made in cut glass and consisted of a tray for hairpins, hair slides and combs, one or two fancy scent sprays, and bowls for face powder or face cream. Compacts for rouge and powder, lipsticks in decorative holders, and ivory or tortoiseshell hand mirrors, brushes, and combs all added to the wide range of items found in many bedrooms of the period. In the eighties cosmetics and beautifying equipment are usually kept in bathroom cabinets, most women preferring to make up in the bathroom where good lighting is often well arranged and all the facilities they require are near at hand. Apart from the extensive and improving ranges of cosmetics for the face, items such as body lotions, skin toners and hair conditioners are found in many more bathrooms and are often used by men as well as women.

Men have gradually become less reticent about using some forms of cosmetics and artifice, after-shave lotions, colognes; dryers to help arrange the shape of hair styles are all widely used by many age groups and are rarely considered effeminate. Fathers are often surprised by their sons' uninhibited attention to their appearance and, although obvious make-up and hair dyeing or tinting is still far from general, it has become acceptable in some homes without parents becoming too concerned over their sons' masculinity; boys' rooms – where designer-named colognes, hair gel and deodorant sprays are openly displayed near collections of manly looking sports equipment – have become quite unremarkable in many households.

Changes have affected nearly every aspect of homes at all levels of society during the turbulent and insecure atmosphere of the 20th century; ideas and attitudes have been subject to constant alterations and revisions over the decades. The leisured and elegantly spacious style of upper-class homes which seemed so permanent and well established 80 years ago has become almost extinct. The living accommodation in general use for the dwindling numbers who still live in palatial mansions has usually been condensed into a few rooms. There are hardly any large town houses occupied by single families in the 1980s; the high value of property in fashionable areas

Two views, above and on the next page, of the author's 17th century cottage home in 1984 after considerable renovations had taken place from his plans and designs

in the centre of major cities such as London, Paris or New York has resulted in the conversion of nearly all sizeable houses into apartments, and a suite of rooms including several bedrooms in a fashionable area has become the height of spaciousness for affluent homes in these cities. Huge country houses used and owned by one family have declined in each decade; today, aristocratic homes in use in the country usually have a museum-like quality and they are in fact frequently used as a kind of monument to earlier periods. The family confine themselves to a smallish area and the rest of the property is often on view to the general public who tend to look at the rooms as interesting examples of how people used to live and admire rather objectively the antique style and value of the décor, furnishings and pictures. Apart from the prohibitive cost of maintaining town or country mansions, the teams of willing servants who used to help run them so smoothly no longer exist even if they could be afforded in the present age.

The 20th century has almost seen the end of the servant population which once formed such a high percentage of the general public and appears to have existed in some form in all the recorded civilisations in history. Automation and labour-saving devices have taken over many of the functions once performed by staff, although gadgets, however modern, have to be assembled, operated, cleaned and put away, all of which is time-consuming and sometimes tiring. Women today, even with the most up-to-date equipment, are kept busy in the home and rarely enjoy the amount of free time that was nearly always available to comfortably-off middle-class women at the beginning of the century with two or three servants in attendance. The return of a more leisured age with plenty of time for well-mannered and stylish social life may well have to wait for the arrival of a totally push-button range of home appliances with a team of robots to operate and maintain them and to run errands and be on call whenever they are required.

Some forms of comfort and convenience have improved considerably during the century and are enjoyed by a far wider range of people than could have been envisaged in 1900. Telephones are standard appliances in most homes and kitchens and bathrooms have developed more quickly and excitingly than any other part of the home and have become the really futuristic features in some houses and flats that were prophesied by advanced thinkers earlier in the century.

Central heating systems, double-glazed windows, and wall-to-wall fitted carpets which were usually thought of as additional luxury features a generation ago have become quite general and are often considered basic necessities by many present day middle-level home-makers.

American prominence and vitality during the century has influenced homes and home life all over the world. Many progressive developments in the home have been pioneered and promoted by America, and the concept of less obviously class-conscious homes continually updated with changing fashions in interior decoration and ever-improving equipment for a wider section of the population have become established trends in many countries, together with the ideal of attaining the most comfortable

The living room in the author's cottage home.

The exterior and interior of a New York luxury apartment in the early eighties

home background possible in which to enjoy a casual and informal way of life. This concept was very different to the style of living aspired to in Europe during previous periods when an elegant but often uncomfortable background provided the setting for a very much more formal type of life.

Possibly the best known contribution to 20th century homes by America and the one most likely to be remembered and recorded is the skyscraper, which has been adopted to some extent in nearly every country in the world. Cities in south-east Asia which have continued to prosper during the recession years, particularly Hong Kong and Singapore, have been transformed almost beyond recognition in less than two decades by the rapid building of high-rise offices, hotels and apartment blocks. The idea of building upwards to save limited and very expensive ground space has been taken further in these cities than in most parts of the world and a medium sized house set in its own grounds has become a highly valued asset usually enjoyed only by the very well off.

New creative designing for architecture, furniture, and interior decoration has stemmed from several different countries during the course of the century and the centre for new style movements has shifted in importance from decade to decade. In the 1900s France and Britain were the source of many important new developments in domestic architecture and furniture design. After the First World War Germany and France became the centres for very inventive ideas on modernistic styling. In the 1940s Scandinavian and American designs gave the lead in new concepts of design for the home.

New fashion trends of the eighties. Italian chairs showing a slight influence of the fifties in shape

During the fifties and sixties Britain produced many exciting and revolutionary ideas and London became famous as the swinging centre for young designers. From the fifties until the present day Italy has been responsible for a succession of inventive and elegant modern designs which have provided an influence and an inspiration to stylists all over the world.

Revivalism has been a recurring theme in 20th century homes and nearly every decade has had its share of popular 'retro' or 'nostalgia' designs. Jacobean influences together with simple country-craftsmen pieces of furniture were very successful middle-class styles from the 1900s to the 1930s. Good reproduction designs from the late 18th and early 19th centuries, particularly English styles, have been safe and well accepted throughout the century. Victoriana décor which was so despised in the early decades came back into fashion in up-dated forms in the late thirties and lingered on until 1960. Edwardian designs and turn-of-the-century cottage styles returned to favour in the sixties and seventies and have remained popular into the eighties. Art deco was liked again in the seventies and became an important design influence as part of the strong nostalgia for the 1920s and 1930s. In the 1980s, revivalism is as popular as ever and some of the latest designs for modern furniture show characteristics of the designs of the 1950s; thin black metal legs are used again for chairs and tables and bright colours, particularly clear reds and yellows, have been revived by many of the trend-setting Italian designers. Habitat, with its well-established classically modern image, have recently included a wall unit in their new ranges with a definite look of the fifties, featuring cupboard doors and rows of drawers alternately in red and white.

For people wanting an opulently rich look in their homes the grandiose features of the neo-classic styles fashionable at the beginning of the century are being used again by interior decorators in the eighties. Classic columns, large gilt framed paintings, ancient Greek or Roman style wall plaques and sculptures together with a selection of neo-classic 19th century furniture are all forming part of yet another resurrected and newly fashionable style for prosperous homes in the late 20th century.

Life in the home has changed as much as the home background

The use and scope of computers inside and outside the home has continued to grow each year

during the last 80 years. Desperate poverty and hunger, although still unfortunately widespread in many parts of the world, have been almost eradicated in the richer countries and despite setbacks and protracted recessions more people enjoy a reasonable way of life than ever before. The gulf between standards which had reached its narrowest point in the sixties has widened again in the eighties but is still far less than most people would have imagined possible in 1900.

Manufactured entertainment, prepared and relayed for mass consumption, hardly existed at the beginning of the century. Families made their own amusements and individual resourcefulness was encouraged and fostered. Today some form of 'canned' entertainment is found in nearly every home and the range is growing all the time, video and computer sales are increasing rapidly; Ken Marks, a director of Debenham Stores, has pointed out that sales of home computers in their shops had risen by 1000 per cent from 1982 to 1983.

The easy availability of push-button style amusements and information in the home can be a mixed blessing; piano playing, reciting, singing, dancing and party games, which were so much a feature of the Edwardian period and helped to create an atmosphere of fun and liveliness within an individual home, have practically died out and have been replaced to a certain extent by a spectator population watching the same range of items on a mass scale. In some cases, however, television has helped to revive interest and participation in various activities. Cooking and gardening programmes with their information and instructive value have stimulated more ambitious and professional efforts in many households, and the almost cult-like following of snooker matches on television has resulted in a considerable revival in active participation in the game.

The size, structure and composition of the family has altered radically since the early 1900s. Infant mortality has been reduced very substantially and through medical advancement and effective contraception, people have been able to have far more control over the size and timing of their families. Fewer children are generally preferred and for couples with problems over fertility, test-tube babies produced from donor banks have become a reality. Less people inhabit the average home and the size of middle- and upper-class accommodation is usually very much smaller. Far fewer grandparents and unmarried brothers and sisters live in their married relatives' homes; resident companions, tutors, nannies and servants who were still a part of many prosperous homes at the beginning of the century are very rare in the 1980s and there are many more single home occupiers.

Formality in the household and between members of the family died out almost completely during the course of the decades. Homes where family prayers and grace before meals were habitually said, and husbands were addressed as 'the Master' and wives as 'the Mistress' and where sons called their fathers 'Sir' – still remembered from their childhood by some elderly men and women today – seem as remote as the world of Shakespeare or Jane Austen to the young generation of the 1980s.

Opposite
The 'high Tech' style very
successfully used for a study/office

Firm parental control and forceful discipline so strongly administered by many great-grandparents and which sometimes included
corporal punishment, also seems incredible and amusing to many of
today's youth. Nowadays older generations tend to be far less fixed
in their ideas and not as uncompromising in their general attitudes;
they usually try to win children's confidence more gently and hope
to become a source of guidance and advice rather than an
intimidating authoritarian force to be feared. The author's mother,
with memories of a pre-1914 childhood, was delighted and flattered
to be told by her grandson that he thought of her as a friend rather
than a grandmother.

Speculation on homes in the immediate future has been a popular
subject in all the decades of the 20th century. Futuristic homes have
nearly always been envisaged as rather austere if not clinical in
character and totally automated with the latest technology. Homes in
1999, although just over a decade away and nearer to us than the
1960s, are still often portrayed in this way; homeliness and cosiness
which seem to have such a deep rooted appeal for many would
appear to be due for total abandonment in an amazingly short space
of time.

Confident predictions on the typical home at the close of the
century would be foolhardy in such an unstable world; the threat of a
catastrophic world war which might wipe out civilisation as we
know it is always a frightening possibility. Fall-out shelters are being
built in ever increasing numbers and in some countries it is now
obligatory for most new buildings to include some form of such
shelter constructed to approved Government specifications.

If world wars and economic catastrophes are avoided in the
remainder of the eighties and in the nineties, many homes will
probably see the fuller development of well-established trends. Some
forms of revivalism and at least a few exciting and unexpected
changes are likely to take place. Further technology and automation
is bound to spread and quickly become a standard feature in the
home, particularly in kitchens and bathrooms. Television screens
and computers will undoubtedly be an even more important part of
day-to-day life. New styles of furniture and interior decoration with
a futuristic look will probably be launched, and after the quieter
trends of recent years they may have a considerable impact.

Too much hard modernisation, however, does not seem to suit the
human race and attempts to promote a cold synthetic background for
home life have so far only been partially successful and have always
been followed by alternative or reactionary trends.

Comfortable and traditional attitudes towards home-making and
home life in general appear to be very deeply entrenched and it seems
likely that the homes of the future will continually adapt new
developments to blend in with the hereditary idea of its being a
warm and enveloping haven for private living, away from the
harsher intrusions and realities of the outside world rather than
allowing itself to be transformed into some stereotyped space-age
unit devoid of any individual character.

INDEX   *Page numbers in italic type refer to illustrations*

Index by
Anna Pavord